# WORLD-CLASS
# GROOMING
## for Horses

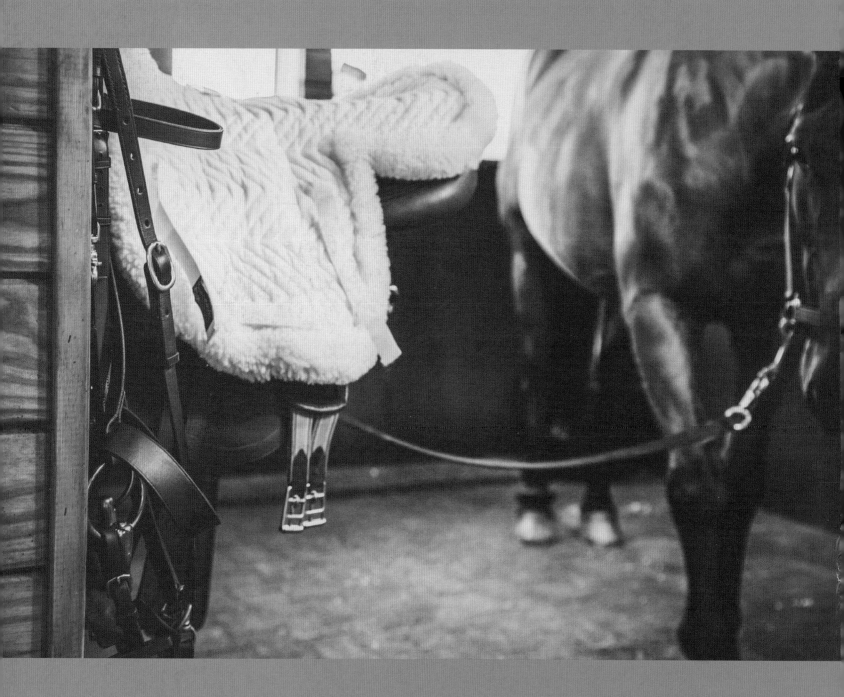

# WORLD-CLASS GROOMING
## for Horses

*The English Rider's Complete Guide*
*to Daily Care and Competition*

## CAT HILL AND EMMA FORD

### WITH PHOTOGRAPHS BY JESSICA DAILEY

Forewords by Phillip Dutton and Silva Martin

TRAFALGAR SQUARE
North Pomfret, Vermont

First published in 2015 by
Trafalgar Square Books
North Pomfret, Vermont 05053

**Disclaimer of Liability**
The authors and publisher shall have neither liability nor responsibility to any person or entity with respect to any loss or damage caused or alleged to be caused directly or indirectly by the information contained in this book. While the book is as accurate as the authors can make it, there may be errors, omissions, and inaccuracies.

The authors and publisher make no warranties regarding horse care products recommended in this book. The authors are not medical professionals. In the case of injury or illness, consult your licensed veterinarian.

Trafalgar Square Books encourages the use of approved safety helmets in all equestrian sports and activities.

**Library of Congress Cataloging-in-Publication Data**
Hill, Catherine, 1981- author.
  World-class grooming and care for horses : the complete resource for English riders /
Catherine Hill & Emma Ford ; photographs by Jessica Dailey.
      pages cm
  Includes index.
  ISBN 978-1-57076-690-9 (PLC Wiro)
  1.  Horses--Grooming. 2.  Horses--Care.  I. Ford, Emma, 1976- author. II. Title.
  SF285.7.H55 2015
  636.1'083--dc23
                              2014026424

**All photographs by Jessica Dailey (www.jesslynn.photography) except the following photos courtesy of the authors:**
1—5 (top), p. 17; 1 (middle) and 1 (bottom), p. 30; 1 (top), p. 31; all, pp. 32–3; 5, p. 34; 1B (bottom), p. 37; all, pp. 39, 42; 2A–F, p. 46; 1, p. 47; 3A, p. 51; 1 (top), 1 (middle), and 4 (bottom), p. 57; all, p. 58; 1–2B (middle), p. 59; 1 & 2 (middle), p. 60; 1 (top left & right), p. 62; 1, p. 63; 3, p. 67; 1, p. 74; all, p. 76; all, p. 78; 1, 3B, p. 79; (top), p. 94; 2, p. 95; 4, p. 96; 2B and 5, p. 98; 1A & B (top), p. 101; 1–2C (middle and bottom), p. 102; 2, 3 (bottom), p. 105; all, pp. 107–8, 111–2; 4, p. 109; 1–3, 5 (top), p. 117; 2 (bottom), p. 119; 2–4, p. 123; 5, p. 124; 6, p. 125; 1, 5A–D, p. 129; 1, p. 139; 2, p. 153; 1–3 (top), p. 164; 1A & B (top), 6 (bottom), p. 168; 2, p. 170; 4A, p. 174; 1, 3, 4, p. 175; 1 (top right), p. 185; 4A & B, p. 186; all, p. 191; 1 & 3 (top) and 1A & B (bottom), p. 193; all, 197–8; (bottom left), p. 201; 1–3 (bottom), p. 202; all, p. 203; (bottom), p. 204; all, p. 205; 1A–C (top), p. 207; 1 (top), p. 210; all, p. 215; 1 (bottom), p. 218; all, pp. 219–20

*Note: The author and publisher made every effort to obtain a release from all persons responsible for the photographs that appear in this book. In some cases, however, the photographer or individual photographed was not known or could not be contacted. Should photographers and individuals photographed be identified, they will be credited in future editions of this book.*

Book design by Lauryl Eddlemon
Cover design by RM Didier
Index by Andrea M. Jones (www.jonesliteraryservice.com)
Typeface:  Open Sans

Printed in China
10 9 8 7 6 5 4 3 2 1

*This book is dedicated to all those horses that took us to the top of an industry we love—especially, our Nicki, Simon, and the amazing Woodburn, who was taken from us far too soon. Without your quirks, your opinions, your talent, and your heart, we would not be the grooms we are today.*

# Contents

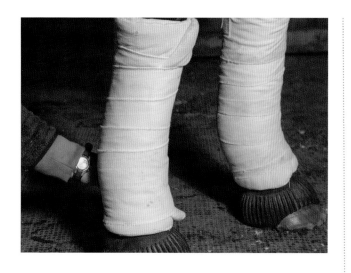

# Foreword
## by Phillip Dutton

Riding and competing (and maybe even winning) are not just about your horse looking fabulous in your lesson or in the show ring. True horsemanship requires possession of essential skills that ensure a horse is kept happy, healthy, and sound. In the pages ahead, you will certainly learn how to superbly groom and present a horse; in addition, you will also gain valuable insight when it comes to giving your horse the care he deserves.

The title of this book suggests that becoming "world-class" is within your reach, whatever your current level or ability. But how is it possible for the average rider to be what I would consider "world-class"? To speak plainly: Learn these grooming and management skills. They will go further in helping you reach riding and showing goals than will a dozen fancy saddles or hours of expensive lessons. And they will earn the respect of others who consider excellent care of their horses nonnegotiable.

For those like me who turn professional and pursue equestrian sport at the very top of international levels, the way our horses are cared for—both day to day as well as before and after competition—directly impacts our success and our livelihood. The simple truth is, you can't ride without a horse. So even if you love to ride "just for the fun of it," the care of the horse through quality management helps to guarantee you will be enjoying your time in the saddle for many years to come.

I and my horses have been very privileged to have Emma Ford support us over the years. She is as good as anybody in the world at caring for horses and ensuring they look tiptop when we compete. Cat Hill has earned my respect as well, with her management of Mara DuPuy's barn while Mara campaigned some of her top horses. Both of these women have taken their careers as professional grooms to another level. The pride they take in their work and the skill they exhibit in both keeping horses at home and preparing them for competition are unparalleled.

We can all learn from them and be better horsemen for it.

*Phillip Dutton*
12-Time USEA Leading Rider of the Year
5-Time Olympian with 2 Gold Medals

# Foreword
## by Silva Martin

As I've told others, for me, not being on a horse is not a normal life.

But being on a horse is only one small part of it, really, because of course it is also the being *with* him, and the care we take to keep him happy and performing his best, that matters even more.

In this book, Cat Hill and Emma Ford teach us how to groom our horses until their coats shine and their legs flash white; how to clip and pull and braid so that when we trot down the centerline, we look and feel like superstars. Sure, we learn techniques for wrapping legs, bandaging tails, adding quarter marks, and polishing the metal on our bridles. But we also meet two conscientious and supremely motivated horse people who put the needs of the horse first in their own work, and do their best to show us how to do the same.

Perhaps what I like best about this book is the enjoyment Cat and Emma so obviously get from being with horses. They take their jobs as grooms seriously, no doubt, and I can attest to the level of professionalism evident in the top turnout of the horses in their charge. But it also seems that, like me, they wouldn't think it a normal life without horses in it. They love what they do.

When you read the personal stories they share, placed throughout the book, you get a real sense of the good humor and perspective they bring to the barn and ringside. I want to make a point of mentioning this because I think attitude matters when you're around horses. I'm a very positive person. This quality has helped me get through the challenges I've faced over the past few years as I've pursued my riding, training, and teaching career. And I believe that having a positive outlook on the ground, when handling and grooming your horse, ultimately affects how he communicates with you and performs movements in the dressage arena.

As Cat and Emma say at the end of the last chapter, "We're all in this sport for one thing—and that is the horse."

Take pride in your horse's turnout. Stay positive. Be safe.

*Silva Martin*
German *Bereiter*
Top Young Horse Dressage Trainer and USEF Developing Rider
Member US Dressage Team 2014 CDIO Wellington Nations Cup

# About the Authors

*Cat Hill* grew up in upstate New York on a working farm. Her first clear memory is of the day her parents got her a pony for her fifth birthday. She grew up on that pony, and the pony was followed by a series of Arabian show horses. In college, Cat started riding show hunters with the intercollegiate horse show team at SUNY Geneseo. After receiving her degree, she followed her love of horses to Ireland to be a working student at Mullingar Equestrian Centre, an hour northwest of Dublin. Quickly promoted to barn manager, she spent half a year working with show jumpers and eventers.

Upon returning to the United States, Cat spent time as a working student for a top Grand Prix dressage rider, a winter working the Winter Equestrian Festival for a Grand Prix show jumping rider, and moved on to manage a AA hunter barn. From there she worked for eventer Craig Thompson, learning the ropes of grooming at events, before being hired to manage top competitor Mara DePuy's barn. After leaving DePuy to move closer to family, Cat began freelancing as a groom in every discipline, as well as teaching lower-level riders in dressage, jumping, and eventing. Over the years, she has worked at almost every type of equine competition, from the local fair to the Pan American Games.

*Emma Ford* originated from North Devon, England, and was raised in the hunt field with her dad as Master of the Foxhounds and surrounded by horses. She grew up in the Pony Club system, receiving her "B" designation and culminating with jumping at the Horse of the Year Show in 1991. After completing her BS at the University of Wales, she moved to the United States to follow her passion for horses.

Emma managed Adrienne Iorio's Advanced event horses for seven years outside of Boston, Massachusetts, then moved on to Phillip Dutton's barn in West Grove, Pennsylvania. She has groomed at almost every four-star event in the world and has been a member of the US Eventing Team at multiple Olympic, World, and Pan American Games. Over the years, in addition to eventing, Emma has had the opportunity to turn horses out at many upper level show-jumping competitions, including the Winter Equestrian Festival in Wellington, Florida, as well as work for a promising young dressage rider at many upper level dressage shows.

*Facing page, from left to right: Photographer Jessica Dailey, co-author Cat Hill with her daughter Adelaide, and co-author Emma Ford with Mystery Whisper and her dog Charlie.*

# About the Photographer

*Jessica Dailey* is the owner of Jess Lynn Photography, located in the picturesque Finger Lakes Region of upstate New York. Jessica's long time love of art evolved into a passion for photography, and then eventually into the growing business that she runs today. Her images have been featured in an international photography magazine and on various photography-related social media outlets. Her work includes commercial, event, landscape, and portrait photography. After her work on this book, Jessica has a new appreciation for the beauty of the equestrian world. See more of Jessica's work at www.jesslynn.photography.

# PART ONE

# At Home

CHAPTER ONE

# "A Day in the Life"

## Cat says

*Many years ago, I became friends with an up-and-coming young jumper rider. Two of his closest friends happened to be professional grooms, and we were regularly horrified by his daily horse management. His riding was fantastic and he was doing a great job of training, but he rarely brushed his horses, never cleaned his tack, and was simply a bit of a mess. In fact, one year, we even bought him a kit of brushes, painted them in his colors so he couldn't lose them, and gave them to him for Christmas in the hope it would convince him to groom a little. It didn't. However, after a bit, he started to have little issues: with tack, the horse's weight, and minor injuries such as cuts that turned into a real problem like cellulitis. So he called me and said it was time to step up, take better care of the horses, and train a groom. I went to his farm, met his new girls and stayed for a few days showing them how to take care of a barn, then went to a show to help them organize their time. I wrote him a handwritten book with notes about management and daily operations. His horse care finally matched his riding and horsemanship, and now he is regularly on the top of the leader board. In fact, the handwritten notes from several years ago were part of the inspiration for this book. It just goes to show that you cannot ignore the daily operations in a barn, no matter how well you ride!*

## DAILY SCHEDULE

Here is a complete daily schedule for any discipline:

### Daily Groom's Schedule

*7:00 a.m.* • Feed horses in the barn.

*7:15* • Bring horses in from fields to eat (check legs and body).
 • Feed outdoor horses (check legs and body).
 • Check water troughs in fields and paddocks.

*7:30* • Turn horses out.

*7:45* • Clean stalls and set up with each horse's hay.
 • Dump, scrub, and refill buckets.
 • Sweep/rake aisle.

*Throughout morning:*
 • Prepare horses to ride.
 • Cool out and aftercare.

*9:00* • Rinse feed buckets.
 • Make up feed for later.

*11:30* • Feed lunch when appropriate.
 • Check water buckets, refill as necessary.
 • Pick stalls.

Morning Routine

*Throughout afternoon:*
- Thoroughly groom horses.
- Care for injuries and other issues.
- Do extra chores such as de-cobwebbing and barn repairs.

*3:00 p.m.*
- Turn horses out for the evening.
- Clean stalls and set up with each horse's hay.
- Check water buckets: refill when clean; dump and refill when dirty.
- Check troughs.

*4:00*
- Feed horses.

*8–10:00*
- Do night check (look for signs of illness including colic; change blankets).
- Feed late-night when appropriate.

The most important part of a groom's job isn't at a show, and it's not the clean tack, the shiny brass, or the perfect braids. It is the day-to-day, nitty-gritty: catching skin issues before they become a problem; noticing something is not-quite-right before it becomes wrong. It's doing a little every day so that nothing gets out of hand. Let's start at the beginning of the day and head toward the end.

**1** Depending on the time of year, on most mornings, horses will either be heading in or out of the barn. Generally, we put horses out at night during summer and in at night during winter. There will almost always

Haltering

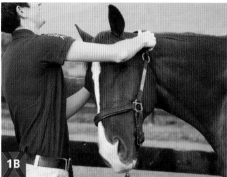

be horses that require monitoring or need measured turnout, as well, but we'll get to them in a minute. How you handle your horses every day sets the stage for how they will handle a stressful situation. You must be calm and in control of the little moments, and that begins by making sure that when you are catching, leading, and letting go of your horse, it is done correctly. This is an area where many people cut corners without realizing how much it affects them in the end!

# THE DAILY NITTY-GRITTY

## Haltering, Turnout, and Stabling

### Haltering
**1 A & B** Wrong: When haltering a horse, never approach from the front, pushing the halter in front of you. Horses have a blind spot immediately in front of them

and often shy away from you when you reach toward that point.

**2** Instead, stand next to the horse's head with the halter nose opened and gently lift it onto the horse's head.

**3** Wrong: A swinging throatlatch can catch an eye, a fence, or whack a horse in the head and cause him to spook, so always do it up. Wrapping a lead rope around your hand is just a bad idea: the calmest horse might trip and take you down; you could be dragged if he spooks; and it creates a "tense" feel to the horse.

**4** When walking your horse, insist that he marches next to you at a good speed.

**5** Wrong: Never drag a horse behind you!

## With a Chain

Some horses lose respect for a normal halter and lead rope. If your horse doesn't stop when you stop, drags you faster than you want to walk, or bumps into you with his shoulders, he is being rude!  Horses should "heel" just like a dog. They should walk next to your shoulder on a loose, relaxed lead. When your horse is "rude," a chain might be necessary to remind him to pay attention.

However, many lead ropes are sold with a short chain, and this can be quite dangerous. There are two issues: First, the chain needs slack to be properly used. When it is held tight, the horse will quickly lose respect for it. A quick, tug-then-release is the correct action for using a chain. Second, a short chain that only reaches across the noseband of the halter is unsafe.

**1** Wrong: Hooking the chain to the noseband of the halter can lead to two problems. It can slip below the chin and when the horse pulls tight, scare him into rearing. Also, the long end of the snap can jam into a nasal passage if pulled too sharply and break the delicate bones there.

**2 A** Instead, thread the chain through the noseband.

**2 B & C** Then wrap once over the noseband and thread through the other side.

**3** When you are out of chain, snap to the top of the cheekpiece.

**4 A** If you have a bit more chain, cross it under the horse's jaw.

**4 B** Snap the chain to the top of the cheekpiece on the other side. This prevents the halter from twisting when you need to use the chain.

With a Chain

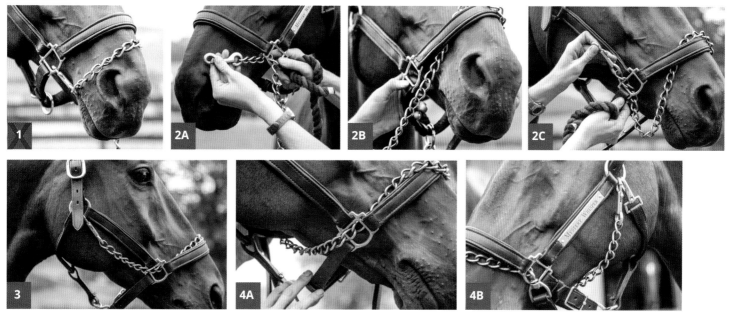

Letting Go

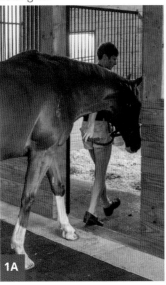

1A

1B

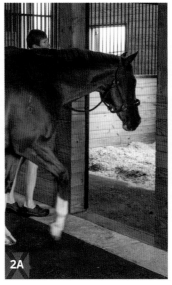

2A

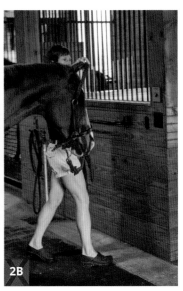

2B

## Letting Go

**1 A & B** When letting your horse go, either in a stall or in the field, you always want to walk him into the gate or door, calmly turn him around, then remove his halter.

**2 A & B** Wrong: Letting the horse walk past you into the door, or worse, sliding the halter off while he's still moving, can cause banged hips, a loose horse, and a bad habit.

Letting your horse go as soon as you walk into the field, without first asking him to turn around and stand quietly, can teach him to dart off as soon as he gets through the gate—dangerous for you and him.

## Hands-On Check-In

First thing in the morning, use your hands to check your horse's legs in the stall. There is no replacement for your hands; just looking doesn't catch what might be brewing under the hair!

**1** Investigate anything out of the horse's "usual." Check legs for heat, swelling, and skin abnormalities.

**2** Check pasterns for the beginning of "scratches."

**3** Don't forget he has hind legs too!

It is a good idea to keep a little log book for a new horse to catalog any splints, windpuffs, scars, or other "jewelry" that are "normal" for him.

## Grooming

We give our horses a good groom every day to promote skin health; loosen muscles; let you find any little skin problem before it gets out of hand; and produce that beautiful shine from deep down.

Hands-On Check-In

1

2

3

Hoof Picking

Grooming Kit

## Hoof Picking

**1** When you get a horse out of his stall, first pick out his feet into a small bucket to make sure mud doesn't fall into the bedding and create dust. Halter your horse and keep the stall door closed while you pick the feet to prevent him from leaving the stall prematurely. This helps to keep the aisle clean and tidy.

**2 A & B** Remember when picking the horse's feet, always point the hoof pick toward the toe and be gentle with the frog. Wrong: Pointing the hoof pick toward the heels can be dangerous. You could catch the hoof pick in the fleshy frog, causing an injury.

## Brushing

**1** Next up, assemble your tools:

- Jelly curry
- Good mud brush
- Medium bristle brush
- Nice soft brush or sheepskin mitt
- Towel
- Scissors
- Comb and brush
- Sunscreen
- Talcum powder
- BB® Double Strength Super Gro (our favorite brand of hair-growth serum)
- Hoof oil and sealant
- Hoof pick
- Witch hazel
- Tail conditioner/detangler
- Coat conditioner
- Fly spray

**2** Start with your curry and rub in vigorous circles to loosen up any dead hair, loose dirt, and give a good muscle massage. Be gentle over areas that don't have a fat or muscle covering, and listen to your horse about how hard you can push—every horse is different.

**3 A–C** While you groom, look for any scratches, bumps, or skin issues to be treated once the horse is clean.

Brushing

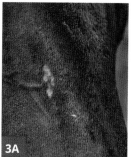

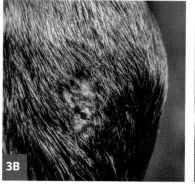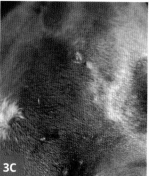

*Continued* ▶

Brushing (Cont.)

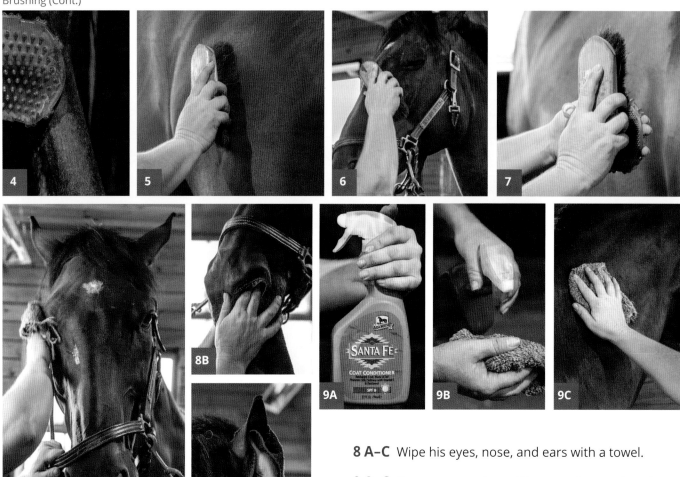

**8 A–C** Wipe his eyes, nose, and ears with a towel.

**9 A–C** Spray your coat conditioner onto your towel or sheepskin mitt to provide the final touch smoothing his hair and bringing up the shine.

Tail
**1 A–D** When combing the tail out, start at the bottom and gently work out tangles as you go on up to the top.

**2** Never rip a comb through the middle of the tail in a hurry; you will pay for it later!

Mane
**1** A pulled mane can be brushed down with a comb or a bristle brush.

**2** Daily, you can also place a hot towel over a horse's mane to help train it to lie flat. A very hot towel will keep most manes lying down for about one-half hour on its own.

**4** Gently use the small bristles of your jelly curry to do the cannon bones of all four legs.

**5** When your horse is quite dirty, use your mud brush to get rid of any really stubborn mud clumps. Your medium stiff brush should be flicked against his skin with short, hard strokes to get rid of any dirt down near the skin.

**6** Don't forget to gently brush his face.

**7** Periodically use the jelly curry to clean the brush as you move from neck to rump.

Tail

   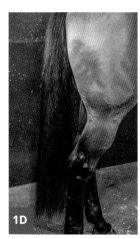 

Mane

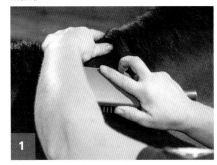   

**3 A & B** When training a mane, use a little beeswax pomade smoothed over the mane daily to help create a nice smooth mane.

## Hooves
You either use hoof oil to help provide moisture, or a hoof sealant to keep moisture out.

**1 A & B** Hoof oil must be applied all the way to the coronary band and on the heels.

**2 A & B** Hoof sealant must *not* cover the soft coronary band or heels.

Hooves

## Treating Issues

Finally, treat any problems you find while grooming.

**1** Thermazene® or SSD (silver sulfadiazine) cream is an excellent strong, gentle antibiotic and antifungal that can be used on many minor skin problems.

**2 A & B** First clean the area with witch hazel on a clean cotton square.

**3 A & B** If necessary, apply the SSD cream.

# GETTING READY TO RIDE

Once your horse is groomed, go ahead and get your tack. However, always be sure to have double-checked the girth area, barrel, and corners of mouth for dryness, chafing, or irritations. Catching these minor issues before you ride helps to make sure they don't become big ones. Girth rubs or spur marks can be treated with a topical antibiotic such as SSD or Neosporin® then coated with Vaseline® or Desitin® to prevent friction. On the mouth, bit rubs or cracked lips can be treated with Vaseline prior to riding and again at the end to keep them soft. If your horse has a skin issue like hives, spur rubs, or a dry coat, place a towel on his back over the saddle pad and under the saddle to protect his skin from being irritated by a leather boot or rider's leg. Next evaluate the plans for your horse that day.

## Leg Protection

For each discipline, there are plenty of leg protection options available. We will go through the best for each activity.

**1** Neoprene galloping or brushing boots: "Brushing" boots are flexible, won't pick up water, and provide shock protection should a horse bang himself or hit an object.

Treating Issues

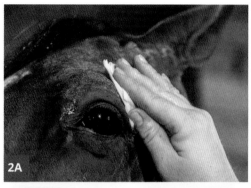
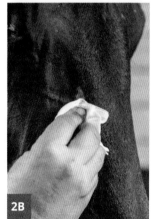
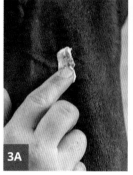

Brushing boots are best used when trail riding, doing fitness work such as trot or canter sets, and flatwork in wet arenas. "Woof Wear" brand classic brushing boots are a great option. We prefer "brushing boots" to "splint boots," which look quite similar, because of the added fetlock protection and lighter weight. You might see "sports medicine boots," which have a strap that goes below the fetlock. These boots were created for Western disciplines to support horses when they slide and spin. While great at providing what is called "rundown" protection to the lower leg, they can cause rubbing and can prevent a horse from full freedom of movement in dressage and are too bulky and heavy for jumping. For cross-country, they absorb water and pick up seed pods and grass, which can cause irritation.

**2** Polo wraps: "Polos" are a long strip of polar fleece with Velcro® at one end. They provide shock protection and a small amount of tendon support. They are excellent for flatwork or dressage in a dry arena or field. Polos should never be used in wet conditions, even an overwatered arena. The polar fleece will absorb water and can create problems. Polo wraps can get wet, stretch, and twist, fall down, or cause "bandage bows," which is a condition where the large tendon in a horse's leg gets swollen or damaged due to being pulled on by the bandage (see p. 13).

**3** Open-front boots: "Open-fronts" come in many materials, including leather, neoprene, and fleece-lined. They cover the back of a horse's tendon and fetlock and have small, thin straps across the front. These boots are used for jump schooling since they give the horse protection from injury while making sure he feels the rails when he's not careful. Leather boots must be cleaned and oiled daily so are usually reserved for show days. Neoprene is easy to clean and is lightweight so is great for daily use. Eskadron® brand boots are easy to put on and are hard-wearing. The fleece-lined versions can provide excellent protection to sensitive skin but must be kept clean and cannot be used in wet conditions since they will absorb water and rub.

**4** Ankle boots: "Ankles" are the hind boots paired with open fronts. Ankles have a small circle of strike protection that covers the inside of the ankle with a small strap that goes around the fetlock to hold the boot in place.

**5** Fleece-lined sport boots: Commonly called "fuzzy boots," these are a strong Cordura® or vinyl exterior paired with a fleece interior that cover the entire lower leg. Fuzzy boots are the easiest choice for dressage and flatwork. In dry conditions they are also good protection for trail riding if your horse has sensitive skin. They provide full strike protection during lateral work and are gentle on sensitive skin. The DSB™ Dressage Sport Boot brand fares really well and is machine-washable, making it excellent for daily work. Like polos, "fuzzy boots" will absorb water and do get very heavy when used in wet weather, so they should be limited to dry conditions.

**6** Stretch or dressage wraps: "Stretch boots" are thin, light, and provide slight shock protection, don't absorb water, and hug the tendon. A favorite of dressage riders,

Leg Protection

    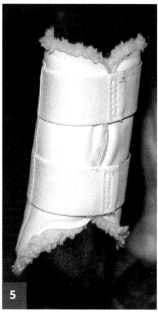

Continued ▶

Leg Protection (Cont.)

## Putting on Brushing Boots

We normally use leg protection on our horses' legs when they have four shoes. If your horse is barefoot or only wears front shoes, you can let him head out with only front protection, or bare-legged.

To apply neoprene brushing boots:

they are a nice option for daily work since they are machine-washable and easy to put on.

**7** Bell boots: "Bells" are bell-shaped rubber or neoprene boots that protect a horse from over-reach injuries, as well as helping to prevent torn-off shoes. Most commonly used on the front legs, many dressage riders use them on all four legs due to the increased lateral work.

**1** Make sure you put them on with the straps on the outside of the leg; pressure should only be put on the *front* of the cannon, NOT the *back* of the tendon.

**2 A & B** Any excess neoprene from the front should tuck under the back of the boot so as you tighten it on the leg, there are no wrinkles against the skin.

**3 A–C** For *double-lock* boots (these boots have two pieces of loop Velcro and one piece of hook Velcro to create a Velcro sandwich), you must still make sure the tension is

Brushing Boots

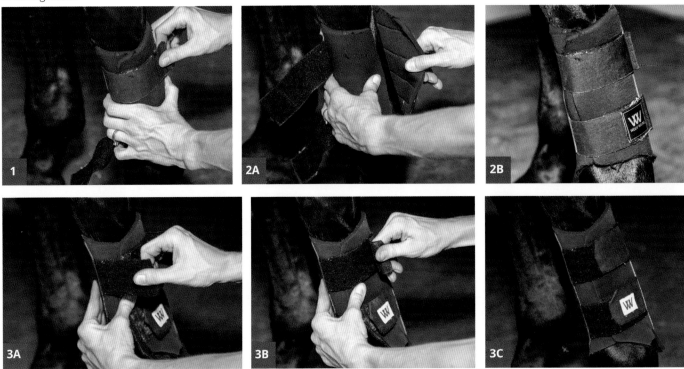

placed on the *front* of the cannon, NOT the *back* of the tendon. This means that the "top" Velcro strap is facing the front of the horse as shown in Photo C.

## Putting on Dressage Boots

Dressage boots are put on the same way as neoprene boots, with the tension on the front of the leg. Be very careful with elasticized fuzzy boots; only pull the tension until snug, not tight. You should still be able to put your finger under the elastic.

**1** Place the boot with the straps at the front, just below the knee.

**2** When there is an overlap (extra boot material), make sure the front section tucks *under* the back section; pull the top strap snug but not tight, then do up the bottom.

**3** The inside of the boot should have the large, round part of the protective area centered over the fetlock. (This photo is of the *inside* of the leg).

**4 A & B** Wrong: Many boots are placed too high. This can cause discomfort as well as decreased protection.

## Putting on Polo Wraps

If you have a horse with sensitive skin (and you will be riding him where it is dry), you can use dressage boots or polo wraps. Polo wraps can also be a lifesaver when you have a horse with boot rubs or scrapes on his legs. A little baby powder dusted on the legs helps to prevent chafing. Polos are an "advanced" technique. Practice makes perfect. Take your time and make sure it is correct because the last thing you want to do is put a bandage bow on a horse's tendon from a bad polo wrap! A "bandage bow" is an injury to the superficial digital flexor tendon that creates a swelling on the back of the leg. It can range in severity from simply looking ugly to a long-term injury.

Dressage Boots

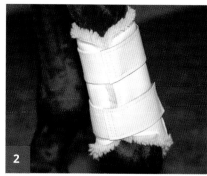
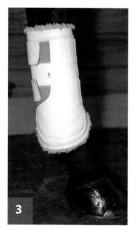

**barn gossip**

While working at a dressage barn, we had a horse come in for training. His fuzzy boots were a bit old and the elastic was stretched out. I put the boots on, pulling quite tight to get the elastic snug enough for the boot to stay on. When he was finished working the first day, I washed him off, turned him out and thought everything was fine. A few hours later, I brought him in to find two perfectly matched swellings on the front of each one of his front legs. I had over-tightened the straps because of the old elastic and caused pressure hematomas under where the straps had been. Needless to say I was horrified. I was lucky that a little cold hosing and liniment took care of the problem, but I am now quite shy of tight boots or old elastic! —*Cat*

Rolling Polo Wraps

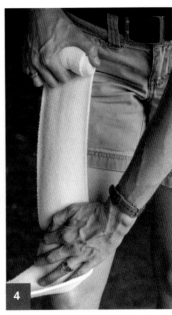

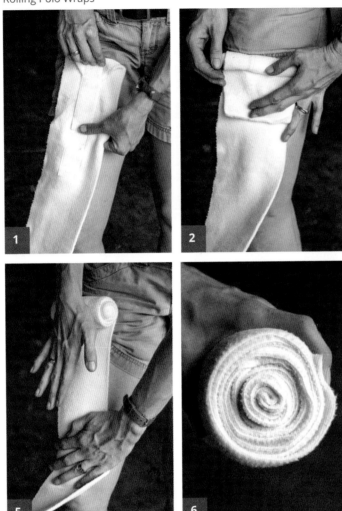

## Rolling Polo Wraps

**1** First, you must roll the polo. A loose, sloppily rolled bandage creates a loose, sloppy wrap! Lay the polo out flat in a clean area. Lay the Velcro end on your thigh, facing up. Fold the Velcro back on itself.

**2** Making sure to keep tension, start rolling the Velcro end down toward your knee.

**3** Once you get to the end of the Velcro, keep rolling with your hand until you reach your knee.

**4** Grasp the roll and pull up while holding the loose end with your other hand, keeping tight pressure.

**5** Open your hand and roll down the polo until you again get to your knee.

**6** Continue until the end. When you are finished you should see a nice, tight roll.

**7** Wrong: If you end up with a sloppy polo that you can easily flatten, you need to start over.

Applying Simple Polo Wraps

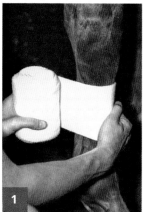 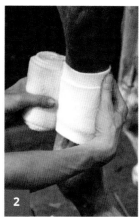 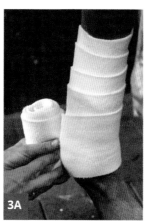 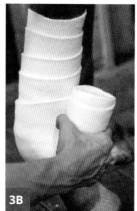  

## Applying Simple Polo Wraps

**1** Start the polo below the knee, with the roll facing you and the horse's tail.

**2** Using a firm consistent pressure, wrap with even (about 1 inch apart) layers down the leg until the ankle.

**3 A & B** Keep the same pressure as you cup the ankle with the wrap.

**4** To change direction, create a "V" at the front of the fetlock.

**5** Use the same consistent pressure as you go all the way back up to the knee. End with your Velcro perfectly lined up and check your work.

## Things to Watch Out For

**1** Wrong: Pulling inconsistently. Never pull strongly as you come around the front. A firm, consistent pull prevents pressure points.

**2** Wrong: Going the wrong direction. The wrap should *never* come from the back of the leg to the front.

**3 A & B** Wrong: Uneven layers.

**4** Wrong: Gaping at the ankle or loose areas of the wrap.

**5** Wrong: A "lumpy" look when you are done.

Things to Watch Out For

Extra-Protection Polo Wraps

  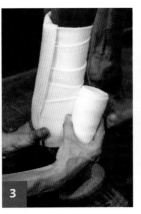 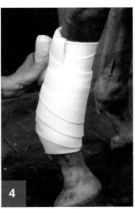 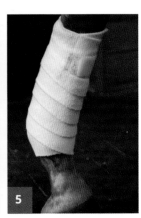

Back Legs

 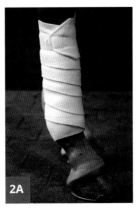 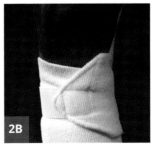

**5** Finish at the top of the tendon with your Velcro straight and even.

## Back Legs
**1** To wrap a hind leg, simply start just below the hock, front to back.

**2 A & B** Wrap the same way down and up as you did the front leg. Due to the hind leg's increased size, when you get to the end of the bandage, the tapered end that attaches to the Velcro may be visible. As long as the Velcro is straight and smooth, do not be concerned.

## Extra-Protection Polo Wraps
Alternatively, you can use a modified method for a horse that tends to kick himself. It has a "tail" going down the back of the leg to provide an extra layer of protection.

**1** Start with a bandage "tail" the same length as the cannon bone. Again wrap front to back.

**2** Carefully wrap down the leg with consistent pressure, leaving the tail out of the way for now.

**3** Wrap to the ankle creating a "V" in the front of the fetlock as you change direction. Carefully smooth the tail down the back of the tendon when you turn the ankle.

**4** Wrap back up the leg, keeping the tail smoothly down the back of the tendon.

## Removing Polo Wraps
**1** When removing a polo, make sure to keep the unwrapped section in your hand as you unroll.

**2 A & B** Wrong: Dropping bits on the ground or having sections hanging creates a safety hazard.

Removing Polo Wraps

## Polo Wraps with Quilts

**1** This form of wrapping is mainly seen in the dressage world where horses do a lot of lateral work. By adding a quilt underneath the polo you add more protection. These are often paired with bell boots to protect the entire lower leg.

**2** Take your exercise quilt and wrap around the leg. Start with the quilt at the front and wrap it snugly around the leg, going front to back.

**3** Take your polo bandage and starting in the middle of the cannon bone, proceed to wrap down toward the fetlock.

**4** Continue to wrap the leg, ensuring even pressure is used throughout and that the Velcro strap ends at the top of the wrap.

**5** A dressage horse ready to be saddled with wraps, including bell boots, all around.

## Bell Boots

### Rubber Bell Boots

**1** These boots are meant to help prevent horses from either taking their front shoes off or "heel grabs" like this one. There are several boot styles, and the biggest concern is that they fit well and are kept scrupulously clean or else they will rub.

**2** Rubber pull-ons are great for horses that need to live in bell boots because they are easy to clean and gentle on skin. First turn the boot inside out. By putting the horse's knee against your thigh and holding the ankle straight, you can pull the boot over the hoof.

Polo Wraps with Quilts

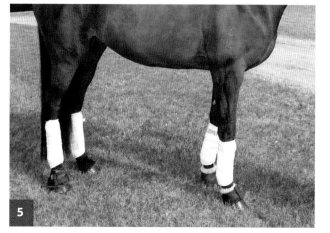

Rubber Bell Boots

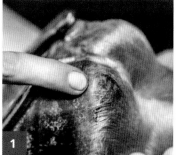  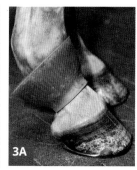  

**3 A & B** Replace the hoof to the ground and turn the bell boot right side out.

**4** To remove, pull the bottom of the boot toward the toe making sure not to drop the hoof as it comes off.

## Velcro Bell Boots

**1** Put the Velcro on the outside of the hoof, with the tab facing the back of the horse.

**2** Press tightly and smooth the Velcro.

**3** The boot should sit just off the ground and have one finger of "wiggle room."

## Fabric Bell Boots

There are two types of fabric bell boots. One type is smooth all the way around; the other has a small knob on the inside of the boot to help prevent the boot from spinning. Fabric boots are appropriate for short use but can rub in long-term or turnout situations.

**1 A & B** Bell boots with knobs should be set with the knob sitting centered above the cleft in the heels.

**2** Velcro should have the top tab on the front of the hoof, facing front to back.

Velcro Bell Boots

Fabric Bell Boots

## Fetlock Ring

A "fetlock ring" or "interference boot" is a simple rubber ring that buckles around a horse's fetlock to prevent injury sustained when a horse steps too close behind and catches himself. It can be used on either leg and a horse can wear it for extended periods of time, if necessary.

**1** First, open the ring and slide it onto the fetlock.

**2** Buckle the ring, keeping two fingers behind it. Tuck away the ends of the strap.

**3** Make sure there are two fingers of wiggle room when you are done.

Fetlock Ring

Water Cooling with a Hose

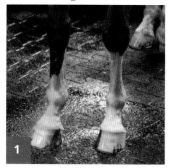

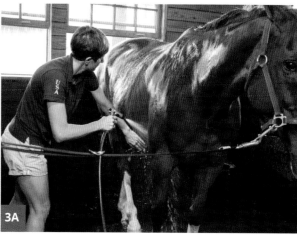

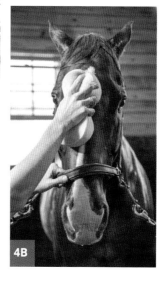

## POST-WORKOUT CARE

After your horse has been ridden, first make sure he is nice and cool before beginning the grooming process. This does not always mean dry! Check his respiration and heart rate (see TPR details on p. 35). Looking at his veins also tells you how he is doing: a horse with his veins still "up" (raised from the skin and easily visible) will likely heat up again if he just stops and stands. The raised veins indicate a horse whose internal temperature is still high. The large muscles in the hindquarters and shoulders retain heat, and slow walking helps to release the heat through the movement of the muscles. When he is warm from a vigorous workout, walking him out until his respiration is down, then getting some water on him, is the best way to cool him out.

### Water Cooling with a Hose

If you have a wash rack and hose available:

**1** Start at the toes if the horse is not used to water.

**2** Rinse him all over from his neck to his tail; use your hands to make sure you are getting all the sweat off.

**3 A & B** Make sure you rinse his armpits, chest, and between his hind legs.

**4 A & B** Rinse off his head if he doesn't mind. Or use a damp sponge to rub out the sweat.

**5** Sweat scrape his body and thoroughly towel off his legs and face. (Never put wet legs into shavings. The fungal skin infection that will follow isn't worth skipping this step!)

Water Cooling with a Bucket

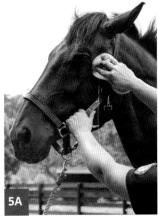

## Water Cooling with a Bucket

If you do not have a hose and wash rack, bucket rinsing is the next best thing.

**1** Fill a bucket with clean cold water and dip your sponge in it. Start at the neck.

**2** Move down the neck to his barrel, spending extra time at the girth area.

**3** Next work toward his quarters.

**4** Make sure to get between his hind legs.

**5 A & B** Go back to his head, getting all around the browband area.

**6** Also, make sure to get the sweat off the back of the ears; be gentle!

When you are finished, towel him off.

# pro tip

If your horse had a jump school, adding a little liniment to his rinse water and wrapping his legs helps ensure he feels good the next day. A horse that has worked really hard on the flat can benefit from a light rubdown with liniment, and wraps if he is staying in overnight.

## Checking for Injury

Now, check his legs all over for bangs, bumps, or cuts. Check his mouth and ribs for rubs.

When he doesn't need to be rinsed, curry and brush him, and reapply hoof oil. Pick his hooves, comb the tail and mane out and make absolutely sure he doesn't have sweat marks anywhere. Common spots people miss are under the belly and next to the ears.

## Standing Bandages

Standing Bandages are a two-part system: First, wrap the leg with a large cushiony bandage called a "pillow wrap," then use a "standing bandage" wrapped snugly to provide support. To wrap legs, we recommend flannel standing bandages. There are many brands, which come in fancy colors. Sometimes they are advertised as "track bandages." However, unless they are made of flannel, they will have stretch to them and although wrapping with stretchy bandages might be easier to learn, it's also easier to do wrong and cause serious damage to a horse's leg.

There are several types of pillow wraps: we use "Wilker's" brand or "no-bows." Wilker's pillow wraps have a foam center sandwiched between a piece of flannel and a piece of cotton. No-bows are made of polyester fleece bonded to a foam center. These are the correct thickness and the right flexibility to ensure proper wrapping. Lumpy, thin, or dirty pillow wraps can cause real problems, and avoid any of the "quick-wrap" options that

have Velcro attached to a pillow. Wrapping is a skill that takes time and practice, and it must be done correctly. Your horse is better off with bare legs and a little liniment than with incorrectly wrapped legs.

**1** Left to right: No-bow pillow wraps and flannel standing bandages.

**2** Start with a nicely wrapped pillow pulled into a tight roll.

**3 A & B** Begin the pillow at the front of the cannon bone, pointing toward the tail.

**4 A & B** Pull evenly and gently on the pillow as you go around, smoothing it out so it lies with no wrinkles.

**5** Tuck the end of the wrap into the pillow right under the knee.

**6** Pull snugly and consistently as you go down the leg, keeping the roll close to the leg and smoothing as you go.

Standing Bandages

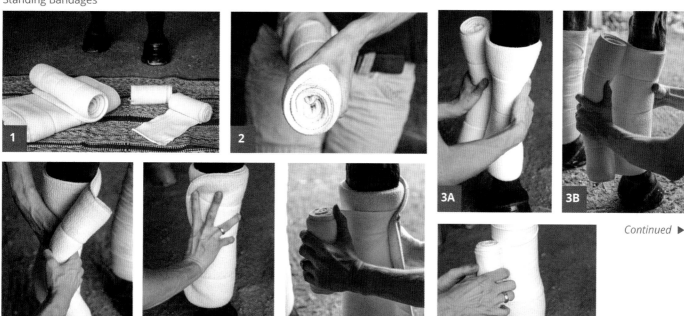

Continued ▶

Standing Bandages (Cont.)

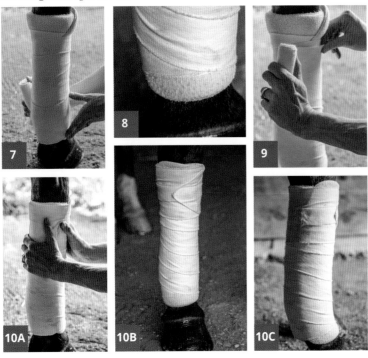

Alternative Method

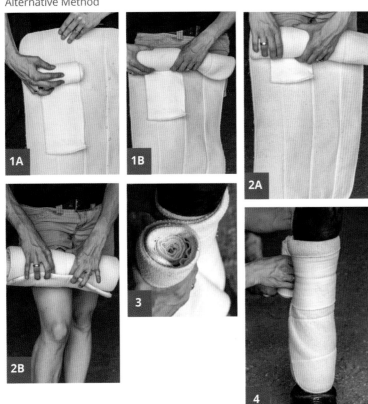

**7** Cup the ankle with the wrap, pulling evenly all the way around.

**8** Create a "V" at the front of the fetlock.

**9** Work your way back up with smooth, evenly spaced wraps.

**10 A–C** End under the knee with your Velcro parallel to the ground and tight.

## Alternative Method

**1 A & B** If you find holding both the pillow and the wrap together complicated, you can start with the tightly rolled flannel wrap inside your pillow. Unroll the flannel slightly and roll them so the tails point the same way.

**2 A & B** Keep rolling all the way down, keeping the pillow nice and tight.

**3** Wrap the legs following the instructions on page 21, or keeping hold of the wrap inside the pillow.

**4** When you get to the end of the flannel, simply begin the wrap at that point.

Complete the wrap as described above.

## Incorrect Pillow Wrapping

**1 A & B** Wrong: Starting in the wrong direction puts pressure on the superficial digital flexor tendon (SDFT).

**2** Wrong: Starting with the wrap low creates an uneven area as you wrap back up the leg.

**3 A & B** Wrong: Pulling at the front of the wrap only or leaving a gap at the ankle can create pressure spots.

**4 A & B** Wrong: A loose, wrinkly wrap is a safety hazard, your horse is better off with bare legs than poorly wrapped ones!

Incorrect Pillow Wrapping

      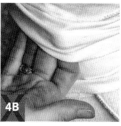

1A · 1B · 2 · 3A · 3B · 4A · 4B

## Unwrapping and Re-Rolling

**1 A & B** To unwrap, undo the Velcro, unroll the wrap close to the horse's leg, and keep loose ends off the ground. Once the standing wrap is removed, grasp the end of the pillow and pull gently, and it will slide off the leg.

**2** To re-roll the wrap, hook the Velcro to itself to make sure you go the correct way.

**3** Using your leg to create tension, hold the end of the roll and pull.

**4** Keep holding very tightly as you roll evenly, using your arm to keep the wrap rolling.

**5 A–C** Wrong: A poorly wrapped, loose pillow is impossible to use correctly.

Unwrapping and Re-Rolling

### pro tip

There are times when you may want to turn out in standing bandages—for a variety of reasons. As with many things horse-related, there are a couple of schools of thought about this and you should go with what makes you feel comfortable. Most horses will do better turned out bare-legged than wrapped. Just moving around keeps the circulation going and prevents inflammation and swelling. But, for horses that have an injury or a circulatory problem, moving around might not be enough, so wrapping is necessary. If you turn out with standing wraps, use a single loop of masking tape around the Velcro to help secure it. NEVER turn a horse out with standing wraps where they can get wet.

      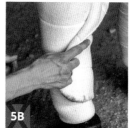  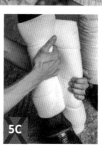

1A · 1B · 2 · 3 · 4 · 5A · 5B · 5C

# BARN CARE

## Grain Room

The other important piece of the day is making sure the barn is tidy and safe. Let's start in the grain room. We like to set up grain for the next feeding prior to meals becoming due. Small, frequent meals are much better for a horse's digestive system, so aim for three or four a day. For people who work and are not at home all day, breakfast (6–8:00 a.m.), dinner (4–6:00 p.m.), and a late-night meal (9–11:00 p.m.) might be the answer.

**1** Using a small bucket with a name label helps to keep things organized.

**2** Putting grain, supplements, and daily medicines into the bucket makes sure each horse gets what he needs.

**3** Keep all grain in bug- and rodent-free containers, and sweep up any spilled grain immediately.

**4** Wrong: Grain left on the edges of buckets will attract flies and rodents. Rinse buckets daily.

**5** If the grain begins to build up on the buckets, they should be scrubbed with a strong dish detergent.

**6** Set them upside down out of the way of horse traffic to air dry.

Grain Room

## Stall Cleaning

Stalls should be cleaned thoroughly as many times a day as you have time for. A working barn cleans at least three times: at breakfast, lunch, and dinner. If you have any extra time, picking the manure out will make your job easier at the end of the day. Ammonia builds up quickly and a dry stall is imperative for horse health.

**1** Looking at a dirty stall can be overwhelming, and it is surprising how many people don't know where to start and end up missing whole sections.

**2** Pick any obvious piles and wet spots.

**3** Then make a pile against the wall and throw a forkful of bedding against the wall on top of it.

**4** Move along the walls, and then work toward the middle.

**5** Manure balls will roll to the bottom where you can easily pick them up and sift out any good bedding.

## pro tip

Pick up manure as soon as it arrives when the horse is on the cross-ties. Leaving it for even a minute will mean a bigger mess to clean up when your horse steps in it, gets it in his shoes, and grinds it to bits!

Stall Cleaning

**6** Turn the whole bed over when cleaning to make sure you have found all wet spots and piles.

**7** Once turned over, rake the bedding back into the center.

**8 A & B** You can either leave a bank along the back and sides for extra bedding and to help prevent a horse getting cast, or you can smooth the bed flat.

**9** Then pull shavings back from the wall under your water buckets and door, and sweep back the door (rake if you have dirt floors).

**10** The end result should be a tidy, inviting stall.

Water Buckets

# How to Rake a Herringbone Pattern

When raking the floor, a herringbone pattern not only looks nice, but also helps to grab all those stray pieces of hay that can slide between the tines of your rake.

**1** First, start by angling your rake 45 degrees from the line of the aisle.

**2** Next, reverse your angle and head the other way.

**3** As you go, periodically rake close to the wall in a straight line to catch any bits left behind.

**4 A & B** Continue until the end of the aisle, then rake a straight line across the end and collect the bits.

**5** The finished product.

## Water Buckets

Water buckets should be dumped, cleaned, and refilled daily. We provide two buckets at all times and fill them throughout the day. You can never provide too much clean water!

**1** Water buckets should be hung at the front of the stall, high enough to be out of reach of pawing front feet, and low enough to be easy to drink out of.

**2** Wrong: When hanging buckets in a stall, never put your snaps facing up or out. They can hook onto horses' eyes and cause major damage.

**3** Snaps should face down or into the wall.

## Grain Buckets

**1** Grain buckets should be hung in a corner where the horse doesn't feel threatened while eating. A wood partition between stalls near horses' grain buckets can prevent fighting between the bars. Ground feeders should be regularly scrubbed and placed on the clean area of the floor.

Grain Buckets

## Hay

**1 A & B** Hay should be either put near the water buckets on the swept section of the floor or hung in a small-hole hay net high enough so that hooves have a hard time reaching it.

Hay

## Miscellaneous Barn Tips

Now let's move to the rest of the barn:

**1** Hay should be stored in a separate building from the horses if at all possible; hay is a major fire risk. A hay cart helps prevent hay from being dropped all over the aisle so you can bring in a bale or two at a time.

Miscellaneous Barn Tips

**2** Water spigots should be located near drains and hoses should always be coiled out of the way.

**3** Exit signs should be located above all doors; in a fire it's easy to get turned around in the wrong direction.

**4 A & B** A barn should have a fire extinguisher at every exit, and a fire ax to add extra protection.

**5** Electrical outlets subject to getting wet should be covered.

**6 A** Wrong: Cross-ties hard-tied to the wall are unsafe...

**6 B** ...so attach to the wall with a loop of baling twine or thread that will break easily. Always put an emergency snap at the wall end of the cross-ties; getting close enough to a panicking horse to undo the snap when it's attached to him could be dangerous.

**7** Once stalls are cleaned, the aisle is swept or raked.

**8** Electrical cords are coiled and taped.

**9** Wrong: Fan loose; electrical cords dangling; hose on the floor; too-low hay net; water bucket on the ground; lead rope dragging.

# CHAPTER TWO
# "Cleaning Out the Corners"

## Emma says

At Phillip Dutton's True Prospect Farm, all horses are jogged up every Monday morning. No matter if we have 30 horses or 60 horses in the barn, our awesome vet, Dr. Kevin Keane, assesses the horses for soundness, from Advanced Level down through the four-year olds. This provides Phillip, Kevin, and me with a wealth of information as to how each individual horse has dealt with week-to-week work as opposed to being at a horse trials or coming off an FEI competition. Occasionally, there are days when the jog is not until the afternoon so I always have the working students jog up any horses that competed over the weekend before turning them out for the morning. I do this for my own peace of mind not wanting to turn a horse out that might be lame. One Monday morning after a CIC competition, I jogged the Advanced horses and they all looked great. Three hours later I had to get them in for Dr. Keane and Phillip. One horse was 3-out-of-5 lame. I was horrified. I think Phillip thought I must have been sleeping on the job. However, with the working student who had jogged him to back me up, Phillip knew I had originally seen a sound horse. After a good work-up it was concluded that he had a little too much fun in the field and knocked himself a bit too hard!

## WEEKLY MUST-DO'S

To ensure a clean and safe environment for your horse there are some chores that should be done weekly or bi-weekly, depending on the season and your own available personal time. If they are kept up on a regular basis, they will be less time-consuming than if they get left to do once every other month. Regular check-ins also alert you to equipment that might need repair before it breaks, as well as make sure that certain items don't become dangerous from neglect.

## Cobwebs

Cobwebs

**1** De-cobwebbing is a major safety precaution in every barn. Cobwebs are very flammable and should be swept down weekly to reduce risks of fire.

Taking a broom, sweep over all surfaces, rafters, stall bars, and around windows to remove them.

Fans

Drains and Wash Rack

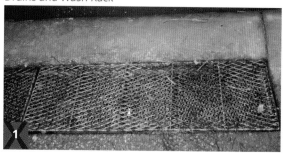

Bedding

## Fans

**1** When buying a stall fan, it is essential to buy one with an enclosed motor so that there is less likelihood of dust building up around the running motor. Also pay extra attention to removing dust and cobwebs around it. It should be hung on the outside of the stall where horses cannot reach it, and have the cord neatly kept out of the way.

## Drains and Wash Rack

**1** Wrong: Clogged-up drain. All drains should be cleaned on a regular basis to prevent a bad odor and clogging up. Many barn drains have a double layer of grills to help catch debris. Both of these should be removed and thoroughly cleared of any debris buildup. Pour bleach down the drain to help prevent odor. Instead of using chemicals when you have an open drain, weekly doses of vinegar are a nontoxic way of preventing bacteria.

The neglected wash-rack muck tub is a pet peeve of most professional grooms. It must be emptied daily, preferably at the end of the day. It should also be rinsed regularly to prevent nasty buildup.

## Bedding

**1** At least once a week all the bedding in the stalls should be banked up to allow the floor to dry.

Sunlight is a great disinfectant; however, with stalls that do not get a great deal of natural light, lime powder (available at most good feed stores) can be added to the floor. The lime helps to remove the ammonia odor that comes from the urine.

## Brushes

**1** Dirty brushes make a dirty horse, so washing all brushes at least once a week is a must. If your horse has some kind of skin condition then brushes should be washed daily with an antibacterial, anti-fungal wash, such as Betadine® scrub. For full effectiveness, brushes must soak in Betadine for at least 60 seconds to kill bacteria and fungi. If

**barn gossip**

At a large hunter barn one year, we had a young rider sent to us for a little "polish." A typical teenage boy, he was a bit of a mess. After a few weeks of pulling my hair out about how to get through to him, I developed a system of punishment to suit the crime. Anytime he left a mess, he had to pick up all the mats from the wash rack, and scrub the concrete, mats, and drain by hand. We have never had such a beautiful wash rack! *—Cat*

Brushes

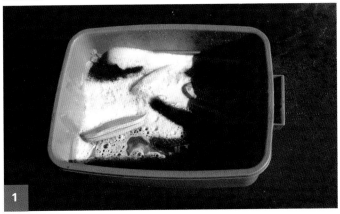

1

you have a lot of horses, it's a good idea to use individual grooming kits to reduce passing on infections from one horse to another. Skin diseases such as ringworm can easily and quickly be passed around a barn when everyone uses the same brushes.

## Feed Room

**1 A**  Wrong: A messy, dirty feed room.

**1 B**  Feed rooms should be swept clean daily; however, if time is usually short, then the feed bins and any portable shelving should be pulled out at least weekly and swept behind. If you have a shop vac it is great for providing that extra cleaning power. When your feed room consists of trash cans in a stall or on a dirt-floor tack room, be extra careful to use a broom and sweep under and around the area to prevent digging rodents.

Take an inventory of feed, hay, and bedding. It is essential to have a good idea of how quickly you go through these commodities in a week. In summer, you do not want feed hanging around in high humidity or temperatures, and in winter you need to have enough to last you for at least two weeks should bad weather affect delivery or pick up of these necessities.

## pro tip

Did you know that the water buckets in your horse's stall pick up ammonia? This is one more reason why water should be given fresh and buckets scrubbed out every day. If you have dirt stalls, when you bank the stalls back, rake the center to help prevent pits and holes developing. It also gives you a chance to check for large rocks that might be "growing up" from the floor.

## FARM MANAGEMENT

### Paddocks, Fields, and Fencing

Checking your paddock fencing is essential to minimize injury from failures in the fencing. Board fences need to be checked for loose nails, broken boards, or loose posts.

Feed Room

1A

1B

# Fencing Options

**1** In an ideal world, all fencing would last forever, but in reality, maintaining fencing can be costly. There are many safe and effective methods of fencing, but they must be maintained. Woven wire makes an ideal fence, but it must be kept free of weeds. Board fence is another good option. Electric fence does a nice job but horses must be properly introduced to it so they do not panic the first time they touch it. With all forms of fencing, we prefer to see a lane between paddocks or fields to prevent fighting or playing over the top board or wires.

**2** Putting a strand of electric wire along the top of a fence can prevent horses from doing damage by leaning, chewing, or "sitting" on the fence. It also can help prevent fighting between paddocks.

**1 A** Wrong: This split-rail fence has missing boards.

**1 B** Wrong: A board has separated from the post.

**1 C** Wrong: The gate has bolt ends jutting out that could catch a horse's body.

**1 D** Wrong: The post has a rotted middle and needs to be replaced.

**2** Wrong: Woven-wire fence should be checked for sagging sections, broken wires, or holes. This picture shows a sharp, cut wire that is sticking into the field.

Vinyl board fence should be checked for sagging, loose post clips, and damage from the sun that results in cracking, discoloration, and weak spots. Electric fencing should be checked for tightness to ensure there is no place where a leg can get caught in the wire or tape. Also make sure any fencing is free from weeds and excessive growth. Not only can weeds short out electric, they can also climb up and "pull

down" woven wire and make it hard to see board and vinyl fence.

**3** Wrong: Large-hole fence like this is just as dangerous as barbed wire. Neither should be used under any circumstances.

**4** Wrong: Walk through the paddocks to check for hazards. Perhaps there is a bit of string that got missed when putting hay out?

**5** Wrong: Has that pesky groundhog made its hole again? Has your horse dug near the fence and caused a hole he could get cast in?

## Poisonous Plants and Weeds

When ingested there are many plants that cause serious illness, even death. If horses are provided with plenty of good grazing they will tend to stay away from such plants, and many of these plants have a "defense mecha-

nism" such as a leaf-oil or sour-taste deterrent. It is not abnormal in certain areas to see horses grazing among buttercups that are toxic to horses but left uneaten when there is plenty of grass around. When your horse is in a dry lot or overgrazed pasture, ensure plenty of hay is given or the pasture is clear of weeds.

Also, watch for your friendly neighbor who thinks that throwing his garden cuttings in the paddock is giving the horses something to chew on. Many oriental garden plants are toxic, oleander and rhododendrons are two examples, so have a friendly chat explaining the situation. If your paddocks have oak, yew, or red maple trees close to the fence line, watch for acorns and leaves falling in because you will need to remove them. Wilted red maple leaves are very sweet and some horses acquire a taste for them, but they can be very toxic. Yew trees are evergreens and carry leaves year round, so check weekly that leaves are not migrating into your pasture. Even the beautiful cherry tree can be poisonous.

Jogging Up

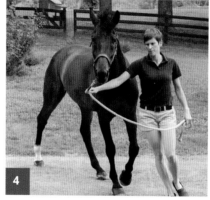

Burdock can be found throughout the country, and while not poisonous, it can be the cause of extreme grooming frustration when the seeds are caught in your horse's mane and tail.

## HORSE HEALTH

### Jogging Up

Whether you are a pleasure rider, competitive amateur, or a professional, knowing what "normal" is for your horse is paramount. Jogging your horse in hand on a regular basis both for yourself or a knowledgeable person (vet or trainer) should be done once a week. For competition horses this should be in the off season as well as during the competition season.

## pro tip

When jogging, you need to evaluate your horse's overall movement, evenness of footfall, and length of stride. Sometimes a horse will take even steps but if you listen, he might not land as lightly on one foot or the other. Have someone jog him for you so you can watch from behind. Does he move evenly behind or does one hip drop more than the other? Once you understand what "normal" is for your horse when you jog him, each week you will start to see if anything has changed. However, consider whether the horse has worked hard the previous day, been stall-bound, or on night turnout. Has his routine changed? Many horses will jog stiffly out of their stalls if they have run a cross-country the day before while if they've been turned out all night, they look fresh as a daisy!

Teaching your horse to jog correctly is important. This makes life easier when your vet or farrier needs to watch his gait when a problem arises. Train him to move forward into a controlled trot while in hand. You might need to use a whip, depending on your horse's sensitivity. Start by using a non-slip surface, such as grass or gravel driveway, making sure your horse is walking forward and beside your shoulder. Use a voice command along with a light touch of the whip at the flank to ask him to jog.

**1** Wrong: Do not get in a dragging match.

The horse is on your right so use the whip in your left hand behind your back. Your right hand should have light to no tension on the rope or reins. When the horse has a positive forward response, do not pull on his head, but allow him to move forward in a straight line.

**2** Wrong: When the horse's head is not straight it can affect how even he looks in front.

**3** The horse should be straight, active, and on a loose contact with the runner by his shoulder.

**4** When turning at the end of a jog strip, move your horse away from you to the right. If he spooks, with luck, he will spook away from you instead of on top of you!

**5** Once your horse can jog sensibly in hand you will need to be on a hard surface to evaluate soundness. Here Dr. Kevin Keane evaluates a horse on a hard-packed driveway at Red Oak Farm in South Carolina.

## Know TPR (Temperature, Pulse, Respiration)

As with soundness, knowing your horse's TPR is essential so you know when your horse is not feeling so good. This information should be known so you can give it to your veterinarian when he comes to examine your horse. By taking his TPR weekly, you are able to assess a situation quickly, which will help you make a decision whether or not to call a vet. Fitness level, air temperature, and the horse's natural temperature can all affect his TPR.

## Temperature

**1 A & B** Taking the horse's temperature is simple with a digital thermometer. Dip its end in some lubricant, such as Vaseline, and place in the rectum until it beeps. If you use a mercury thermometer it should stay in for three minutes for accuracy. Be sure you hold on tightly to the end of the thermometer; to be safe you can use string to tie it to the tail.

Temperature

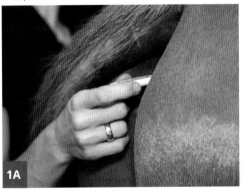

1A

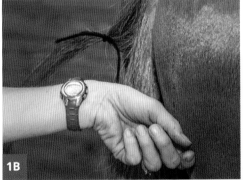

1B

## Normal TPR Guidelines

**Temperature:** 99–101 degrees F (37.2–38.3 C)

**Pulse:** 28–44 beats per minute

**Respiration:** 10–24 breaths per minute

You should take the horse's TPR in different situations: at rest, after light work, after a gallop, on a humid hot day. Knowing this information is vital in understanding your horse's health.

## Pulse

**1 A & B** For those without a stethoscope the easiest place to read a pulse is by finding the lingual artery on the bottom side of the jaw that crosses the bone. Use your middle and index finger; your thumb contains a pulse that can misrepresent what you are feeling. Count the beats for 15 seconds and then multiply that number by four to get the beats per minute.

Pulse

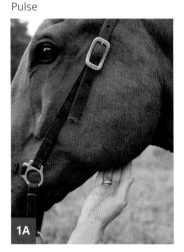

## Respiration

Watch the horse's flanks move in and out for 30 seconds then multiply that number by two for breaths per minute. Do not put your hand over the nostril as this can worry the horse and cause him to breathe more heavily.

## Hydration

**1 A** Simply take the skin of the horse's neck between your thumb and forefinger, and gently pinch to tell if your horse is dehydrated.

**1 B** The skin should snap back within two seconds; when slower, he might need water.

**2 A–C** Mucous membranes should be wet and a salmon-pink color. When gums are pressed, the capillary refill should be within two seconds. Again, dry gums and slow refill can be signs of dehydration, but can also indicate infection or shock. Notify a vet if your horse is showing these signs.

## Eyes

**1** Healthy eyes should be bright and shiny with no discharge. Continual water-streaming or cloudiness is abnormal.

## Nostrils

**1** Healthy nostrils should have no discharge, or if they do, it should be clear; a yellow or green discharge, and/or with a foul odor, are signs of infection.

## Gut Sounds

**1 A & B** Having noise in the gut is a horse's best friend. When you are

Hydration

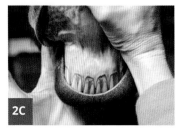

Eyes

Nostrils

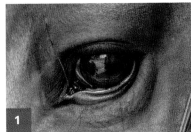

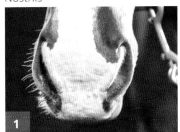

concerned your horse might be showing signs of colic, put your ear to both sides of the belly, high and low. No gut sounds, meaning neither a gurgle nor a rumbling, is *not* a healthy sign.

## Manure

**1 A** Check manure daily. A healthy pile should be free of grain with soft balls that break on impact. Every horse is different; a general rule is when stalled for 12 hours, you should see around 7 to 10 piles.

**1 B** When you find hard manure check your horse for dehydration; when manure is very soft and loose, assess your routine over the previous day or so.

Ask yourself has his diet been changed? New supplement added? Turnout routine altered? Medication given, or dewormer? Has there been a stressful event at the farm: a new horse, construction, or change to his workout regime? Occasionally, horses develop runny manure when they travel. When none of these has occurred, check his temperature and hydration level in case he is developing an infection. If all appears normal, try adding a handful of dry bran to each feeding to regulate his digestive system and return manure to normal. If this does not change, try adding a probiotic to his diet. If the problem persists, watch his hydration levels and check in with your vet.

Gut Sounds

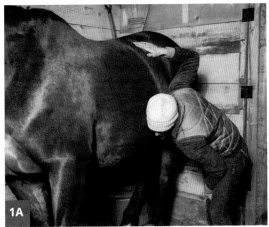

Manure

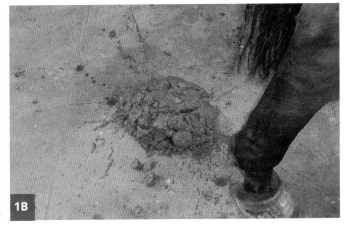

# CHAPTER THREE
# "Like Clockwork"

## Emma says

*True Prospect Farm was originally built by a Dutch family in the 1980s. At the time, the barn was the height of technology, including an underground manure system, an automatic feeding system, and all stalls outfitted with automatic waters. The feeding system has long since gone, the underground manure system has since been replaced with the good old–fashioned wheelbarrow, and the automatic water system continues to be problematic from time to time: some horses choose to rub on the water bowls, and others will sometimes kick the pipes (which are protected by mats) and loosen the plumbing. So when not caught quickly, the barn can become flooded.*

*The first Christmas I worked at TPF I came down in the morning to feed to find water flooding the aisle. I had no idea how to turn off the water main, so I proceeded to wake up the many employees and working students who live in an apartment next to the indoor to try and solve the problem. You needed a special tool that was hidden under the stairwell, then had to uncover some wooden slats to get to the taps to turn off the water. Now, when new people come to work at TPF I show them exactly where and how to turn off the water supply, but I also make an effort to check the waterers for potential failure on a regular basis.*

## PERIODIC CARE

While day-to-day and weekly care is incredibly vital to making sure we stay on top of our horse and stable care, there are certain things that must be taken care of periodically and routinely. Because they aren't done daily, these items can often get away from you. Make sure you have a calendar that outlines when these deadlines are coming due. Make appointments in advance because vets, farriers, and bodywork professionals get their schedules filled far ahead.

## Veterinarian

Vital to any horse are periodic vet evaluations. A good working relationship with your vet helps in so many ways. In veterinary medicine, there is shorthand "NQR," which means "not quite right." When a vet doesn't know your horse, and you tell her the horse is not quite right, she can't help you determine what is wrong with as much conviction as a vet who sees the horse regularly.

There are two categories of veterinary visits, *well-visits* and *urgent care.* Let's split them up.

Well-Visits

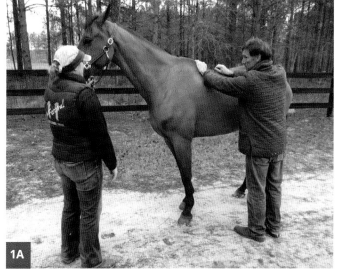

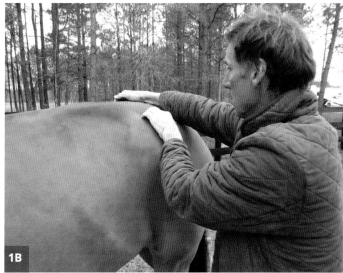

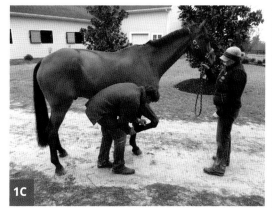

## Well-Visits

Well-visits are your vaccination visits. These are necessary for all horses in the spring or fall, whether or not they compete. So when the vet comes to give shots, ask her to do a well-horse evaluation, as well. This entails running her hands over the whole horse, asking about his habits, and maybe watching the horse move at the walk or trot. Sometimes, when we see our horses daily, it's easy to miss a little weight loss, or a sore spot that has been slowly getting worse; an expert can catch problems before they get out of hand.

We recommend monthly well-visits called "soundness checks" for actively competing horses during the competition season. Dr. Kevin Keane does regular check-ins on Phillip Dutton's horses, and is shown here performing a general wellness exam.

**1 A & B** During these visits the vet feels all over the horse's body.

**1 C** He carefully checks legs.

**1 D** Wrong: Make sure you stay on the same side as the vet, not the opposite as I'm doing here. If the horse should spook when you are on the other side of the vet and you pull the head, your poor vet will get run over.

**2** The vet watches the horse trot out.

Often, the vet will also do flexions of the horse's joints then ask you to trot him off. Little changes to the horse's gait and body can herald big problems, so having your vet catch them early can keep your horse sounder for longer.

For a number of winters, I worked as Dr. Kevin Keane's assistant in South Carolina. One of the most respected soundness veterinarians in the industry, travelling around with Dr. Keane was one of the most educational experiences I have ever had. Something that astounded me was the number of people who were afraid of early intervention in their horses' soundness. When a horse is competing in a strenuous sport, some maintenance might help the horse to feel his best, so Dr. Keane would often recommend preventive maintenance in the form of Adequan® or Legend® injections for horses competing heavily. If a horse had been diagnosed with degenerative arthritis, he might recommend intra-articular joint injections. Arthritis has been found in wild mustangs, so it is a naturally occurring part of the equine aging process. Modern medicine has created some wonderful ways to help slow down the process and help a horse feel more comfortable well into his competitive career. In the past, this procedure caused joint degradation, but that is no longer the case. While it is absolutely necessary for it to be performed under aseptic techniques, when done properly it does nothing but assist the horse.

Remember, any time a horse has a painful area of his body, he will compensate for it somewhere else in his body. Additionally, an old campaigner most likely needs a bit more help to keep him comfortable even when doing lower levels. *—Cat*

At-Home Medical Kit

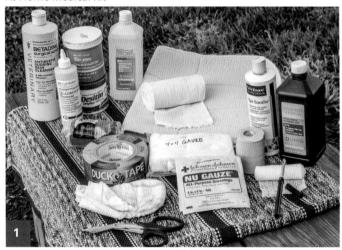

### Urgent Care

Periodically, you may need to call your vet for an urgent care or emergency visit. It is important to know the difference, since vets often cover a large area and need to know which horse is in a life-or-death situation and which can wait a few hours. *Urgent care* can be everything, from hives, coughs, minor injuries, or a mild colic. An *emergency visit* will most likely be an acute injury or a serious colic. First, before you call your vet, do a little triage. When you have a horse with a giant gash bleeding everywhere, it's an *emergency*. Or, when you have a horse with hives or a dry cough, it's an *urgency*. Stating the condition of your horse as truthfully as possible ensures that the vet has all the details to react accordingly. Make sure you have a well-stocked first-aid kit for both home and the trailer so you can help keep things under control until your vet arrives.

**1** Your at-home medical kit:

- Betadine® scrub (to clean wounds)
- Alcohol (to disinfect)
- Hydrogen peroxide (to clean dead tissue)
- Epi-Soothe® (a cortisone shampoo to soothe skin issues)
- Desitin® (cream to keep moisture out of skin problems like scratches)

- SSD (powerful antibiotic, antifungal, antipruritic cream, also very gentle)
- Quadritop™ (steroidal antibiotic topical medicine)
- Thermometer
- Scissors
- Gauze roll and non-stick squares
- Vetrap™ (4 inches wide)
- Standing wrap
- Diaper
- Duct tape

Discuss with your vet whether or not to have Banamine® (flunixin meglumine) a non-steroidal anti-inflammatory on hand. The oral paste tube is great for easy administration and is safe. Banamine can help to relieve the pain of colic and keep a horse comfortable until the vet arrives.

## Body Care

Consider saddle fit and body care: any horse that wears a saddle should have one that fits well. Just like us, a horse with a sore back feels bad everywhere. An experienced saddle fitter is the first key to a pain-free horse. You must be aware that as a horse goes through the year his back muscles will change from work, so periodically check to make sure the saddle doesn't need slight adjustments to prevent back issues from developing.

A good bodywork professional is vital for horses that work hard. Whether you use a chiropractor, acupuncturist, massage therapist, or some combination of them all, your horse will be the better for it. The best person to tell you if the professional is good or not is your horse: when he "fights," resists, or needs to be strongly restrained during treatment, he is not reaping the benefits the therapist has to offer. Some bodywork can be uncomfortable for a moment, but once the release is triggered, your horse should relax into the work and allow the treatment to help him (see more on body work on p. 220).

## FEI Rules

For FEI competition, an equine passport and drug administration sheet are necessary. There are very strict rules regarding the administration of vaccinations and your vet is an integral part of making sure that the passport is kept up to date. Passports are tricky. The vaccinations that are required must be given at certain intervals. Missing one can mean having to do several at the correct intervals to get back up to date. This delay can cause disqualifications and missed competitions. We always have our vet double-check our passports at the beginning of the season to make sure we are on schedule. Drug administration rules currently require all FEI-controlled substances to be recorded, so work with your vet to make sure pain management, injections, and even antibiotics are noted. Since FEI rules seem to change with the wind; always stay on top of changes and requirements before administering vaccinations and drugs!

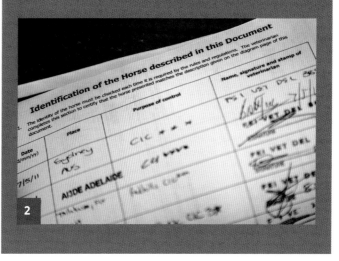

Body Care

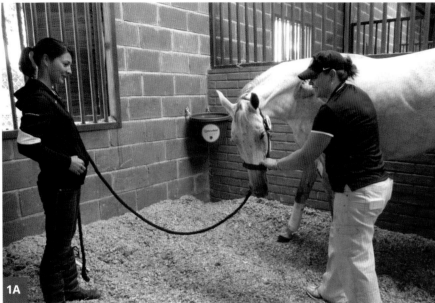

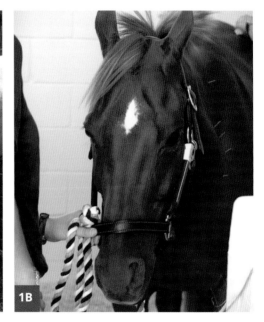

**1A** Angie Cooney, the US Eventing Team masseuse, working on Michael Pollard's "Hanni" at the 2011 Pan American Games.

**1B** Teddy O'Connor getting acupuncture at the 2007 Pan American Games, where he won the gold medal.

## pro tip

A good massage can make or break a performance horse's moment in the spotlight. For the dressage horse, having a pre-test workup can help him relax his back so he can truly "give" his back to the rider. For a jumper or hunter, a rub down after a hard class can make sure he stays loose in the back and careful in the hind end day after day. For an eventer, a rub down after cross-country at a tough event can make the difference between jogging up sound and jumping well on show-jumping day, or getting eliminated in the final jog evaluation.

## Dental

Every horse needs his teeth worked on regularly. Getting him checked every six months makes sure nothing gets out of hand, and in our opinion, once a year is mandatory. Since horses chew in a sideways motion, they create sharp points on the edges of their teeth that can cause ulcers in the side of their mouths. This mouth pain can create problems under saddle as well as prevent good mastication of feed and hay, which can cause choke or poor condition.

Dental

Parasite Control

1A

1B

1C

1D

**1 A**  A good horse dentist uses a speculum to hold the horse's mouth open and head up while he looks into the horse's mouth.

**1 B**  The dentist uses a variety of tools to carefully rasp the points off sharp teeth, as well as check for loose or broken teeth, or any other issues.

## Parasite Control

We've all heard the old standby of rotational deworming— the problem being that rotational deworming for decades has developed some "super worms" in some areas that are resistant to standard drug treatments. In addition, more and more, we are being warned to medicate only when necessary, and that refers to deworming, too! While rotational deworming had its place, the best way to achieve a parasite-free farm is to do fecal testing. Your local vet should be able to do this for you: all you need is a zipper-lock sandwich bag and a brand new pile of manure. Do not use manure found in the stall that could have been sitting out, flies will lay their eggs in it and confuse the results.

**1 A**  Label the bag with the date and horse name.

**1 B**  Turn the bag inside out with your hand inside.

**1 C**  Remove one ball of normal manure with the bag.

**1 D**  Zip the bag, call your vet, and find out where you can drop it off!

*Continued* ▶

Parasite Control (Cont.)

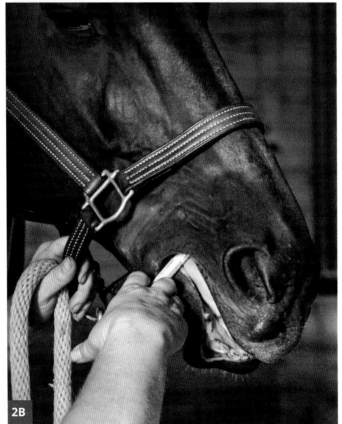

**2 B** Put the syringe inside the cheek and as high as you can get it.

**2 C** Depress the plunger. Hold the horse's head up for 10 to 15 seconds to help him swallow.

If managing your deworming program by fecal counts is not possible—for instance, at some boarding barns, regular deworming is required because of the large number of horses coming and going throughout the year—it is important to understand which dewormer to use and when.

Strongid® C is a popular *daily* dewormer that is supplemented twice a year with either Quest® or Quest Plus: one in the spring and the other in the fall. It is still highly recommended to do a fecal count at least twice a year to make sure your horse is in good health. Using the daily dewormer might form a resistance, so long-term it may not provide the protection against parasites that is required.

If you decide to do a rotation of dewormers, your year should look similar to the following:

**January:** Anthelcide® EQ
**April:** Quest or Quest Plus
**July:** Anthelcide EQ or Strongid paste
**November:** Quest or Quest Plus

In spring and fall, Zimectrin® should be given to cover bot larvae.

Always make sure that you discuss the best plan for your individual horse with your veterinarian.

**2 A** When you do need to deworm, take the cap off and turn the dial to the desired positions.

It is important to realize that in warmer southern climates, you should give the Quest one month earlier where worm infestations arise sooner. The reverse is true for northern climates.

## Farrier

Farrier care is vital to a horse's health. Whether your horse is an active athlete or a quiet pasture pet, without solid feet, he will not be comfortable or happy. How frequently your horse gets cared for depends a little bit on his workload, time of year, and individual animal. Horses grow hoof based on the blood flow to their feet. Blood flow increases with work and temperature: higher temperatures and more work equal more blood flow and more hoof growth. So a horse in the summer in heavy work might need his shoes re-set every four to five weeks, while a barefoot horse in light work can go eight weeks. Here are some signs to evaluate when your horse needs to be shod or trimmed:

**1** Do the nails look tight and the hoof fits the shoe well (the shoe should be easily visible)? This is a recently shod horse.

**2 A & B** Are the nails loose or sticking up? Does the hoof wall hang over the shoe? This horse needs to be shod.

**3** Is the hoof wall breaking away, long in the toe or uneven? This unshod horse needs a trim.

### Pulling a Shoe
You may find yourself needing to remove a shoe. If your horse has stepped on his own shoe and bent it (referred to as "springing" a shoe), or has managed to shift

# Deworming for "High Shedders"

Some horses are known as "high shedders." This means they continually have a high egg count and when in pasture with others can be the catalyst for some of the other horses also developing a high fecal count. Once this horse has been recognized, he will need to go on a strict deworming program with fecal counts taken to ascertain when the parasites are under control. In this situation, a good dewormer rotation consists of the following:

- Start with a Panacur® paste
- Follow in eight weeks with Zimectrin®
- Follow four weeks later with Strongid®
- Follow four weeks later with Zimectrin®

Farrier

1

2A

2B

3

Pulling a Shoe

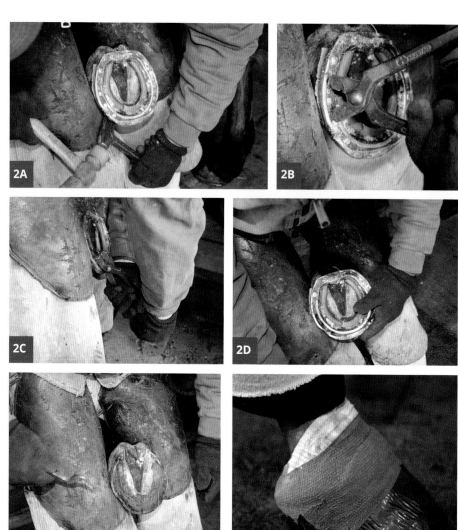

it so he is stepping on a clip, the shoe has to come off. Prolonged standing on a "sprung shoe" will cause lameness and when a horse is standing on a clip, he can puncture his sole. Farrier Russ Young shows us the correct way to pull a shoe.

**1** You need on hand: nail pullers, shoe spreaders, and a rasp.

**2 A** First stand with the horse's leg between your legs, grasping firmly with your thighs.

**2 B** Use the nail pullers to grasp the nail.

**2 C** Then rotate along the shoe to pull the nail out.

**2 D** Repeat on every nail; the shoe should just slide off.

**2 E** You will end with a clean hoof, with very little damage to the walls.

**2 F** Follow the directions on page 227 to wrap the hoof up until your farrier can attend to your horse.

## Sheath Cleaning

Many people find sheath cleaning to be their least favorite horse duty. However, it is a necessity for good health in the domesticated male horse, geldings in particular.

A male horse collects *smegma* in his sheath over time. This is actually a natural process used to provide lubrication for his penis. Over-cleaning this area can in truth do more harm than good because the sheath contains naturally friendly microorganisms that main-

Sheath Cleaning

 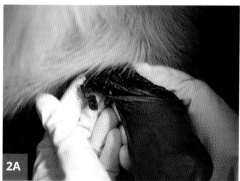 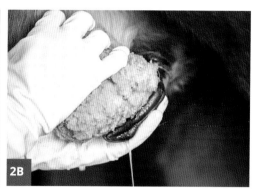

tain a healthy environment. Too much cleaning can cause damage and upset this balance. If you think about it, horses in the wild never have this process done and they seem to live and reproduce just fine. Some research shows that wild stallions actually have better reproductive percentages than those domesticated that have their sheaths cleaned three to four times a day depending on their breeding schedule.

Since geldings do not breed, however, they can build up more smegma than is healthy.

## Frequency

**1** The most you should need to clean a gelding's sheath is twice a year. Using warm water is ideal, and on some horses necessary, in order to prevent getting kicked. Dedicated cleaners such as eZall® sheath cleaner are best; never use antibacterial or harsh cleaners such as Betadine scrub or dish soap.

## How to Clean

Be very careful doing this job. Some horses tolerate it while others will not let you get near their sheath. Obviously, it is easier when a horse relaxes and lets his penis hang down. Take note of the times of day when this happens so that you can make the most of him already being relaxed.

**2 A** Using a glove, place a large amount of sheath cleaner into your palm, wet the shaft, and gently rub the area until the smegma is loose.

**2 B** Hose or sponge the area off with warm water until it runs clean.

## The Bean

**3 A** Now you need to feel for the "bean," an accumulation of smegma that forms in the small pocket at the end of the penis.

**3 B** It can get as large as a lima bean and if not removed you might find the horse has trouble urinating comfortably. Gently feel for the bean and you should be able to squeeze it out the tip of the penis.

The Bean

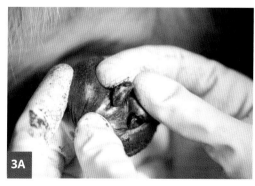 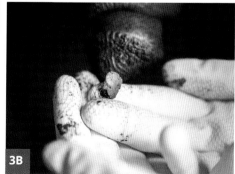

## pro tip

Some horses secrete smegma onto their legs on a regular basis, so use baby oil in these areas to help prevent the smegma from sticking to their legs. When it is necessary, just use a mild dish soap that cuts through the grease, such as Dawn® or Ivory®, to remove the oil and debris.

If your horse does not "drop down," no problem. Slowly insert your hand into the sheath area and gently work away at the sheath walls. The penis sits pretty high up so you will go as deep as your elbow. If possible, ask your vet for a couple of long gloves; this makes your job a little less messy. If your horse allows, slowly insert the hose into the sheath to wash away loose debris. Always use warm water and let it run until nothing is falling from the sheath. When your horse does not tolerate this process, ask your vet to sedate him for you, or have your vet do the process in conjunction with another procedure that requires sedation. Always be aware of your horse's behavior; never put yourself in a position where you can get kicked.

# CHAPTER FOUR
# "The Full Monty"

## *Emma says*

For me, clipping horses is an extra source of income. I started doing this when I was 14 years old and some of the first ponies I clipped did not look so pretty! Years on, I have improved my technique so, on a regular basis, you will find me clipping out two to six horses a day during the winter months. However, even with all this experience, I still make mistakes. I had been clipping at this hunter barn for a couple of years and on this particular visit they gave me an 18-year-old, pure-white pony to clip out. Without checking my blade length first, I started to clip the pony as always, beginning on the shoul-der, then realized that the blades were the wrong length and cutting the hair very short so it looked as if I had surgically clipped him. I changed the blades to medium length and these proceeded to make terrible track lines. In short, I did a horrendous clipping job. The more I tried to correct the track marks, the more lines I made. Luckily for me, the pony wasn't showing anytime soon. Obviously I didn't charge for the job but I will never forget the embarrassment of having to tell the owner about my mistake. I haven't clipped a pure-white pony since!

## CLIPPING

### Why Do We Clip?

In their natural environment, horses produce enough coat to protect them from the harsh elements. As you all well know, we have changed their environment in many ways: with ever-improving blankets; work and training; heated wash stalls; and for many, moving them to warmer climates to continue training in the winter.

Removing the hair by clipping makes it easier to keep the skin and coat condition in good shape during the winter months. However, the main reason for clipping is to ensure the horse can work efficiently, then be cooled off in a timely fashion so he doesn't get chilled while drying. When he gets the chills, it can lead to sore muscles, and, worse still, serious illness.

It can actually be very difficult to keep good condition on a horse that is in moderate work and not clipped. Excess sweating, as well as being too hot, whether standing in a stall or during exercise, can both lead to a horse losing condition. A clipped horse that is not kept warm enough will end up using his fat reserves to maintain body heat. In warm climates, you may need to clip year-round if your horse has a heavy coat. In cold climates, you should be careful to clip appropriately to your horse's workload, and make sure you have the right blankets.

You may find that you will need to clip your horse several times throughout the year. Some horses, no matter how well you blanket them, will grow a coat as quickly as you can clip it off! A *trace clip* that works well in the fall may need to be increased to a *hunter* or *show clip* as the horse's workload increases. (See p. 60 for a list of clipping styles.) Although many people in the northern climates believe clipping a horse after the winter solstice is a bad idea, when your horse grows a heavy coat in April, you might not have an option but to re-clip and help your horse to be as comfortable as possible while working.

## Deciding When to Clip

Answer these questions to decide *when* to clip:

*Where does your horse live?*

For example, if you live in Massachusetts all the time, you may only need to clip your horse for the winter. However, if you live in North Carolina, you may need to

### pro tip

In upper-level eventing, year-round clipping out your horse prior to a big competition is paramount to the all-important efficient recovery after cross-country. Taking off the extra hair can reduce cool-out times by 10 minutes. Your horse's internal temperature can rise by as much as 4 or 5 degrees, depending on fitness level, air temperature, and workload. A fast cool-down cuts down muscle fatigue and heating up of internal organs, which can have serious detrimental consequences when not taken care of properly.

do a clip year-round. If you move your horse from New York to Florida for the winter, you will certainly need to clip him since he will have grown a northern coat for a southern winter.

*What is your horse's workload?*

How much work your horse is doing and how sweaty he gets is a big factor in determining when to clip. Dressage horses doing an hour of heavy work, jumpers working on big jump courses, or eventers doing gallop sets in warmer climates need to remain cool and not overheat while working.

*How long does it take for your horse to dry after his workout?*

Remember how you feel after a long run on a chilly morning. The quicker you dry, the warmer and less stiff you feel, so if your horse is taking a long time to dry, he might need a clip. A good rule to follow is the "one-third rule." If your horse is not cool and dry in one-third the time it took you to work, he needs a clip. For example, if you ride for 30 minutes, it should not take your horse more than 10 minutes to be cool and dry. If you ride for one hour, it should not take more than 20 minutes for your horse to be cool and dry.

*What is your horse's turnout schedule?*

During the winter months in the northern states, many ridden horses remain on 24-hour turnout. If yours is one of them, always leave his legs and face unclipped. Your horse will need his hair to protect him from the elements. With the blankets available now, keeping your horse warm and dry while outside during the winter has never been easier.

*If competing, when is your first show or event?*

For readers in the north who pleasure ride or do not start competing until mid-April, you may not need to clip your horse at all. For those who compete earlier in the

Preparing for Clipping

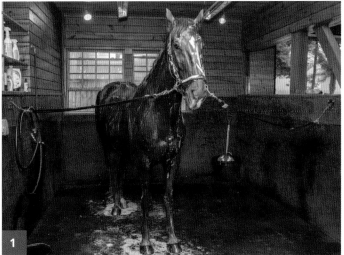

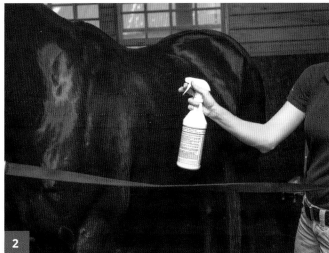

year at indoor shows or go south to get a head start on events, you will probably find that a clip is required to maintain a healthy coat and condition, and for your horse to be show-presentable.

## Preparing for Clipping

**1** First, give your horse a good shampoo bath. Pay attention to the top of the rump, legs (if clipping them), and the head. These areas tend to be the worst and a dirty horse causes clipping blades to become dull and sometimes the motor to overheat. Your horse should be completely dry before clipping. Nothing dulls blades faster than wet hair.

**2** Next, spray and towel your horse with a coat-conditioning product such as Cowboy Magic® Super Bodyshine®. This helps to provide sheen to the coat, which allows the clippers to move through easily.

**3 A & B** If you don't have the luxury of a heated wash stall and it is too cold to bathe him, curry him really well, spot clean really dirty areas, then wipe a hot damp rag in circles over the area you are clipping. If there is one available, use an equine vacuum. It does a great job at getting the deep-down dirt up. Apply a coat conditioner and towel it in.

Tools Needed for Clipping

## Tools Needed for Clipping

**1** Assemble what you need:
- Large clippers
- Small clippers
- Size 10 or 15 blades
- Extension leads
- Clipping oil
- Coolant
- Rubbing alcohol in a tub wide enough to dunk clipper
- Blades
- Brush
- Towel
- Witch hazel
- Step stool
- Non-fleece clothes (for you!)

### Clipper Blades and Sizes

**1** The small Andis® clippers that have interchangeable blades are very popular and a good way of saving money as you won't need two sets of clippers.

**2** Blades come in different widths and lengths. Both the T84 Blade and Oster® Wide Blade are as wide as a regular

## New to Clipping?

If you have decided a trace or blanket clip is the way to go, you can help yourself by drawing lines on the horse using chalk or by applying tape (see p. 60 for clipping styles).

large blade, and therefore, can be used to body clip. The narrower blades could be used to body clip but it takes a long time: they are really useful for the head, legs, and any tight places. The number on the blade indicates how short the hair can be clipped: the *lower* the number, the *longer* the hair. A 10 or 15 blade is the correct length for body clipping.

**3** Large clippers are really useful if you have several heavy-coated horses to clip or have multiple horses to clip in one day. The Lister® brand clippers are our favorite because they are sturdy, quiet, and clip without leaving lines.

Clipper Blades and Sizes

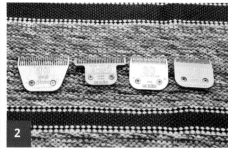

Preparing a Safe Clipping Area

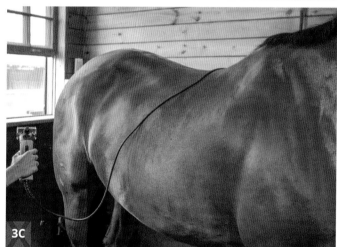

## Preparing a Safe Clipping Area

If it is the horse's first time, it is safer to have someone hold him rather than cross-tie him. The last thing you need is your horse spooking, then hitting the cross-ties and getting into trouble.

Pick a time to clip when you have at least two to three hours available. You don't want to feel rushed. (Remember though, bathroom breaks might be necessary for both of you within that time period.)

**1** Your clipping area should be free of clutter and large enough to allow you to move around the horse easily.

**2** A shelf should be available to lay out your equipment so it's out of reach of the horse but in an efficient place for you.

**3 A–C** Wrong: Ensure that your extension leads are long enough to get around all of the horse *without* having to go over, under, or through his body or legs as demonstrated in these photos. There should be enough slack that the wire can lie out of reach.

It is wise when clipping for the first time to have someone else in the barn with you in case there is an incident.

## Getting Started

**1** Wrong: Non-parallel blades like those shown on page 54 will cause bad track lines. Make sure the blades are on straight.

**2 A & B** Using clipper oil, follow the manufacturer's instructions as to where to place the oil. Most clippers

Getting Started

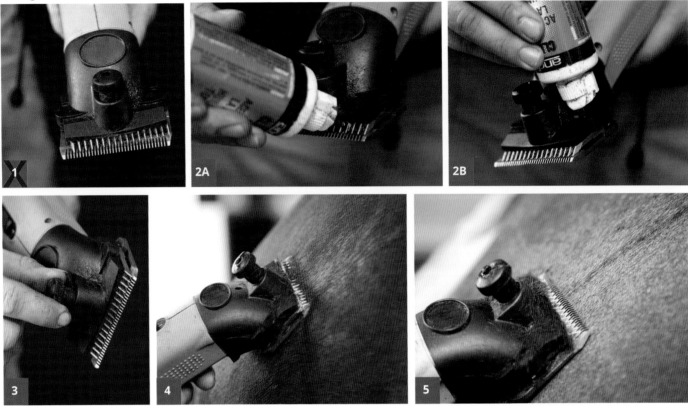

have about five holes in which oil needs to be regularly placed. Oil should also be placed on the underside of the blades. Excess oil should be wiped off with a towel to prevent it passing onto the horse's skin.

**3** Most large clippers have some form of tension mechanism. Follow manufacturer's instructions.

**4** Always use even pressure, moving the clippers against the natural growth of hair. With a nervous horse, run the clippers over the horse's entire body with them turned off. Do this until your horse shows signs of relaxing.

**5** Your first strokes should be on a big muscle, such as the shoulder. The horse's ticklish areas include: behind the elbows, belly area by stifle and sheath, and around the ears. Leave these areas until the horse is quiet and relaxed.

## Things to Remember

**1** Check the motor and blades for heat. Hot blades can easily burn you or the horse. To cool them, use a coolant spray or dip the running clippers into rubbing alcohol (this also helps to clean the blades). You may need to turn the clippers off for a while. If possible, switch to smaller clippers while waiting.

**2 A & B** Brush excess hair from the blades and air vent on a regular basis.

**3** Be careful around the elbow and stifle area. The skin can easily be cut here if you dig the blades in too deep.

**4 A & B** On the elbow area, use one hand to stretch the skin out flat to prevent lines and nicks.

**5** On the chest area, pick up the leg you are working on and float the clippers over the sensitive folded skin.

Things to Remember

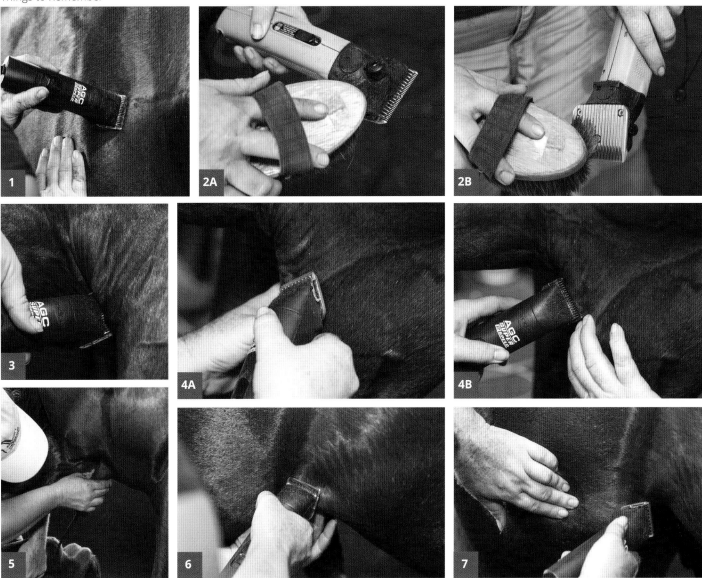

**6** Use your free hand to smooth the skin underneath the flap of skin joining the stifle area to the barrel to prevent nicking the skin.

**7** Stretch the skin tight to help make sure you've got all the hair.

Be aware of your horse's behavior. Some will let you know when they are losing patience. When your horse is unhappy about being clipped in a certain spot, redo an area that he doesn't mind, then go back to the "bad" area when he is more relaxed.

## Clipping Legs

**1** Use either the large clippers or the wide blades on the small clippers down to about the knee. For fine-boned horses such as Thoroughbreds, small clippers tend to be better for the lower limbs. Still clipping against the hair, use your free hand to stretch the skin over the bone so you can remove the hair between the tendon areas.

**2** If your horse is a little touchy on his leg, pick it up as if picking out a foot. Use your free hand and knee to steady the leg. The tendon area will be in a relaxed position and should be easier to clip cleanly. Be careful not to point the clippers straight down; you can easily cut the sensitive skin on the leg.

### Leaving Legs Unclipped

**1** You want to leave a clean, sharp line at the top of each leg. With the front legs you follow the muscle line between the bottom of the shoulder and top of the leg.

**2** You are aiming to make an inverted "V" where the top of the leg meets the chest.

Clipping Legs

**3 A & B** For the hind legs, visualize a line that starts at the point of the stifle and runs in a diagonal line to the bottom of the horse's hamstring.

**4** You want to make a clean "V" at the back of the leg.

Leaving Legs Unclipped

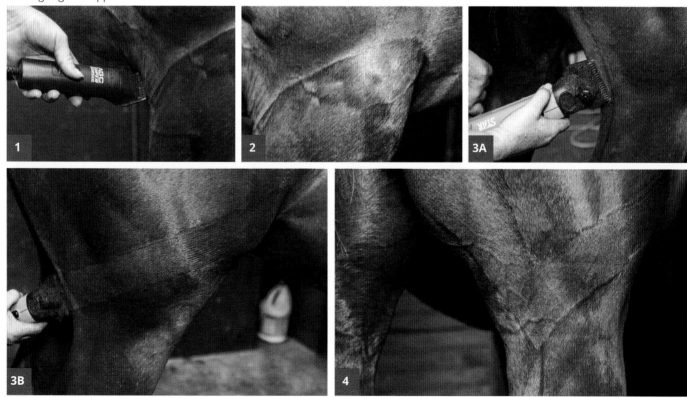

## Clipping the Head

How much of the head should you clip? Much like the rest of the horse, this depends upon a variety of factors. Horses that will be shown while clipped should have the front of their faces clipped. Horses in steady work, living in a cold climate and not showing should be clipped under their chin and cheeks. Horses that live outside in the north should not have their heads clipped unless a full, insulated face hood is worn.

Use the size blade that is closest in length to the large clippers: size 10 or 15 would be typical. Try a test area low on the belly to see the result. Many horses have had an unfortunate scalping of their head (or legs) when size 30 blades have been used by mistake.

**1** When clipping only to the cheek line...

**Clipping Entire Head**

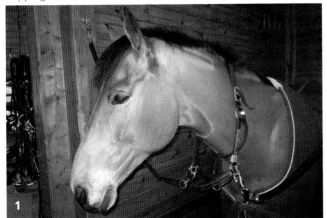

Clipping Only to Cheekline

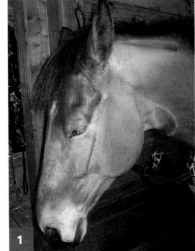

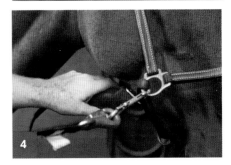

**2** ...hold the skin at the bottom of the jaw and push the clippers toward the cheekbone.

**3** Continue down the face, drawing a line between the lips and cheekbone and ending there.

**4** Clip under the chin and muzzle.

### Entire Head
**1** When doing the entire head...

**2** ...start by doing the ears first. Carefully squeeze an ear in the palm of your free hand.

*Continued* ▶

Clipping Entire Head (Cont.)

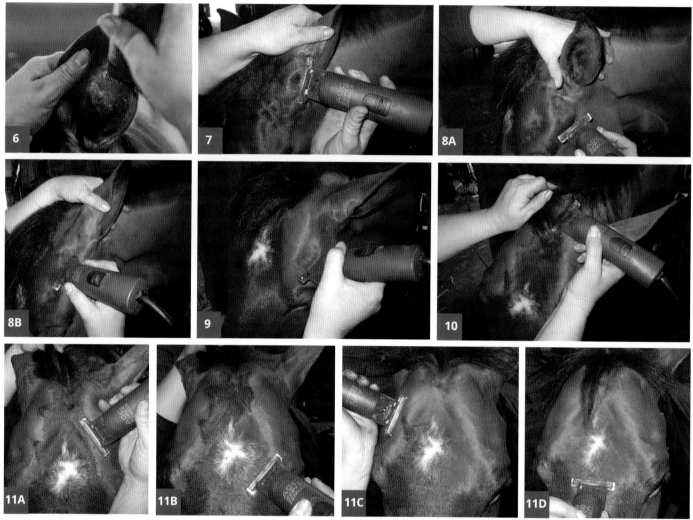

**3** When not doing the inside of the ear, run the clippers from the tip of the ear to its base.

**4** For the outside of the ears, start at the tip and clip down the outside of the ear.

**5** Run your clippers down the edges of the ear.

**6** When clipping the inside of an ear, run the clippers from the top down, being careful as you approach the bottom not to stab the clippers down.

**7** At the front of the ear the hair grows across it, so clip from the outside to the centerline.

**8 A & B** Carefully work down the face toward the eye, taking note of the direction of hair growth.

**9** Be extra careful at the eye sockets. The horse has a pocket above each eye that you will need to carefully scoop out.

**10** Clip until you reach the forelock, being careful not to catch the forelock in your clippers.

**11 A–D** Take note of whorls and the way in which the hair is growing. You will need to clip into the center whorl from each direction.

Top of the Tail

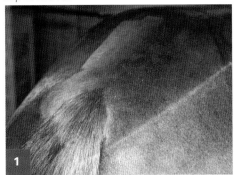 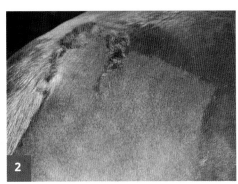 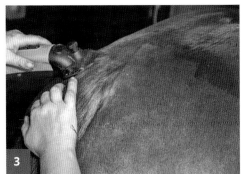

Removing Track Lines

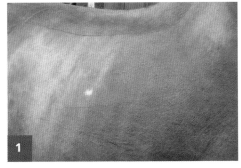 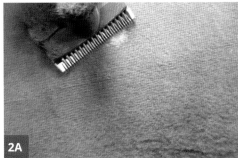 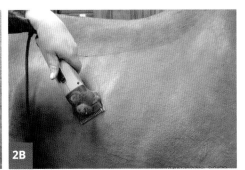

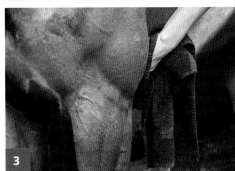 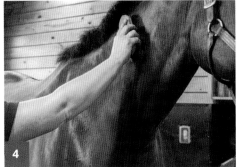

Please do not clip your horse's long eye whiskers. They provide a vital warning to a horse when his face is getting close to an object. Without them, your horse can damage an eye.

## Top of the Tail

**1** To leave a cleanly clipped finish, the final touch is to create an inverted "V" at the top of the tail.

**2** From the outside edge of the dock, clip a line toward the dorsal line.

**3** Repeat on the opposite side making sure the angle is the same.

## Track Lines

**1** Removing the dreaded track lines.

**2 A & B** These can be caused by a dirty horse, inconsistent pressure, and hot and/or dull blades. When trying to remove the lines first go against the track line, then reverse the direction you are clipping. Think about making a cross or "X" pattern across the line. Then go back over it against normal hair growth direction.

**3** Take your witch hazel and towel and wipe over the area, and hope the line has disappeared!

**4** When weather permits or you have a heated wash stall, give your horse a bath after clipping. This helps to remove any residue oil from the coat and reduces the likelihood of him having a skin reaction. If bathing is not an option, dust cornstarch on a medium-bristled brush and flick it all over your horse to help make sure that there is no clipper oil left on the skin. This also helps to remove the short, sharp, clipped hair pieces.

## Types of Clip

### Belly Clip

**1** Good for lesson ponies and horses in very light work. You remove hair from the belly and up through the legs, to the underside of the neck. You can finish at the top of the throat or you can also remove the hair on the underside of the jaw line.

### Trace Clip

This clip can take various forms: It's very useful for horses in moderate work that sweat at the bottom of their necks and flanks; also great for ponies and horses turned out at night during the colder weather. They stay warm—not too

Belly Clip

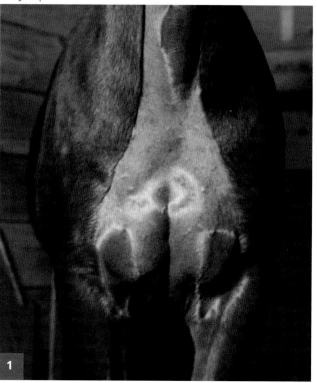

Trace Clip

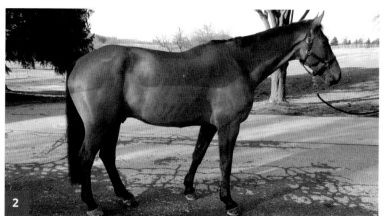

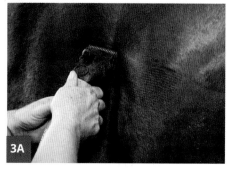

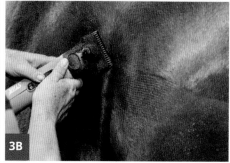

Continued ▶

Trace Clip (Cont.)

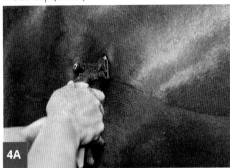

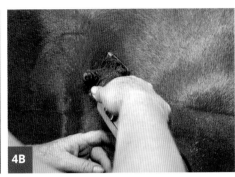

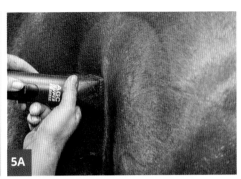

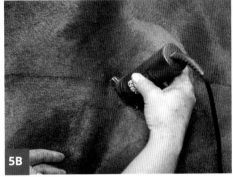

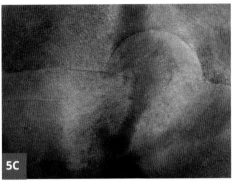

much blanketing is needed—but they dry more quickly after work. There are a few ways to do trace clips. The most commonly used ones are the *steeplechase clip* and a *high trace clip*.

**1** To do a *steeplechase clip*, start at the bottom of the flank and take a diagonal line up across the belly and to the base of the ears; you can leave it there or remove the cheek area of the face.

**2** A *high trace clip* is for a horse in regular work and on a lot of turnout. He can work without getting excessively hot and will not need heavy blanketing. Remove the hair from the lower part of his quarters, half of the belly, and half of the neck. How high you go is your choice and the decision should depend on where your horse sweats the most. For instance, if you have a horse that sweats heavily at the flank, clip more from that area. If he sweats more on the neck, clip higher toward the crest.

**3 A–C** The tricky part of the *high trace clip* is the flank area. This is where a chalk line or tape helps. Start behind the flank, point your clippers up, and gradually draw an arc toward the center whorl.

**4 A & B** Next, move your clippers to the other side and repeat the arc in reverse.

**5 A–C** Grab your small clippers to clean up the area, cutting the hair toward the whorl from all directions. You will end with a smooth arc.

## pro tip

When you need to clip for a particular show, plan on doing it at least two weeks beforehand. Some horses are very sensitive to clipping and may get a skin reaction: you will need the time to calm the skin and get it back in shape. If you have to deal with this, I recommend using Equifit® shampoo and talc products; SSD cream is great to use on the legs to help skin recover. An apple cider wash is also beneficial in these cases. I took care of Phillip Dutton's four-star horse, Fernhill Eagle, for years. No matter what oil, clippers, or coolant I used, he would always break out after being clipped. Knowing this, I had to be on the ball when deciding when to clip him: too close to a competition, he would have very sore and sensitive skin; too far out, he would regrow his coat to the point that he would need clipping again! *—Emma*

Blanket Clip

Hunter Clip

**Blanket Clip**

**1** Think of putting a quarter sheet on your horse. Except for the legs, everything outside of the sheet is clipped. It's a good clip for horses that work throughout winter and do some hunter paces, paper chases, or indoor jumper shows.

**Hunter Clip**

**1** To be used when a horse is in full work. It takes a lot of blanketing too: the horse cannot be left "naked" anytime during winter because you have removed his line of defense against cold. Sometimes a quarter sheet

# Blanket Rubs

When you have a horse with the beginnings of a blanket rub, it is important to treat it immediately before it gets out of hand.

**1** First, treat the symptom of hair loss with a skin protectant and softener to help the hair regrow and prevent skin irritation.

**2** Rub it in well, leaving a little extra there to prevent friction.

**3** Next, switch blankets to find a better fit. Often, putting a silky sheet under a turnout blanket helps protect the shoulders.

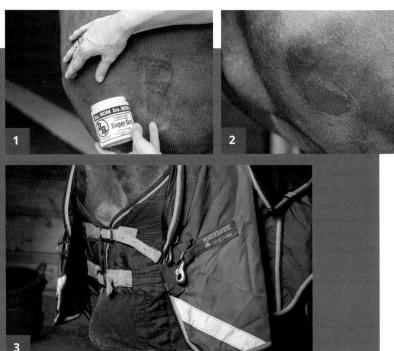

Show/Full Body Clip

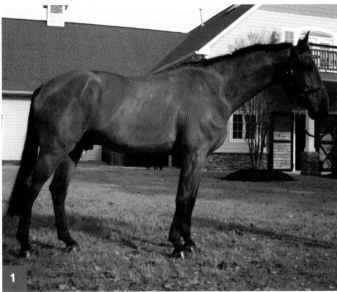

**Show/Full Body Clip**

**1** Used when your horse is in full competition mode—especially during the winter. His entire coat is removed from the tips of his ears to hairs around the coronet band. You need a good stable-management program for fully clipped horses: blankets need to fit well to prevent rubs, and they need to be changed during the day to accommodate changes in weather. Extra care must be

## pro tip

When you leave a "saddle patch" of hair, take your regular saddle pad, position it in its normal place, and draw its outline on the horse. If you try to clip around the pad itself, you risk the pad or the horse shifting as you try to clip and, before you know it, you have no saddle patch left!

## Sedation

Remember, if you need the help of sedation to clip your horse prior to competition, be sure you know the drug rules and "withdrawal time" for that particular sedative. Never sedate your horse without first consulting your veterinarian.

taken with boots and bandages to prevent a rub that could develop into a nasty infection. For horses living in the colder winter climates, night turnout is impractical, and if your barn is on the cold side you might need to bandage your horse's legs at night to help him to maintain his warmth.

A full clip might be needed in summer so your horse can cool down more efficiently. But there is another reason for a full body clip: Cushing's Disease, where a horse cannot shed his coat sufficiently to regulate his own body temperature.

## CARING FOR A CLIPPED HORSE

For this section, let's assume it is winter and you live in the colder regions of the United States. Common sense plays a major role, and the style of clip decides how you should groom, wash, and blanket your horse.

### Grooming

**1** During the winter, bathing a horse is only an option when hot water and heat lamps are available.

Prior to riding, fully groom your horse as detailed on page 6; however, a blanket- hunter- or show-clipped horse should retain his blanket while being groomed. Be sure that belly straps and hind-leg straps are undone and properly reattached as soon as you start grooming. This way you won't forget to undo them when you go to remove the blanket—it's a safety issue.

is required to warm up or cool your horse down so his muscles can stay warm and relaxed. By leaving the legs unclipped, you protect him from bad weather, mud, cracked heels, and scratches.

Grooming a Clipped Horse

2A

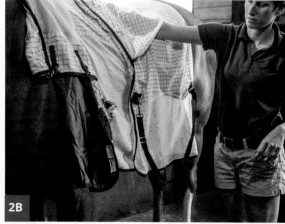

2B

3

4

## pro tip

**1** One of my pet peeves is blanket leg straps being left undone. Due to their length and position on the blanket, they dangle much more than belly straps.

**2** I am always telling working students to reattach these before taking off a blanket. On one occasion, I was holding a horse for the vet, while a friend went to put on a blanket. The leg straps were free and proceeded to catch on a ceiling fan. Needless to say, the horse was very spooked, and I got a little trampled. The students watching then understood why I was always nagging about such a simple, yet important task! —*Emma*

1

2

**2 A** Wrong: The leg strap in this photo was forgotten, and could cause the horse to panic as I pull it off him. You can see him cocking his hind leg at me, preparing to kick at the leg strap.

**2 B** Here the leg strap has been undone, then safely done back up on the outside of the leg. This prevents trailing leg straps from being caught up.

**3** Fold the blanket in half toward his tail and groom the front end first.

**4** Then reverse it, covering the shoulders and back, and groom the hind end. This allows the horse to stay warm. Leave the blanket covering the quarters while you tack up.

## Quarter Sheet

**1** Remember to use a quarter sheet when you start your initial warm up, then have it at hand for cooling out. When doing a light workout, use a wool quarter sheet during the entire ride to prevent chills and tension.

# Cooling Out/Washing Off

## Coolers: Knits and Woollens

There are many options for coolers to help keep your horse comfortable in cold weather. "Cooler" simply refers to any breathable, wicking sheet used during the cool-out process to maintain warmth. Catalogs call them by many names, so let's clarify.

**1** A *net* is exactly as it sounds: an open weave net that is used to help keep dust and flies off.

**2** A *scrim* is the next lightest weight in coolers. Little more than a *net*, a *scrim* is also used to help keep dust and flies off but will also provide a small amount of warmth on a windy summer day.

**3** *Irish knit* refers to a loosely woven cotton cooler. With air holes and a light weight, this is used for moderate weather or as an under-layer used with a heavy cooler to help promote air circulation.

Quarter Sheet

Coolers

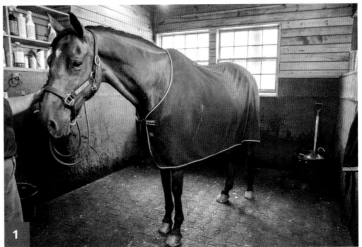

Continued ▶

**4** A *fleece cooler* is made of either cotton sweatshirt material or polyester fleece. These range in warmth rather dramatically based on thickness and quality. We use the cotton-sweatshirt ones to keep a horse warm between classes in moderately cold weather. We prefer the high-quality, heavy-weight, polyester fleece coolers for cold

Coolers (Cont.)

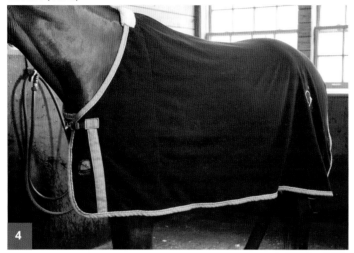

4

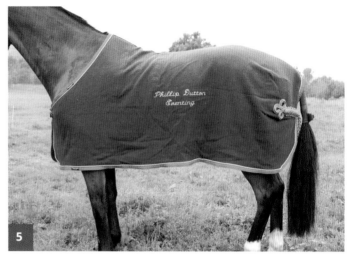

5

Placing a Cooler

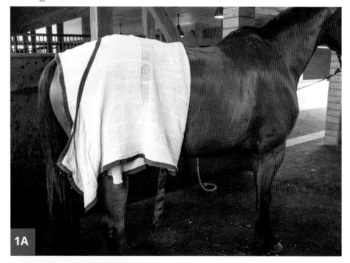

1A

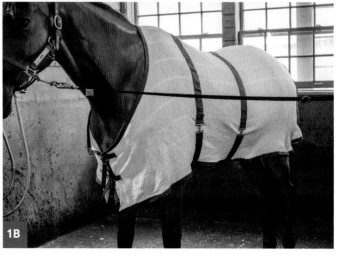

1B

weather. Easy to wash and quick to dry, a polyester fleece cooler is a staple item in a northern barn to help a horse cool down and dry off after getting sweaty in the winter. Many even come with a shaped neck attachment that is perfect for keeping the entire horse warm. Avoid the large, square coolers, though. Since they are not close fitting, they can get a draft underneath and create a chill.

**5** A *wool cooler,* sometimes simply called a "woolly," is a heavy cooler made of pure wool. Woollies are invaluable to have because they are warm even when they get wet with sweat—they help to wick sweat without allowing a chill to reach the muscles. We use them ringside to keep a clipped horse warmed-up and ready, as well as using them at home to keep him warm in extreme cold. A woolly is a great choice for shipping a clipped horse; it breathes well and keeps him toasty.

## Placing a Cooler

**1 A & B** When you get back to the barn after riding, place a cooler over the horse's quarters while untacking. When removing the saddle, place the cooler onto the horse fully so the saddle area does not get chilled.

If your horse is only slightly damp, spray witch hazel or rubbing alcohol on the damp areas, and rub dry with a towel. Once dry, you can fully groom and blanket your horse.

Washing Off

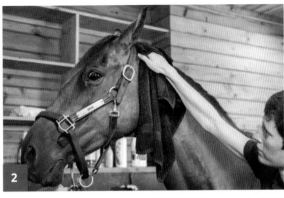

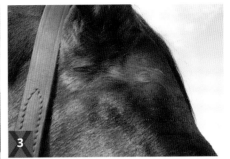

## Washing Off

**1** However, when your horse is sweating, place witch hazel and a squirt of Ivory® soap in a bucket of warm water.

**2** Wet a towel and dip it in the solution. The small amount of soap will help to pick up dirt and sweat spots without foaming, so rinsing off won't be required. Rub vigorously to get the sweat from the skin.

**3** Wrong: Pay attention to the horse's face; you should never find dried sweat marks, as shown here, on his brow!

**4 A & B** When he is not completely dry, use an Irish knit or scrim as an under layer with either a woolly or fleece cooler on top (see Blanketing, p. 68). This combination helps to wick away moisture.

## pro tip

**1** When removing coolers, it is a major pet peeve to see people just fling them off and throw them on the ground. A clipped horse often creates static electricity, and pulling the cooler off him quickly over his rump can give him a nasty shock.

**2** Instead, fold the coolers to the center of the horse's back and lift them off one at a time.

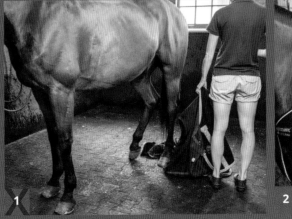

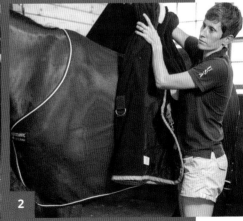

Blanketing

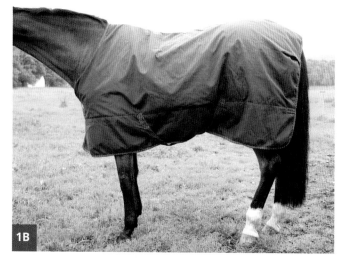

When using a fleece cooler, you should change the top layer if you see vapor sitting on the outer blanket. Fleece does not retain warmth once it is wet. Wool will continue to keep him warm even if it looks wet. In Photo A, you see a combination of an Irish knit and woolly, and B is a scrim and fleece cooler.

## Blanketing

When *you* are wearing 10 layers of clothing, it is reasonable enough to assume your horse might need a heavier blanket to stay warm if he has a hunter or body clip. Now, knowing your horse well will come into play here; some horses definitely run hotter than others, so experimenting with blankets might be needed to help keep your horse comfortable. Years ago, it was very common to have day blankets that were breathable and turnout blankets that didn't breathe at all but were waterproof. Nowadays, you can buy a complete set of quality waterproof and breathable blankets that will stay in good shape for use inside and out. For a complete set, you want waterproof blankets in three weights:

**1 A** A lightweight one with a neck attachment, sometimes referred to as a rainsheet.

**1 B** A mid-weight one.

**1 C** And, one that is heavyweight with a neck attachment. This way when it's quite cold out, you can layer the lightweight with the neck over the medium-weight should the heavyweight blanket get too wet to dry quickly. If you are working on a budget, a layered blanket system can be a lifesaver. These systems come with a breathable liner and a waterproof, breathable exterior blanket that attaches to the liner.

**2 A–E** The Rambo® Duo is one of our favorite blanketing sets. The liners come in many different weights and are not normally meant for use without the over-blanket. You can buy a few extra liners that can be easily laundered and switched out so your horse can have on clean "underpants"!

The Rambo Duo

2A

2B

2C

2D

2E

## pro tip

Blanket snaps should never face out. Many people don't understand why this is important. I have had the misfortune of seeing many horses in tough situations: I have found a panicked horse hooked to a wire fence by the chest strap where he had been rubbing. I have seen a horse rip his lip to bits from biting at an itchy flysheet and getting caught in the chest snaps. It's a simple thing to do: just point the clips in! —*Cat*

**1** Wrong!

**2** Right!

1

2

Specialty Blankets

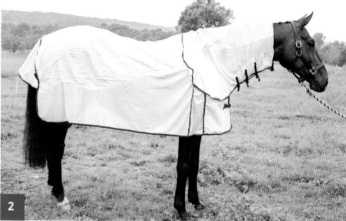

the neck and often under the belly. It can be a necessity for a sensitive horse's turnout during the summer.

**4** A *fly mask* is a must when you clip the inside of a horse's ears to protect him from biting insects.

## Blanket Care

It is very important to re-blanket your horse daily. Even if you are not riding and only have time to pick out his feet, reset the blanket so that its pressure points that are created by shifting are released. This reduces rubbing of shoulders and withers. It also lets you assess the blanket and buckles for any weak or broken spots.

Blanket Care

## Specialty Blankets

In addition to a quality set of blankets for everyday use, there are many others that are useful to have:

**1** *Stable blankets* come in several weights but are not weatherproof, so are used inside. They are great to have for horse shows because they are easy to launder and keep looking nice.

**2** *Sheets* are another option for use in the barn and at shows. A sheet can be used in warm weather to keep a horse clean; as an under-layer to everyday rugs; and to help prevent a rub developing on a shoulder. For horse shows, there are sheets with a neck attachment to help keep the entire horse clean.

**3** A *fly sheet* is made of mesh and generally extends up

Folding a Blanket: Method One

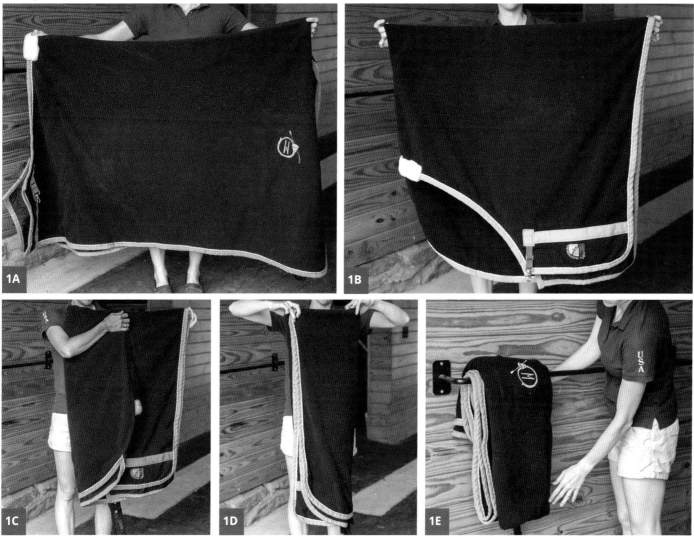

1A 1B 1C 1D 1E

**1** Wrong: Here the Velcro on the tail flap has ripped. This should be fixed since it will cause a draft from behind.

## Folding a Blanket

A blanket should always be folded neatly and hung up. Blankets chucked over the wall or railing are not only not very nice to look at but potentially dangerous. Belly and leg straps hanging down can get tripped over or get caught on a horse; then, suddenly, you have a loose blanket attached to a horse! A blanket touching the ground can host mice overnight; as a consequence it gets holes or stains in it. There are two ways to fold a blanket:

**1 A** Method One is used for lightweight coolers and sheets.

**1 B** First, fold the blanket in the middle with the chest and tail lined up. Make sure the belly straps are inside the fold, and the leg straps are hooked up.

**1 C** Next, fold each side of the blanket into the center, starting with the neck...

**1 D** ...then the belly.

**1 E** Finally, hang with the folded edge facing out.

Folding a Blanket: Method Two

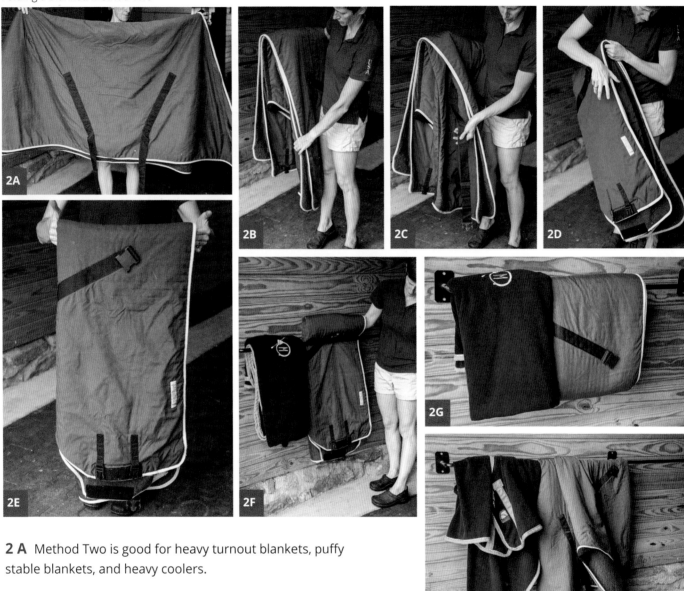

**2 A** Method Two is good for heavy turnout blankets, puffy stable blankets, and heavy coolers.

**2 B** First, fold the blanket in half widthwise.

**2 C** Check that the belly straps are inside the fold.

**2 D** Fold the blanket in half again lengthwise, using your arm as a guide.

**2 E** Line up the neck with the tail.

**2 F & G** Finally, hang with the folded edge out.

**3** Wrong: Hanging blankets haphazardly not only looks a mess, but also creates a hazard for horses to get tangled in.

# CHAPTER FIVE
# "Bits and Pieces"

## Cat says

At the Pan American Games in 2011, Buck Davidson was our leading event rider out on course. The first few riders out had trouble, so we were all a little charged up for him to come home clean. As all the grooms waited at the finish to catch his mare and cool her out, we saw them come over the last fence and knew they were clean and within the time. We were all going a little crazy cheering for him, doing this ridiculous little dance we had come up with over the week, and Buck comes through swearing and grimacing. In the commotion, we were all so con-fused and he wasn't making any sense: the course was filled with terrain and his mare was quite green at the level, so we knew it wasn't an easy ride, but he should be so happy! He had set a great mood for the day! We finally got out of him that his stirrup had broken at the very beginning of the course, and he had ridden the rest of it one-legged. His leg was so cramped he could hardly straighten it to dismount. Turns out, the composite stirrups he was using must be kept out of a hot environment or they will weaken. One of them had simply given out!

## TACK

Other than your horse, tack can easily be one of the biggest investments you make. Good quality tack can last a long time with the correct care, and your safety often depends upon maintaining it.

### Everyday Care

Whenever you use tack, plan to take care of it. Cleaning prevents mold and rot, dryness, and the buildup of sweat, which can break down the fibers of the leather.

**1** Cleaning supplies include:
- Glycerin saddle soap
- Oil or conditioner
- Saddle balsam
- Saddle cleaner
- Scrub brush
- Towel
- Sponge
- Scrub sponge

Cleaning Supplies

Cleaning Bridles and Strap Goods

## Cleaning Bridles and Strap Goods

**1** When you finish riding, hang your strap goods on a hook clear of the wall.

**2** Fill a small bucket with warm water, put your bit in it and leave it to sit.

**3** If it was a really humid day, also take all the straps out of their keepers.

**4 A & B** Using a glycerin-based soap, scrub all of the leather, paying special attention to the inside of the noseband, cheekpiece, and browband.

**5** Rinse out your sponge or use a damp towel to wipe off any excess soap or suds.

**6 A & B** Using a conditioner or oil, lightly coat the leather, doing up the keepers as you go.

**7** Use a dry towel to wipe off the bit and any metal buckles and reattach the bit, being careful that it is on correctly.

**8** For a bridle with rubber reins, use the "scrubbing" side of a sponge to get sweat off or else it will break down the rubber.

**9** When you've finished cleaning the bridle, wrap (or "figure-eight") it for the night (see below). This keeps the tack room looking tidy and is an easy way to tell which pieces are clean or dirty.

## Daily Storage

**1** With the bridle hanging neatly by the crownpiece, smooth the reins to the buckle, take the throatlatch across the front of the bridle, then around the back, threading through the reins as you go.

**2** When you get back to the front, cross the other end of the throatlatch across the bridle and thread through the keepers.

**3** Next, take the noseband to the outside of the cheekpieces and cross the ends behind the bridle.

**4** Buckle the ends or thread securely through the keepers.

## Storing a Flash or Figure-Eight Noseband Bridle

Follow the first two steps above.

**1** Then take the flash and thread it through the bit, tucking the reins between the mouthpiece and the flash.

**2** Come back around to the front and buckle the ends or thread securely through the keepers.

Daily Storage

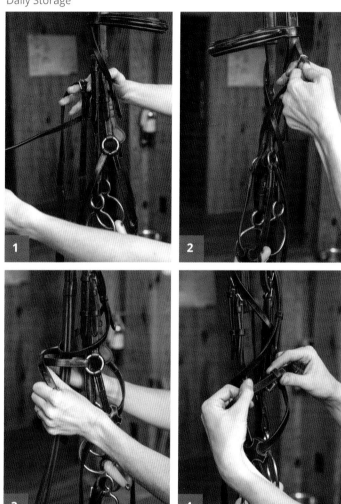

Storing a Flash or Figure-Eight Noseband Bridle

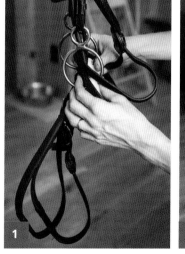

Storing a Double Bridle

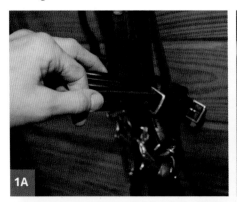

1A

1B

2

3

## Storing a Double Bridle

Follow the first step on page 75 unless you have a rolled-leather throatlatch. Rolled leather tends to twist when stored in a figure eight so, instead, simply slide it between both sets of reins at the back of the bridle and buckle the ends or thread securely through the keepers—it should sit exactly as it is on the horse.

**1 A & B** Follow the second step on page 75 unless you have a padded crank noseband. These often don't reach all the way around to the front of the bridle, so simply buckle the ends, or thread securely through the keepers without crossing in front of the bridle.

**2** Finally, take the curb chain behind the reins, smooth the links, and secure the hook.

**3** All set!

## Cleaning the Saddle

**1** Brush out the treads on the stirrups with a stiff brush.

**2 A & B** Use a glycerin-based saddle soap and a sponge to clean off the skirt, flaps, and seat.

**3 A & B** Then clean the stirrup leathers and panels. Wipe away any residue or bubbles.

**4 A & B** Make sure to get under the skirt and billets.

**5** Use a good conditioner like Effax® Lederbalsam.

Cleaning the Saddle

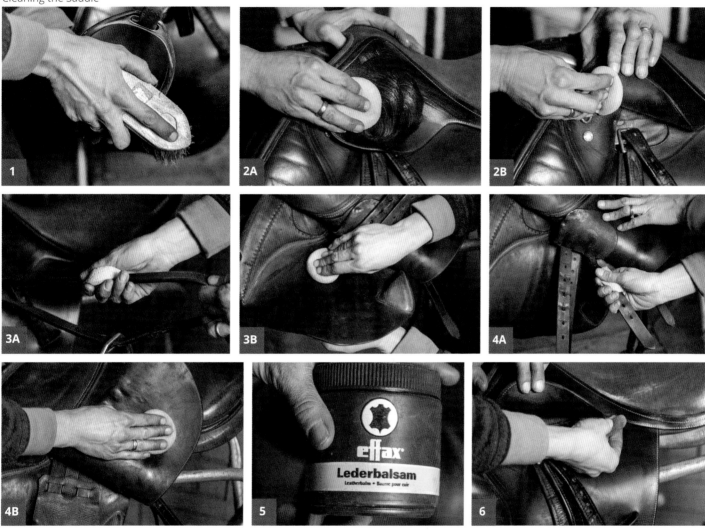

**6** Put a light coat over the entire saddle.

**7** Make sure to get in the crevices under the flaps and skirt.

## Regular Deep Cleaning and Conditioning

Periodically, even tack that is cleaned lightly every day needs a deep clean and conditioning. How often depends on how hard it is used. Tack that is used daily on sweating horses needs conditioning more often, as does tack that isn't used at all! The ways to

# Long-Term Storage—The Emma Ford Way

**1** Do you have that box of old, unused, or spare leather goods? Very often these items mold and get quite stiff, sometimes to the point that the leather cracks and is unsafe to use.

**2** My favorite way to take care of these items is by using Ko-Cho-Line®. This leather-cleaning product leaves tack soft and supple. When put away in an airtight container, tack comes out ready to use after months of storage.

**3** Take the tack and place it in water with ammonia added. Using a sponge or cloth, remove all mold and dirt from the leather. Bridles should be taken apart.

**4** Allow the leather to dry.

**5** Using latex gloves, rub cleaner into leather with your hands. Avoid getting on brass buckles.

**6** Place individual pieces of tack into newspaper. This helps to remove moisture and prevent mold. Use tape to keep the entire same bridle together.

Now place in an airtight container until you need it. I like to place a list in with the tack so I know at a glance what is in the container. I use this method especially at the end of the season when all show equipment needs to be well-conditioned and stored for a couple of months.

Deep Cleaning

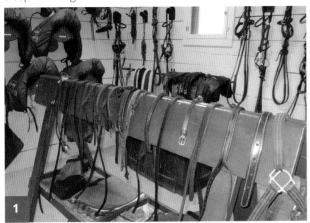

tell if you are nearing the need for a deep clean are stickiness or dullness in the leather. Dry, stiff, or pale leather might also need conditioning.

To deep clean:

**1** Take bridles and strap goods apart. If you are new to this, make sure you note what pieces go where, and in what hole, for reassembly. Remove stirrups and leathers from saddles.

**2** Dilute a small amount of ammonia or white vinegar in warm water. Use a scrubby sponge to wipe any soap residue off the leather.

**3 A & B** Allow the leather to completely dry, then use a thick oil to coat the leather, rubbing it in as you go. Use your hands to work the leather back and forth as you rub the oil in. Most heavy oils will damage stitch-

ing so never soak leather goods in it.

**4** Allow to dry, then use a dry, lint-free cloth to wipe away any excess oil.

## Brass and Metal

The final touch to a truly sharp look is the metal bits on your tack. You clean all metal parts, especially if they are brass. Make sure you *do not* shine the mouthpiece of a bridle, only the bit ends!

Polishing Brass and Metal

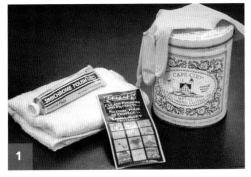

*Continued* ▶

Polishing Brass and Metal (Cont.)

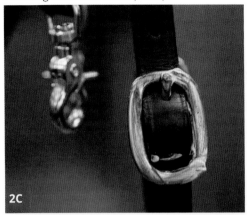

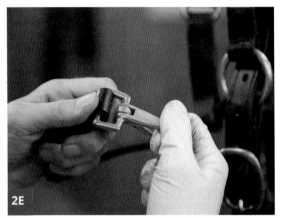

Tidy Tack Room

**1** Supplies:

- Cape Cod® wipes
- Lint-free cloth
- Peek® silver polish
- Glove
- Simichrome polish

**2 A–F** Start with dry metal; use a metal cleaner to fully coat the metal, working it in.

**3** Using a dry cloth, rub until no more black is picked up by the cloth.

**4** You may have to repeat this several times the first time you clean it; regular cleaning keeps it from getting out of hand. You can see the difference on this buckle.

## Tidy Tack Room

**1** There is nothing nicer than a tidy tack room with all the bridles cleaned, wrapped, and hung, and all the saddles oiled and stored.

# CHAPTER SIX
# "Get Ready, Get Set..."

## Cat says

Recently, I found myself teaching a group of after-school lesson kids who wanted to compete. Having an instructor who is a groom, the kids who worked with me knew they had to turn their horses out impeccably. I had two of them going to a small dressage show: one girl with a gray mare, one with a very white pinto mare. After months of preparation, clinics, and mini-shows, the day of the show arrived. Both girls had the routine down pat, with their gear all cleaned, packed, and checked off. The horses' manes were pulled, tack was cleaned, and the girls were bouncing with excitement. They even worked out a wash-rack schedule to make sure both horses would gleam. The morning of the show went like clockwork as all their preparation came into play. When they pulled the mares off the trailer, these two horses looked ready to go "trot down centerline" at Devon: I could recognize them from across the field simply by looking for the blinding reflection of their coats. The girls knew right where their supplies were and barely needed my help. Both of them did very well that weekend, and the pictures of their big day show a record of the hard work they put into that whole summer.

## PREPARING FOR THE SHOW

Your regular routine helps to prepare your horses for competition, setting the stage for success. You have an athlete that is sound, fit, and gleaming from the inside out. Your tack is well taken care of and in good repair, and you have eliminated many of the pitfalls that could waylay your plans at the last minute. Now it's the week leading up to the show, and it's time to prepare. Early preparation makes sure that the stress level in the barn stays low, as well as giving you time to organize and evaluate before the day of travel.

## pro tip

Evaluate where your horse is in his training and his fitness. If you entered a big show this week, but you haven't ridden him enough or his training was interrupted, you should reconsider whether or not to ride. Good horsemanship is putting your horse first, not your goals.

## SUPPLIES

The first thing you want to do is make sure that all the supplies you are taking to the show are ready. This way you can head to the store to replace anything damaged or wash any items that were accidentally put away dirty. Here's a good list of what to check over:

## Tack

Make a list of all the items you will need and check all the pieces on it. Take tack apart the week before the show, scrub really well and then oil. The last thing you want is for a rein to break in the middle of your jumping round, or your girth elastic to give out on the first "halt, salute."

## Soft Goods

All horse items that are washable go into this category. Make sure you have clean standing bandages, show saddle pads, and a couple of work saddle pads. If you don't have the money to have two separate outfits for your horse, don't worry, just launder them the week of the show so they are as clean as possible. Then buy one really good sheet with a neck that is your "show sheet." When you "dress" your horse at the show, simply put that sheet closest to your horse to prevent his regular blankets from getting him dirty.

**1** Weatherbeeta® makes a sheet called the Kool Coat, which is a great option because its sides are mesh so it doesn't add much warmth when you layer it.

Soft Goods

Hard Goods

## Hard Goods

**1** Buckets, wheelbarrows, tack trunks, pitchforks, and brooms fall into this category. Give everything that will be going to the show a good scrub the week before you go.

It's a good idea to mark each item so a neighbor at the show doesn't accidentally pick it up and walk off with it. Eventers like to use electrical tape in their cross-country colors to mark their stuff, but a permanent marker and your name work just as well.

## Feed

**1** Preparing your grain depends a lot on how long you are going and how busy the show will be. If you are only taking a couple horses for a few days, pre-bagging the grain in large Ziploc® bags clearly labeled makes feeding time easy and quick. For longer trips, take grain bags and a scoop. Have a clear chart of which horse gets what so if an emergency arises a friend could feed, if necessary.

**2 A** Smartpaks™ are an amazing invention for supplements, especially for horse shows. Simply grab however many you need and off you go!

Feed

2A

2B

Containers

Cleaning

**2 B** If you use loose supplements, measure them into Ziploc baggies labeled "AM" and "PM" to make your life easier.

## Containers

**1** Trunks, bins, and portable shelves make your life so much easier! Packing into a bin helps to keep you organized and clean. If big, fancy tack trunks are out of the question, head to your local home-improvement store and buy a few cheap rubber bins. It gives you a nice neat spot to keep all your soft goods and small supplies.

## THE ATHLETE

### Cleaning

**1** Let's move on to your horse. You want to spend the week leading up to your event making sure he is clean and tidy to make show day that much easier for you. In Part Two (see p. 93), we will discuss how to pull his mane and care for his tail appropriately. Look him over and tidy

Bubble Bath

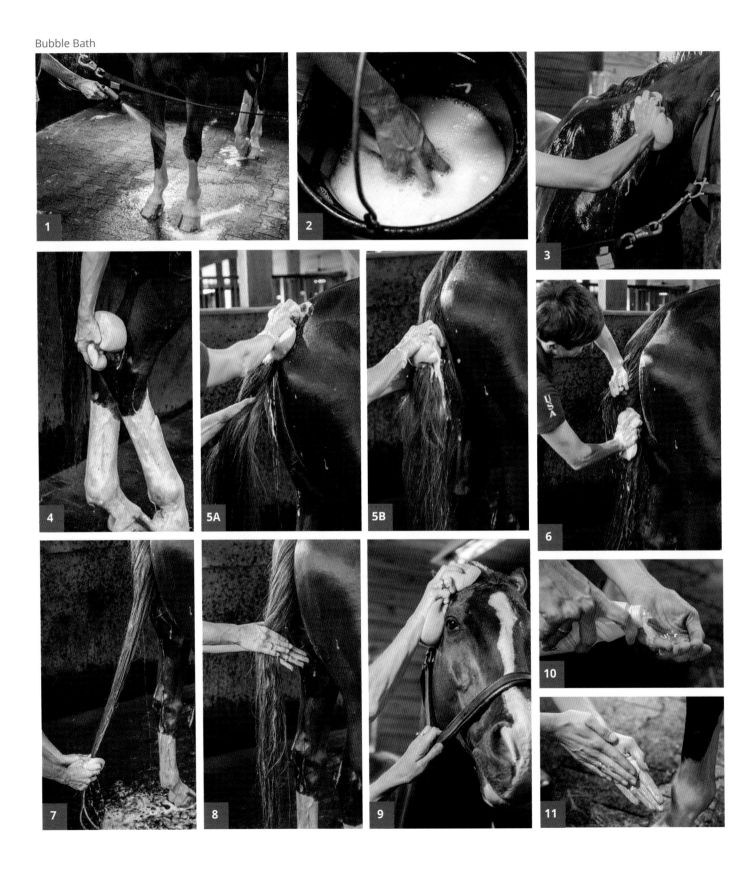

Bubble Bath (Cont.)

Continued ▶

up any long hairs in the tail, and even out the length of his mane, as needed.

## Bubble Bath

Now is the time to give a few really good "scrubbing" bubble baths.

**1** Start by spraying the legs, then hose off the whole horse.

**2** Fill your bucket with water and shampoo.

**3** Use a sponge to scrub the entire horse.

**4** Pay extra attention to the top of the hindquarters, knees, and hocks.

**5 A & B** To scrub the tail, use the sponge to get the entire dock wet.

**6** Pay special attention to the bottom of the dock, where the hair gets really thick and oil can collect.

**7** Run your sponge down the entire tail.

**8** Then scrub the hair between your hands.

**9** Move to his head, and use a damp sponge with just a tiny amount of soap on it to wash the face.

**10** For all horses' legs, put a little soap directly onto your hands.

**11** Rub your hands together to make foam.

**12 A & B** Then rub the soap on the legs and scrub with your fingernails.

**13** If you have a light-colored, pinto horse, or a horse with white legs, you will need to schedule several baths with whitening agents prior to the show. Make sure not to use these more than two times a week because they can irritate skin. Instead, alternate between a gentle shampoo and a whitening agent.

**14 A–C** Use either a bit of OxiClean® detergent or bluing shampoo. Put a very small amount of water into the mixture.

Bubble Bath (Cont.)

**15 A–C** Sponge onto any white legs, knees, hocks, elbows, and tails. Then scrub the area with your fingers. Let the shampoo sit for 5 to 10 minutes. Don't be tempted to think more is better: a long soak can result in a purple horse!

**16 A** Once you have scrubbed the horse all over, start the rinse. Again start with any areas that have bluing shampoo on them.

**16 B** Then, move on to the rest of the horse. This is the most important part of bathing, and the most commonly rushed. You must rinse

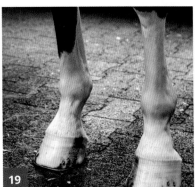

the horse until the water runs clear. Otherwise, the scrubbing you did to get all the dirt up from the skin was for naught. Rinse, scrape with your hand to see the water clarity, and rinse more.

**16 C** Don't forget to rinse the horse's face, either with a hose or sponge.

**17** Make sure you scrape the horse off and towel the legs thoroughly, a wet horse is sure to roll and ruin your hard work.

**18** Comb the mane down while it's wet to help it lie down nicely once dry.

**19** Once the horse is dry, check the white areas, they should look like snow.

## Trimming

Next you need to trim the horse up for the show. How much you trim depends on a few factors such as the riding discipline and its level that you participate in—and your individual horse. For the show hunter, even at the lower levels, you need to trim every part of the horse, whereas for the lower levels of show jumping, dressage, and eventing, it is perfectly appropriate to only trim the long feathers on the legs, cut a bridle path, and clip the muzzle. However, at the upper levels of these disciplines, you should really trim him all over. If you have a horse that goes out at night though, scooping the hair out of the inside of his ears means you must buy him a fly mask with ears to prevent gnats from chewing them. Never clip the long whiskers around a horse's eyes; he uses these at night to prevent himself from bumping his eyes into things.

**barn gossip**

I once had a working student show up from the Midwest to spend the winter with us. On first glance, she seemed to be a very hard worker; however, Kassidy and her horse Umi were a mess when they appeared. The mare was very tricky to handle, and it is a credit to the girl that they got as far as they did together. If you tried to force the horse into a task she didn't approve of, she would remember it and things would escalate if her owner even so much as thought about doing that "terrible" thing again!

When Kassidy first arrived at the barn, Umi was full-body clipped—except for her head. This did not look like it was done on purpose, ending neatly at the cheekbones, but instead, it was a frantic mess that ended at various heights near the top of her neck. Underneath the terrible haircut, this mare was stunning to look at, and I couldn't imagine letting her go around and not showing off her gorgeous face. So, we used a tranquilizer to clip her head, and we got to her muzzle. This turned out to be the root of the whole problem. She absolutely hated to have her muzzle clipped. After almost a year of forcing the issue using every imaginable trick in the book to prevent her from completely losing her mind, Kassidy discovered that if she used a wet razor every couple of days she was able to keep Umi's muzzle tidy. But, after two years, even that "trick" went out the window so the decision was made to let her grow full whiskers. Now, she doesn't get them clipped even for big competitions since she looks better with full whiskers than with half-grown-out ones! *—Cat*

Face

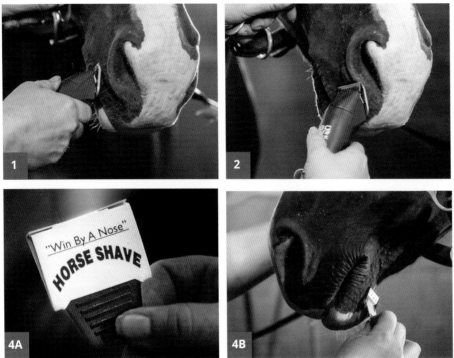

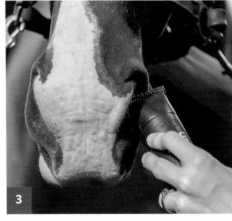

### Face

The horse's face is the first thing people look at, so make sure it's nice and tidy!

**1** Start by trimming the muzzle. Use 30 blade clippers in the summer for a nice tight shave. In the winter stick to a 15 blade to prevent track lines (see p. 52 for more on clipping).

**2** Make sure you get the entire muzzle area, especially the edge of the nostrils.

**3** When you are going to a major competition, or if you show in the hunters, you should scoop out the inside of the nostrils.

**4 A & B** For a horse that hates the feel of clippers on his nose, "Win By A Nose" Horse Shave razors are wonderful. These razor blades have a guard on the back to help protect the horse's skin. Grasp them by the end of the handle and let them glide over any bumpy spots.

### Jawline

**1** Then move on to the horse's jawline to get any long "goat hairs" that hang down. Use a 10 or 15 blade on your clippers. Run the clippers down the jawline at a 90-degree angle to the bone.

Jawline

Bridle Path

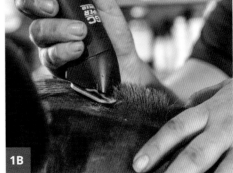

## Bridle Path

**1 A & B** Next, you want a nice, short bridle path. Ideally, the first braid will sit just behind the crownpiece of the bridle, so put two fingers on the mane. Using 10 or 15 blade clippers clip only to this spot. Point the clippers toward your horse's withers and press down gently so they are parallel with the crest.

## Ears

**1** Do the ears last, since many horses do not like this part. It can be helpful to have someone hold your horse's head steady.

**2** Gently cup the outside of the ear in your hand.

**3** Squeeze the sides together.

**4** Run the clippers straight down the ears.

**5** Then, let go of the ear and tidy up the edges by running the clippers down the outside edge of the ear.

**6** When you are going to a major competition or showing hunters, you should scoop the hair out of the inside of the ears. Hold the ear flattened out and run the clippers down the inside edge.

**7** When all is done, the ear should look very tidy and have no long visible hairs.

**8** Here's a "before-and-after" shot of just how much clipping the ears will make a horse look civilized!

Ears

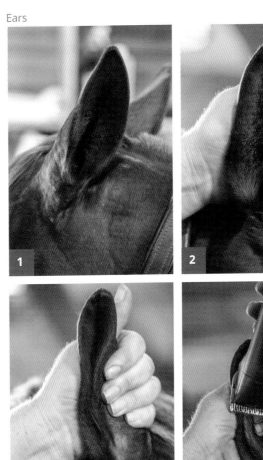
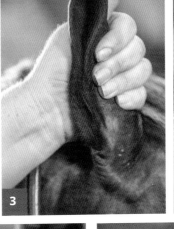

Legs

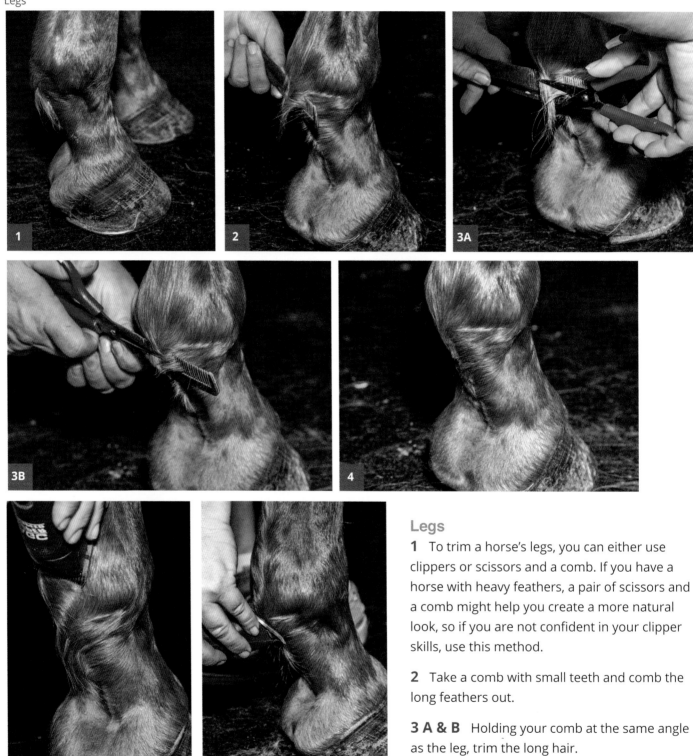

## Legs

**1** To trim a horse's legs, you can either use clippers or scissors and a comb. If you have a horse with heavy feathers, a pair of scissors and a comb might help you create a more natural look, so if you are not confident in your clipper skills, use this method.

**2** Take a comb with small teeth and comb the long feathers out.

**3 A & B** Holding your comb at the same angle as the leg, trim the long hair.

**4** When you are done, it should look clean but natural.

Coronary Band

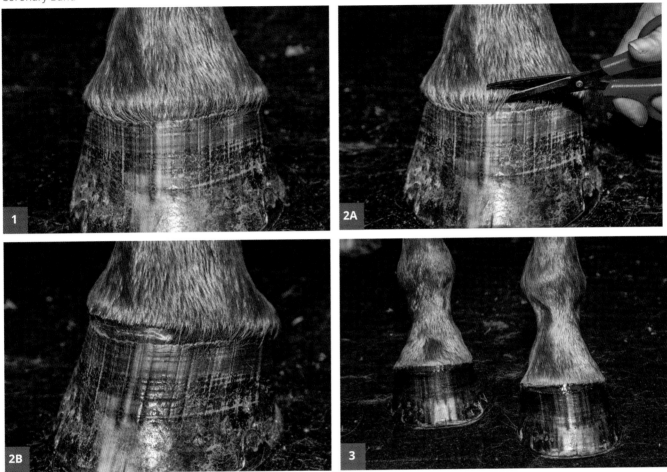

5 Using clippers for the same job, put on a 10 or 15 blade. Run your clippers down the back of the leg with the hair growth.

6 Continue down the back of the fetlock and pastern.

## Coronary Band

1 Then move on to the horse's coronary band.

2 A & B Scissors create the cleanest look; simply snip any hair that hangs below the hoof line.

3 The end product should be a clean line that doesn't get in the way when you are oiling the hoof.

Clean and Trimmed

## Clean and Trimmed

**1** Now your horse is all ready to head to the show!

PART TWO

# The Competition

# CHAPTER SEVEN
# "Closing the Tailgate"

## Emma says

> In 2009, I flew with three horses out to Montana. Used to flying internationally, where horses fly in a cargo area and the grooms fly in the passenger area, I was not quite prepared for this national flight where the horses and grooms all fly together. The horses are in the front of the plane, while at the back, regular seats are set in place for the grooms. Since there is no division between the horses and people, maintaining the right temperature for the horses means the people are freezing! The horses create a large amount of body heat so the air conditioning runs constantly.

*Believe me when I say woolly hat, puffer jacket, and sleeping bag were all required to stay warm. The horses had it much better...but then again, they generally do.*

## TRAVEL

For some of you, putting your horse on a trailer is only an occasional occurrence; for others, you might be shipping to lessons, competitions, or schooling on a regular basis, or even occasionally flying places. Either way, you, your horse, truck, and trailer should all be prepared for the journey. This chapter covers basic rules of travel and gives you checklists that we hope lead you to safe, smooth, and hazard-free trips.

### General Maintenance

#### Truck Safety

**1** It goes without saying that your truck (or tow vehicle) should have an annual, if not twice yearly, full inspection.

In between these, check your oil, water, and brake fluid on a regular basis. Before trips, check all tires to make sure the tread and air pressures are good before taking off for that long haul. Remember the spare tire on both the truck and trailer; if you have a blowout, you want to be able to get the tire changed easily. You should also carry spare oil and diesel exhaust fluid (for the newer trucks).

**2** A health certificate is required, by law, when you are crossing state lines. This needs to be filled out by your vet prior to departure and is valid for 30 days.

**3** An up-to-date negative Coggins certificate for each horse being shipped should also be in the truck. It is important to know different states' require-

Truck Safety

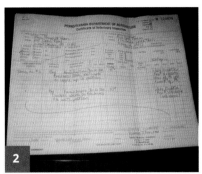

ments: some allow a negative Coggins test within the past year, while others require it within the past six months. Your vet should be able to tell you the relevant rules. When shipping to Canada, health certificates have to be done by your home state offices instead of your local vet. Many times this can take up to three weeks, so planning ahead is a must. Just remember to get things organized ahead of time.

Check Windows and Bars

## Trailer Safety

Whether you have a bumper-pull, two-horse slant-load, or five-horse head-to-head, it is essential to make sure your trailer is in good shape to provide a safe ride. Like your tow vehicle, the trailer should get an annual full inspection. Brakes, wheel bearings, tires, wiring for lights and brakes, the hitch, and the floorboards should all be well maintained.

When it comes to the inside of the trailer, rubber mats should be removed and washed two or three times a year. This will give you the chance to check the flooring underneath to ensure it is in good condition.

**1** Check all windows and bars for broken metal edges.

Some horses are very sensitive to noise. With all the metal latches and partitions banging around, a nervous horse can turn into a wreck by the time you get to your destination. When you have a free stall, remove any loose trailer ties that can clang around; this will also protect your trailer from getting extra scratches.

Emergency Travel Kit

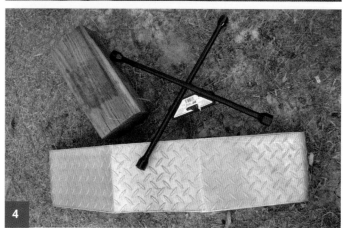

**barn gossip**  Mara DePuy's Nicki Henley was a notoriously unhappy shipper who would rock back and forth and exhaust himself on trips. To try to sort out the issue, I rode with him a few times and discovered that the noise of the trailer and vehicles passing by really worried him. We started stuffing his ears with sheepskin and it immediately lessened his anxiety. Nowadays, he ships in a small trailer with no extra stall dividers that make noise, and he travels like a dream. —Cat

## Emergency Travel Kit

**1** Always have the following items in a box that is easily accessible:

- Wrap and bandage
- Thermometer
- Betadine scrub
- Vetrap
- Square gauze
- Scissors
- Antibiotic cream or SSD cream
- Duct tape

Some people like to carry some form of mild sedative in case a horse needs to be calmed down. Sedatives such as Acepromazine and Dormosedan® can be given easily in the muscle. If you are not comfortable carrying around or giving injectables, don't do it: your own safety must come first.

Never put yourself in a position where you might get trapped by the horse in the trailer.

**2** Carry a spare halter and lead rope in case one gets broken.

**3** Always take a container filled with water and a small bucket—even on a short trip. If there is a breakdown or a traffic issue, you want to be able to provide water for your horse.

**4** Ensure that all tire-repair equipment is accessible: jack, chock, emergency-hazard cones, and lug wrench. It is a good idea to carry a small fire extinguisher, too. You can never be overprepared.

## pro tip

Join USRider Equestrian Motor Plan (www.usrider.org). Belonging to this company has saved me from a few of what could have been disastrous trips. I haul Phillip's horses anywhere from one to 13 hours on a regular basis. Sometimes I have two horses, other times eight. On one occasion, I had eight horses, including two stallions, heading to Aiken, South Carolina, from Pennsylvania. A tire blew on the trailer while on I-95. A co-worker and I changed the tire successfully but went to restart the truck and it wouldn't! To say I was a little anxious is an understatement. USRider came to the rescue and had us towed to a rest area where the horses could be transferred to another trailer and taken to Aiken. The truck got towed to a mechanic.

Even if you don't want to be a member, its website has invaluable information on safe travel as well as a state-by-state transportation-regulation list where you will find what each state

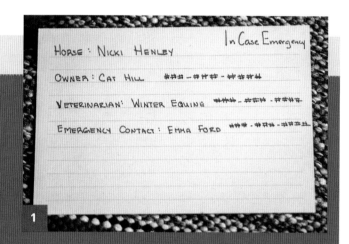

requires, including the state veterinarian's contact information.

**1** One tip they mention is called "ICE: In Case of Emergency." They recommend you carry an information card in your glove box or console with not only all your own emergency contact information, but also a contact number of someone who knows your horse and your vet's number. Should an accident occur, first responders, who might know nothing about horses, will at least have someone to call to get your horse taken care of. *—Emma*

Once the Horse Is Loaded

## Once the Horse Is Loaded

**1 A & B** When ready to go, follow this two-minute safety check before pulling out of the driveway: Check that the hitch is fully down on the ball and that the mechanism is locked. All trailers have a form of lock; this trailer has a lever: *down* means locked (Photo A), while *up* is unlocked (Photo B).

**2 A & B** Be sure the safety chains are attached. On a bumper-pull these should be crossed below the hitch.

Should the hitch and ball separate, the chains prevent the tongue of the trailer from touching the ground.

**3** Check that the breakaway cable is attached...

**4** ... lights, indicators, and running lights are working...

**5** ...windows are open...

**6** ...and latches are double locked.

**7 A & B** Don't forget to raise the jack!

Shipping Boots

## Shipping Gear

There are many discussions over what protective gear a horse should wear while being shipped. It comes down to the horse's comfort and your personal choice. Whether traveling a short distance or across the country, some protection can be the difference between a sliced tendon or clean legs on arrival. Your protective choices are as follows:

- Shipping boots
- Pillow wraps and standing bandages
- Galloping boots and bell boots
- Bare legs

### Shipping Boots

**1** Probably considered the most convenient, there are many brands of differing quality. They basically all offer similar protection from above the knee and hocks—downward. There are some that are short, thus not protecting the knees or hocks. These are great for ponies! The more expensive brands like Lende® are made with stiff materials than some of the cheaper brands. Lende boots are very hard-wearing; they provide great protection and do not slip down the leg—that is, when put on correctly!

*Continued* ▶

**2** As with most horse boots, always pull the Velcro across the front of the cannon. Do the middle strap first, then the top and bottom.

**3** There should be even pressure on all straps.

**4** The boot should sit just off the ground.

**5 A & B** Wrong: Upside down.

Shipping Boots (Cont.)

**6** Wrong: The Velcro can be rubbed loose when it faces the inside of the leg.

**7** Hind boots have four straps.

**8** Set hind boots a bit high when you put them on because they often "sink" a bit as the horse walks onto the trailer.

**9 A & B** Do the middle straps first, then the bottom and top.

**10** Set correctly.

When the horse walks, you might see "spider legs" behind. A horse not used to these boots sometimes lifts up his hind legs very high and awkwardly before taking a step forward. Be patient with him, he will normally figure it out pretty quickly. Some brands of shipping boots are made out of softer material that is more form-fitting to the legs. You must be careful with these since the material can get weak, causing the top part of the boot to collapse. Not only have you now lost protection of the hocks and knees, but the boots are likely to slip, which can aggravate the horse, making him kick or dance around.

### Shipping Boots in Hot Weather

Some people question whether to put these boots on in hot weather. We are constantly aiming for cool, tight legs, especially after a hard workout. It seems counterproductive to ice your horse's legs after competition and then stuff him in a trailer with shipping boots on to add to the heat. But, there is significant risk of injury when he is unprotected in the trailer since you never know if you will need to slam on the brakes. You can always do a cool-out session when you get home.

## barn gossip

Phillip Dutton's Connaught ("Simon") hated shipping boots. He would refuse to walk in them. I even tried putting them on once he was loaded, but this made him even more nervous. So he always traveled in quilts and bandages—as well as bell boots all around—due to his moving around a lot in the trailer. I eventually found soft-padded hock boots that I could put on once he was in the trailer. He would tolerate these and they prevented him from getting hock rubs caused by his occasional bucking sprees while being shipped! —*Emma*

## Taking Care of Shipping Boots

**1 A & B** Shipping boots, especially the hind ones, should be scrubbed off with a detergent after use. This helps them have a longer life. Accumulation of sweat and manure weakens the materials over time. Too much machine washing and drying breaks down the foam and creates limp boots.

## Pillow Wraps and Standing Bandages

**1** If you prefer to wrap your horse, thick pillow quilts like Wilker's and flannel wraps are the best option. You need to have extra-long wraps that cover the pastern as opposed to regular standing-wrap length. Due to their non-elasticity, flannel wraps are safer to use for long hauling. They cannot get over-tightened and cause damage to the leg.

**2** With bell boots already on, start with your big pillow quilt right below the knee: it should go to just above the coronary band. Remember, anytime you wrap, it's front to back on the outside of the leg.

**3** Start the flannel wrap at the top of the leg toward the front of the cannon.

**4** Due to the quilt's long length, you will need to leave extra space between each turn of the wrap.

**5** Wrap all the way to the fetlock, then go one more wrap so you are past the ankle joint.

Taking Care of Shipping Boots

**6** Head back up the leg, being careful not to have lumps or creases at the turn.

**7** End your wrap squarely across the top of the quilt.

Pillow Wraps and Standing Bandages

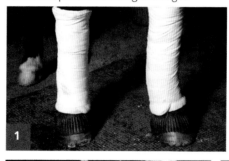
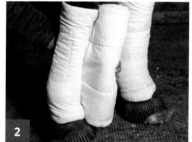

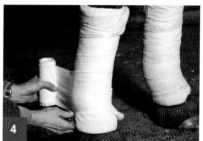
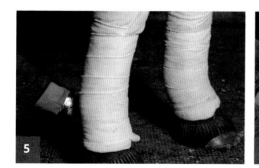
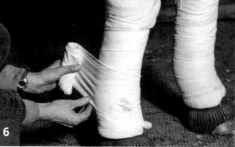
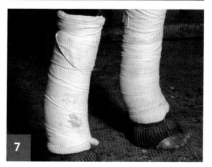

Galloping Boots and Bell Boots

Temperature Control

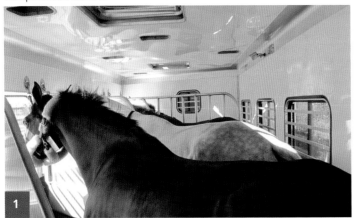

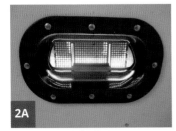

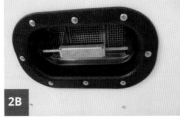

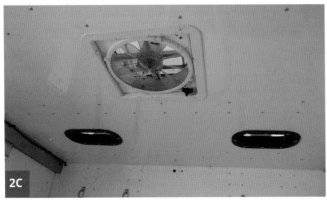

As an extra safety precaution you can use masking tape around the Velcro at the end. Remember not to place the tape on tighter than the bandage because it will cause a pressure point.

## Galloping Boots and Bell Boots

**1** When traveling short distances, maybe to a dressage lesson or jumping school, using work boots and bell boots is an option. This is not recommended for long trips due to lack of air flow around the tendons that can cause considerable heating up of the area.

## Bare Legs

A horse that does not wear shoes can travel relatively safely with no leg protection. With a young horse or inexperienced shipper we recommend getting him used to wearing protective gear before you load him on a trailer. Putting shipping boots on him at home in his stall helps to desensitize him to the sensation of "something" on his legs. There are situations where shipping a horse with no leg protection is the only option: some horses simply do not learn that protective gear is good for them and will paw, kick, buck, or otherwise act out when you put anything on. If he will tolerate bell boots, you can at least help prevent shoes from being torn off. At the end of the day though, a quiet horse is less likely to do himself damage than a worried or stressed horse.

## Temperature Control

Clothing your horse during shipping depends on a few different factors:

### Outside Temperature

If you are beginning your trip in Vermont and heading to Florida in January, think about layering your horse so that as the weather warms up, you can remove a layer to keep your horse comfortable. An Irish knit with a good woolly on top is a good option (see p. 65). Be careful that attachments are in good working order so that slippage doesn't occur, and never put

Tail Guard

 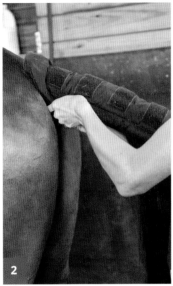  

on a blanket that doesn't have a belly strap or tail strap: a blanket can easily fall around your horse's neck, causing him to step on it—and panic.

## Number of Horses Traveling

**1** Take this into account because horses produce a lot of their own body heat: a two-horse bumper-pull with two on board generates more heat than a trailer with just one horse, so blanket accordingly. You will find many of the commercial rigs with 12 horses loaded ship "naked" in the winter because the horses maintain enough heat, amongst themselves.

## Amount of Trailer Ventilation

**2 A–C** Trailers vary in the amount of ventilation they provide. It is important to have plenty of good air flowing: it's better to add a blanket than close all vents and leave the horse uncovered.

## Tail Protection

You have the option of using protective tail guards or tail wraps to keep your horse's tail in good shape when trailering. You can create an inexpensive tail wrap using an Ace™ bandage, or purchase a sturdy, stretchy one from a tack supplier. For a long trip, use a tail

guard rather than a wrap. When you are sure your horse does not sit on his hindquarters while being shipped, nothing is required, but most people protect the tail in some fashion.

## Tail Guard

**1** These can be made out of nylon, cotton, or neoprene, and all have Velcro fastenings. Some have an attached bag to cover the entire tail length, which is not a bad idea for that grey tail on the way to a show!

**2** Put the tail over your shoulder, and get the tail wrap as high up the tailbone as possible.

**3** Do the top strap up first.

**4** Work down the tail guard, making sure the wrap is snug but not tight.

**5** The last one should be pulled quite snug.

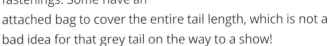

## barn gossip

When we came home after the Pan American Games in Brazil in 2007, the five US Eventing Team horses had a seven-day quarantine in Miami to check for ehrlichia (a tick-borne disease common in Brazil). My charge, Mara DePuy's Nicki Henley, was injured so I was asked to stay in Miami and take care of the quarantined horses since my horse needed the most "tender loving care."

Quarantine is a tough place: only one person is allowed in the stables at a time and only for an hour. Our gold-medal winning equine team went from four or five meals a day of the highest quality grain and constant care and intense exercise routines to concrete boxes with no windows, cheap hay, and one scoop of straight oats twice a day.

I would literally run into the aisleway and fly through getting Nicki into an ice boot, race through the other horse's stalls to put my hands on them, check legs, and run a brush over them, change Phillip Dutton's Truluck's hoof wrap (he had pulled a shoe on cross-country), to finally get Nicki out of ice and re-wrapped.

The last day we were there, Truluck ("Milo") wasn't acting like his normal, cuddly self. I talked to the vets on staff and told them I thought he might be colicking. A vet came, took his temperature, and said he was fine. After a great deal of persuading, I convinced her to let me come back in two hours to check on him.

Many phone calls to Phillip and the United States Olympic Committee, and two hours later, Milo certainly was colicking, but since he still wasn't running a temperature the vets weren't buying my urgency. After much handwringing I was allowed to walk him in the aisle. He settled a little and I was asked to leave for the night. So I did what any sane, rational groom would do: I sat in his stall and refused to leave. I screamed, I swore, I was physically dragged out of the barn yelling that I was calling the news and exposing abuse. I then called Phillip, crying, apologizing. The vet ended up checking on Milo and deciding (once he had a temperature) that he needed more specialized care and they transferred him to Wellington Equine where his colic was treated.

So, after being up all night with this situation, I was thrilled to see the rigs pull in at 9:00 a.m. to take us home to Virginia! We loaded all the gear and horses into the semi-trailers, and I asked the shippers where the hay was. They looked at me blankly and said no one asked them to bring hay. Luckily, the Canadian team was loading their horses at the same time and they were able to spare half a bale. That was one flake per horse!

I then attempted to climb into the cab and the shippers obviously thought I was crazy; they had not expected me to ride up front with them. So I bunked down on some trunks that were stacked in the back with the horses and settled in for the long ride home. We sat at a standstill in traffic during a wicked thunderstorm, but finally made it to the Florida border. The horses were out of hay, wet, and miserable, and I was about the same. When we stopped in line at the agricultural stop on the way out of Florida, I jumped out of the truck and visited every livestock trailer there, asking if I could buy some hay. I ended up buying two bales for an absurd sum of money. A long 10 hours later we made it to Virginia. I can honestly say I have never been happier to see High Acre farm in my life. —*Cat*

Tail Wrap

## Tail Wrap

**1** A tail wrap protects but also shapes your horse's tail. It is a necessity with a braided tail, and when you remove it at the show, all hairs should be in place! Please refer to page 158 for step-by-step instructions on applying a tail wrap.

**2** Make sure the wrap is not applied too tightly. Circulation can be cut off and eventually hair will start to fall out. It can also cause sores—not something anybody wants to happen.

## Shipping Halter, Fly Mask, Head Bumper

**1** Shipping halters are very useful when your horse is traveling long distances where the repeated movement of a regular halter could rub and cause hair loss or sores. They can either be purchased with full sheepskin covering (the best for long trips), or you can get sections of synthetic or real sheepskin to put on the cheekpieces, noseband, and crownpiece of your horse's regular halter during transport.

**2** With good airflow can come flying debris. When you ship in a trailer that has large vents and no screens, a *fly mask* can help make sure nothing gets into your horse's eyes.

**3** The *head bumper* gets placed over the ears and through the halter. When your horse is tall or known for tossing his head, a bumper is good protection for the poll.

## Commercial Shipping

When using a commercial shipper, make the job as easy as possible for the drivers. Put your horse's name, destination, and contact information on the halter. This way there can be no mix up! Have all the necessary documentation. If possible, use boots rather than wraps

Shipping Halter

Fly Mask

Head Bumper

Safe Trailer Loading

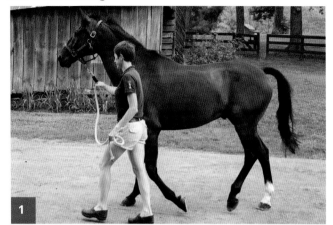

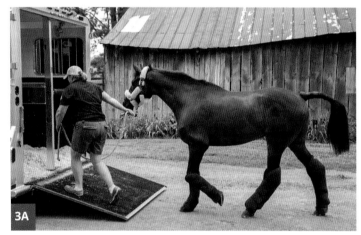

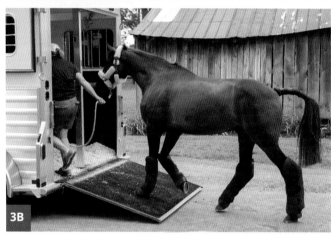

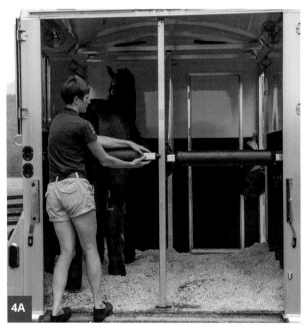

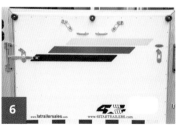

for protection because the drivers are not responsible for removing or resetting a wrap that has slipped. If you need to send equipment along, put it in a well-marked trunk. Do not have multiple individual pieces that can easily be left behind when unloading.

Commercial Shipping

**1** This horse is wearing a protective fly mask as well as an information tag.

## Safe Trailer Loading

When you know your horse has not been loaded very often or you have never done it before by yourself, it is very wise to get help from a trainer or knowledgeable horse friend when starting this task.

**1** Your horse must move forward happily at your shoulder. Practice hand-walking, clucking to ask him to move up and forward a little ahead of you.

**2** When using a two-horse trailer, make the stall as big as possible: If the trailer has a center partition that moves, unhook the butt bar on both sides and swing the center partition all the way to the side. When there is a center post at the back, leave the side doors open, and the escape doors also, to provide light at the front of the trailer, thus making it seem larger. Make sure the open doors are secured to the sides of the trailer so they cannot swing. Be certain the trailer's ramp is level and all the way down.

**3 A & B** Approach the trailer and as you get to the ramp give the horse a cluck to ask him to move forward.

**4 A & B** When he walks on, have a friend quietly do up the butt bar behind him. Never tie up your horse until you are certain the butt bar has been securely fastened.

If your horse tries to step back and hits the end of the rope, a struggle might occur, causing him to break free and hit his head as he reverses out of the trailer.

**5** Once he's on, put the ramp up so he can't slip backward underneath the butt bar.

**6** Immediately do up all the latches; one good kick would have this ramp down!

### Self-Loading

Once your horse is confidently walking onto the trailer with you by his side, you can try to teach him to self-load. In the long run, this is safer for you because you are then not confined in a small space with a large animal while waiting for the trailer to be closed. It also

Self-Loading

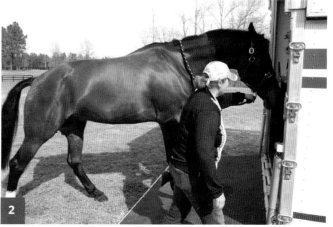

*Continued* ▶

Self-Loading (Cont.)

allows you to load by yourself without help; you can fasten the butt bar once your horse has walked in by himself, and once that is done, go in and secure his head.

**1** This is where that clucking cue comes into play. When loading on the driver's side, stand on the horse's left; on the passenger side, stand on the right. Place the rope over his neck.

**2** Walk him up the ramp, using your clucking cue when he reaches the opening. This is where you let him go in by himself.

**3** Once he is in, fasten the butt bar. You can encourage him to take an additional step forward with one hand on his hip.

**4** When first teaching self-loading, have a friend ready to catch him at the front, but don't do up his head until the butt bar is up!

When training such tasks as these, it is essential you have enough patience to do so and allow time. Do not begin doing this at a show! If you become impatient your horse will pick this up and get nervous about being loaded. He needs to associate loading and being in the trailer as a positive experience, not an anxious one.

Make sure there is someone else to give you a hand.

When you are only shipping *one* horse, he should always be put on the driver's side.

## Unloading

**1** Remember: *always* untie the horse before removing the butt bar.

**2** When you have help, ask the person to stand beside the ramp so as you come back with your horse she can help to keep him straight and not step off the ramp awkwardly.

**3** Back him up all the way off the ramp before you ask him to turn.

**4** If you know you will be by yourself much of the time, then your horse needs to understand when to back up off the trailer. Practice at home with help. As someone

Unloading

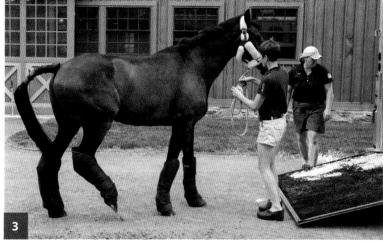

holds your horse and asks him to move back, take a light hold of his tail. Make sure you are standing just to the side of the ramp so if he comes back quickly you are not in the way, but you can also try to keep him straight. Practice this enough and your horse will eventually understand the cue to reverse as his tail is gently pulled.

## Cautions
• Never put yourself in a position where you can get trapped by your horse.
• Never tie up your horse until the butt bar, ramp, or door are closed.
• Always untie before opening the ramp or rear doors.
• Always give yourself plenty of time to load; never rush your horse onto the trailer.

Tricky Shippers

## Tricky Shippers

There are many reasons some horses do not ship well. Here are some solutions:

### Number of Horses

Some horses prefer a companion on board; if one is un- available, try placing a plastic mirror mounted in front of him so he can see himself.

**1** Other horses hate having company; using a bite guard (a small gate that extends in front of the standard divider) so they do not feel crowded by the other horse can be helpful.

### Noise

Pay attention to the noise level. Minimize clatter by secur- ing all loose chains and bars. You can try plugging his ears with sheepskin if your horse will tolerate having it put in and taken out (see p. 173). You can also stuff cotton into the ears of a fly mask.

### Boots

Some horses dislike wearing shipping boots and cannot get used to them. Try different ones or use wraps with bell boots.

### Positioning

**2** Depending on trailer type, a horse might prefer traveling backward instead of forward, or prefer standing on the diagonal. Another can be claustrophobic, so putting this horse in a spot where he can look out the open side window may help. Occasionally, a horse will try to climb out of this side window, so make sure he is tied up snugly with a good chest bar in front.

## Air Transport

Air Horse One? Sounds like a joke, doesn't it! It is the real name of one of the companies that flies horses nationally. Horses that fly around the United States—primarily racehorses, show jumpers, and polo ponies—travel on a jet that is specially kitted out for horses. For those who have watched the 1978 movie *International Velvet*, not much has changed!

**1 A & B** These planes are dedicated to moving animals and have a crew that is used to handling anything—even

**barn gossip** Phillip Dutton's Fernhill Eagle was not the best shipper. He hated having company next to him and would let everyone know he was displeased. I would always try to ship him without a side companion or with a bite guard placed between the two horses so they couldn't aggravate each other. If we were not shipping a large number of horses, we could make the front of the four-horse, head-to-head trailer into a box stall by removing the center partition, which was the best solution but a rare luxury since Phillip normally rides a number of horses at every event. —*Emma*

Air Transport

1A

1B

2A

2B

Continued ▶

loading about 30 horses per hour. The horses are taken to the cargo plane area of an airport, where the trailer's ramp is maneuvered onto the base of another long ramp that goes uphill to the plane. Once in place, the horses are led up the ramp into a large, empty space.

**2 A & B** One by one, a stall is built around the horse. Once the horses are all in, it is quite a full plane. Horses tend to travel this way really well. The plane engines' "white noise" cancels out any sudden sounds and there is very little motion. Once they arrive, they simply wait their turn, their stall gets dismantled, and they walk forward down a ramp. Humans, however, have a bit less luxury: we fly at the back of the plane with no windows on very old seats. There is generally a cooler strapped in the front of the seat section with some beverages and snacks, and once you are in the air you can get up to check on your horse, and peruse the refreshments.

When traveling internationally, your horse could be in the cargo area of that jumbo jet you are flying in! Internationally, there are only a few US airports where horses can arrive and depart: Newark, JFK, Chicago, Miami, Los Angeles, and Atlanta. The horses must arrive six hours

Air Transport (Cont.)

prior to flying for a short quarantine so the Department of Agriculture vet can draw blood and ensure they are healthy prior to exportation. The containers they are shipped in are similar in size to a large two-horse, bumper-pull.

**3** The horses get loaded into a shipping crate directly from the horse trailer. Each crate holds two horses.

**4** The crate is then taken to the plane via a small tug truck. Here is the crate once it is loaded onto the plane.

**5** The worst part of getting them onto the plane is the scissor lift. This is the piece of equipment used to take cargo from ground level to the bulkhead area. It's obviously not specifically made for lifting animals; the lift is not a smooth ride and often the horses get jerked around a little bit to be put into position. Once in the plane and the crate is locked down, the ride is pretty smooth.

**6** Typically the horses' crates are the last to go into the plane so that they are the first cargo to come off. This picture shows a row of shipping crates in the plane; you can see there is not much room to maneuver when you need to check on the horses.

**7** Takeoff and landings all depend on the pilot! Some do this more smoothly than others. For the most part, the horses brace themselves in either direction as needed. As soon as the plane levels off they relax and munch on hay till they arrive at their destination. Here are McKinleigh and Connaught waiting on the tarmac with Emma prior to going to the 2008 Olympics.

CHAPTER EIGHT

# "Go"

## Cat says

*It can be easy to arrive at a major competition, start "spectating" and forget to pay attention to time. Unless your horse lives in a stall at home, standing in a stall at the competition without leaving it all day can be very stressful and can affect performance. At the American Eventing Championships in Georgia one year, the horses were being evaluated for the World Equestrian Games a few weeks later. One of the horses at the very top was not running cross-country because he had already done enough to qualify for a team spot. The rider had several horses competing in various other divisions. However, he was without a groom at the moment and was making do with a working student who was busy watching the event and caring for the horses running cross-country. In the afternoon, a spectator was walking through the barns and started to enquire about who was caring for a specific horse, because he was completely out of water. It turned out he had not been checked on throughout the very hot day. Fortunately, he was just fine, but it was a tough learning experience for this student. No matter how busy the day is, there are certain necessities that must not be overlooked, so write down a schedule to help you get through the day.*

## ON THE SHOW GROUNDS

### A Sample Daily Horse-Show Schedule

#### Stabling on Grounds

When you are stabling at a show for several days, you must establish a routine with your horse. No matter what discipline, he should be taken for a hand-graze or hand-walked a couple times a day so he gets to stretch his legs.

Feeding your horse when stabled at a show can be complicated. "Little and often" is the best rule of thumb. Your horse needs three hours between grain feedings to ensure proper digestion. At the lower levels make sure he has finished eating one hour prior to being ridden. At the upper levels of all disciplines, it should be four hours between finishing grain and heavy exertion.

This will take some creativity in your schedule. If you have an early start, feed a small portion of breakfast and then give a "brunch" once you have a break in the day. If you are competing later in the day, feed him a small dinner a little earlier than usual and add a late night snack when he gets back to his stall for the evening.

When developing a day schedule, allow adequate time for braiding, grooming, and tacking up prior to the competition. Horses that are braided the night before should wear a hood to help prevent rubbing and damage to their braids. Remember, when using rubber bands, braiding must be done the day of the competition since these braids don't hold up well to overnight wear.

6:00 a.m.
- Feed breakfast.
- Check legs and body; unwrap legs if necessary.

6:15
- Clean stalls, set up with hay.
- Dump, scrub, and refill water buckets.

7:00
- Comb shavings/straw from the tails and knock off any major dust.
- Hand-graze and walk.

Throughout day: Keep up with the manure by picking out the stall as it occurs. Groom horse every time he leaves the stall, wash him when returning from work, as necessary. Take a white/gray horse to the wash rack, set up a cot, and live there!

11:30
- Feed lunch (depending on what time you ride).
- Check water.

12:00 p.m.
- Hand-graze and walk horse.

3:00
- Clean stalls.
- Check water.

4:00
- Feed horse.

4:30
- Hand-graze and walk horse.

8–10:00
- Do late check (check for signs of colic or illness; change blankets).
- Feed late-night, if necessary.
- Check water.

## Trailering-In

Things to consider:

• Ride times: For dressage and eventing you will know your times in advance and can plan accordingly so you can have your horse ready at their appointed time. However, for hunter and jumper shows where the day can be determined by the whim of the ring, you must be able to think on your feet, have a "loose" schedule, then react according to how the day is running.

• Exercise and feeding: Horses should not do extensive work on a full stomach, so make sure you pull the hay

net away when you start to tack your horse up. For an event horse competing at Preliminary Level and above, hay should be removed two hours prior to warming up for cross-country so he is not running on a full stomach.

• Cooling out: In every discipline, horses must be completely cool prior to trailering home. Refer to page 199 for complete instructions on a proper cool-out.

5:00 a.m.
- Feed breakfast.
- Pack any final items into trailer.

5:30
- Groom horse. Check braids if put in the night before.
- Wash gray horse and white legs.
- Spot wash as needed.

6:30
- Wrap tail.
- Put on boots/shipping wraps.
- Load horse.

7:00
- Pull out.

8:00
- Arrive at show.
- Check horse.
- Offer the horse a drink.

45 minutes prior to competing:
- Take horse out; tie to outside of trailer.
- Groom.
- Stud when necessary (see p. 192).
- Tack up.
- Head to the ring.

If there is a long break between classes or ride times:
- Tie horse to outside of trailer when warm.
- Leave horse on the trailer when cold or rainy.
- Untack, remove studs, and groom.
- Tie a hay net high near him.
- Hang a water bucket out of reach of pawing forefeet.

Preparing for the next phase or class:
- Groom.
- Put studs in when necessary.
- Tack up.
- Head to the ring.

*When finished competing for the day:*
- Make sure horse is fully cooled out.
- Tie horse to outside of trailer.
- Untack, remove studs, and groom.
- Check all over for scrapes, bumps, and lumps.
- Follow aftercare instructions as necessary.
- Put boots on.
- Wrap tail.
- Load up.

*Arrive at home:*
- Unload horse.
- Check horse all over.
- Note how much water the horse drank through the day.

Follow normal evening feeding/turnout routine. If your horse didn't drink well all day, offer some bran mash or soaked grain for dinner. If he normally gets a lunch feeding and missed it at the show, feed a late night snack between 8:00 and 10:00 p.m.

So you've made it to the competition and are preparing to show off all of the hard work done at home. The first thing you must do is make sure your horse looks the part. In the previous section, we discussed getting a horse's skin and coat to look good from the inside out. Now, we'll discuss the details necessary to wow the crowds!

One of the first things to note is that when you are in public, you never know who will be around the corner. So from the minute you unload your horse, be prepared to run into David O'Connor, Beezie Madden, George Morris, or Robert Dover! Bathe your horse before you leave home, making sure he is trimmed and tidy. When stabling at the show, make sure you brush bedding out of tails and smooth nap marks out of coats before heading out for a walk.

**barn gossip**

Recently, I moved back to my hometown and started teaching between my freelance grooming jobs. A group of kids who had only shown at the local fairs and shows trained with me to go to a small, unrecognized event. I was working with their regular instructor, who was a good horseperson but not well-versed in the various scenarios that present themselves at competitions. I altered some of my normal routines to fit their program, and they altered some of their practices to go with mine. One of the biggest culture shocks for them was the sensation of showing "off the trailer" as opposed to using a stall.

Most of our local shows provide stabling—except for eventing, which very rarely has stabling for small events so most people ship in, even if that means trailering to and from the grounds on both weekend days. Imagine my shock when I discovered that the children and their regular trainer were not very comfortable tying horses to the trailer, or leaving them on the trailer while they walked away. The idea of tying a horse to a trailer worried them since they had only ever walked a horse from the stall to the ring.

During a planning meeting the trainer asked what we would do about the lack of stalls, and it was decided that we would try tying horses to the trailers with hay nets and water—but only if they were constantly monitored. An enormous group of kids and adults were required to make sure there was someone with every horse every moment of the day.

In addition, things that seemed a "given" to me, like carrying water for the day, were foreign to the group at large; they were used to stables with water at hand and wash-racks equipped with hoses. However, with thorough packing lists and double-checks, we were able to make sure all of the necessary supplies made it to the show. Overall, the day was a huge success, but the sheer amount of manpower necessary to pull it off was exhausting! After that experience I resolved to teach all of my students how to be independent, so they would know how to handle *any* show situation. —*Cat*

Trailer as "Home Base"

## Show Base

Now that you are at the venue, what do you do?

### Trailer

If you are using your trailer as "home base," decide if you are going to tie to the trailer or leave the horse on it. Since a horse can accidentally get loose when tied to the trailer, there should always be someone close by when he is tied outside and make sure you have done a dress rehearsal at home.

**1** When leaving your horse inside the trailer, be sure he has good ventilation, hay, and water.

**2 A & B** When the trailer can be watched and the weather is nice, go ahead and tie to the outside. Tie a piece of bailing twine to the rings provided on the out-

side of the trailer, and provide access to hay and water (see p. 118 for tying advice).

**3** When trailering in for the day, make sure to carry enough water. Some places provide water, but you never know how far away the supply will be!

### Stabling

**1** When stabling at the showgrounds, you need to set up the horse's stall. If stabling in a tent, get your water buckets hung then put the horse in the stall *on* the grass because he will dig up any bedding you put down to get to it anyway, so you might as well let him munch on it first.

**2** When housed in permanent stabling, bed the stall down, hang your water, then unload the horse.

**3** Once the horse is in the stall, unload the trailer neatly into either the tack stall or aisleway. Give your horse some hay and make sure he is settled before you leave him.

Now, make sure your area is tidy and neat. Have as much as possible in trunks or tubs.

**4** To hang bridle racks, first lay a clean towel over the bars, then the rack.

**5** Blankets should be neatly folded.

Stabling

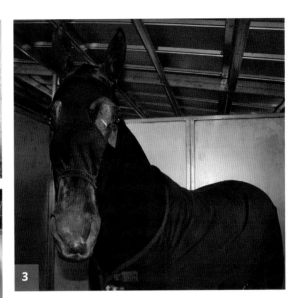

## pro tip

At FEI-monitored events, there is an evaluation when you arrive referred to as "in-barns." While they vary slightly in each discipline, the basics are the same. The veterinary panel will evaluate each horse to check that the horse matches the passport description, that the passport is up-to-date, and that the horse's vitals are all normal.

To do in-barns properly, your horse should be groomed, with tail combed and feet picked. You need your passport and controlled medication chart.

I cannot tell you the number of times I have scoffed at people showing up to the in-barn inspection looking a mess. During my freelancing days, I traveled out to Richland Park CCI with a rider whose standards were not quite as high as mine. He had important business to attend to when we arrived, so he unloaded the four horses and drove away. After a 14-hour drive, I had five minutes to get to "in-barns"

before it closed and we were eliminated. The rider had driven off with all the brushes, combs, and towels. I ended up having to take the four horses to in-barns with travel dust all over them and straw in their tails. Luckily, a good friend saw me walking up, ran out with a comb and damp towel and groomed my horses while I held them in line. I have never wanted to hide my face so badly as at that moment—standing in line with four filthy horses! —*Cat*

Securing the Tacked-Up Horse

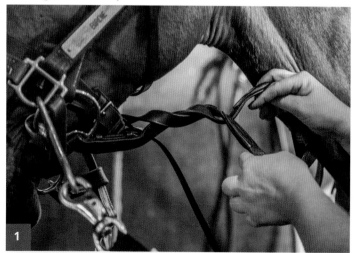

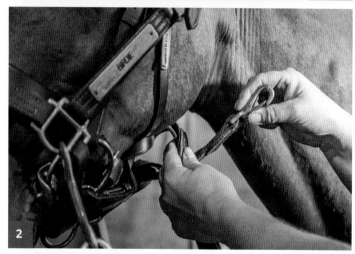

## Safety Issues

### Securing the Tacked-Up Horse

**1** If you ever need to leave your horse once he's all tacked up, make sure you do so safely. Never tie a horse to his bridle. Instead, slide a halter over it and twist the reins around themselves.

**2** Thread the throatlatch of the halter through the twisted reins.

**3** Do up the throatlatch.

### Tying a Safety Knot

A *safety knot* is a slipknot that is easily undone should the need arise. It should also be a knot that does not over-tighten if a horse pulls back on the rope. It should be secured to a piece of string and never directly to the trailer or barn. If the horse panics and you aren't there to pull the tail of the quick-release, the string will break and release him.

**1** Cross the rope over, left to right...

**2** ... bring the tail of the rope up to create a loop...

**3 A & B** ...then fold the tail in half and thread through the loop you just created.

**4 A & B** When you have a long rope, you can keep the end out of the dirt by looping it through itself repeatedly. Be sure to leave the tail free since that it what you need to grab if you have to undo the knot quickly.

### Hang It Tidily

**1** Make sure your halter is hung neatly. If you have a hook available, roll the lead rope and attach it to the halter.

**2** When no hook is available, use a double-ended snap to neatly hang the halter. Snap both side rings to the stall then hook the lead rope to the snap as

Tying a Safety Knot

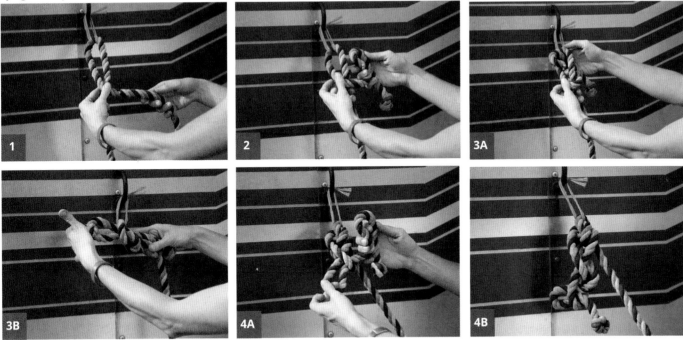

Hang It Tidily

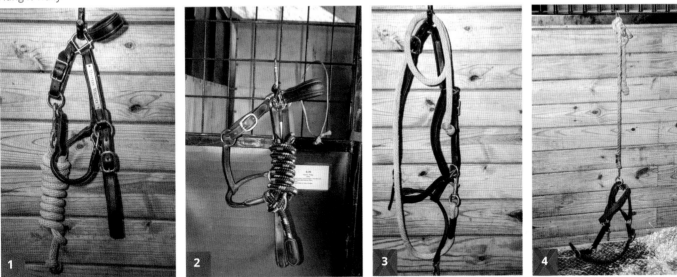

well. If the bars are too wide for a snap, loop a piece of string around the bars so you can snap the halter to it instead.

**3** Wrong: It is never acceptable to leave the halter and lead rope jumbled in a mess.

**4** Wrong: Make sure the halter gets picked up immediately when removed. A halter dangling from the wall is not only unsightly, it also becomes a safety hazard should a horse get his leg through it.

Roll a Lead Rope

## Roll a Lead Rope

**1** Fold the lead rope so that about one foot of the loop lies parallel to the section attached to the snap.

**2** While holding the rope in place, wrap the excess tightly around the two parallel pieces.

**3** When you get close to the bottom, push all the coils up toward the snap, and put your finger through the loop at the bottom.

**4** Tuck the end of the rope through the loop.

**5** Pull the tail tight. Success!

**6** Wrong: If it looks like this, you folded the lead rope too far down and need to start over.

## Roll a Leather Lead Shank

**1** Thread the end of the leather through the connection at the base of the chain.

**2** Create a circle.

**3** Follow the leather to the end and roll the lead rope tight, making sure you are rolling toward the inside of the circle you created.

**4** Keep rolling; make sure it's quite tight.

**5** When you get to the circle, tuck the roll inside it. It should be a little tough to push in.

**6** Snap the chain to the opposite side of the roll. Nice and neat.

Roll a Leather Lead Shank

## CHAPTER NINE
# "On the Crest"

### Cat says

*I had returned to the United States after a stint working at a stable in Ireland and began working toward my Masters in Education when I decided instead that horses made me much happier. So I responded to an ad on Yardandgroom.com as a lark. I emailed the week of Christmas for a position in South Carolina for the winter, taking care of four competition horses. Little did I know my boyfriend would propose at Christmas, I would get a job offer the day after, and I would be heading south five days after that! By the time I arrived in Aiken, four horses had turned into eight, and I was in over my head. At our first competition a few weeks later, I had eight manes to braid. I thought I had things under control, since I had worked as a braider at hunter shows where I would braid all night. So at one in the morning, I walked out to the barn and started braiding so we could be ready to leave at seven. I was on horse number three at four o'clock, panicking because I had no idea how I was going to get them all braided—as well as get them washed, stalls cleaned, and trailer loaded to go without being late. Out of nowhere a voice asks "Would you like help?" A groom named Danielle was staying in the house across from our barn; she saw my light on and here she was, standing there in her pajamas offering to braid a few. Between the two of us we got everything done and the horses were ready to roll at the required time, with Danielle long gone and my boss none the wiser. I, however, learned a few important lessons that night. First, get faster at braiding. Second, braiding the night before and sticking a hood on a horse is really quite all right. Third, and most importantly, always offer other people your help when you have time, because there will be so many times you need theirs!*

## MANES

How you take care of the horse's mane depends on the breed, the discipline your horse is being used for, and your personal preference. In this chapter, we discuss taking care of the mane, braiding for different disciplines, and ways to keep the mane the most appropriate length for you.

## Length by Discipline

### Eventing

1 Most often a horse's mane is braided for the dressage phase but not for the cross-country and show jumping phases. However, in the upper levels, you see many horses braided for the show jumping if an awards ceremony is held at the end.

Mane Length

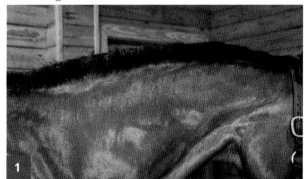

The length tends to be a personal preference and usually depends on how the rider likes the horse to be braided. You mostly see 15 to 25 small-diameter *button braids* (see p. 130) in the dressage phase, and for these, the mane is best kept at approximately 3 to 3.5 inches long.

## Show Jumping

**2** You see a slightly longer mane in show jumping, which is usually only braided for special shows. The norm is 11 to 17 medium-diameter button braids. You will also see a horse with a trimmed mane instead of a pulled one. The length of the mane is longer than the eventers or hunters, but shorter than the dressage horse; it ranges from 4 to 6 inches.

*Continued* ▶

## Dressage

**3** In dressage, the horse is always braided for competition. The mane is kept longer (5 to 10 inches) than in any of the other disciplines to allow for just 5 to 11 large-diameter button braids that best show off the arch of a horse's neck.

**4** Breeds such as Friesians, Andalusians, Lusitanos, Morgans, and Arabians show with a naturally long mane. This is generally braided by using a running braid (see p. 140).

Mane Length (Cont.)

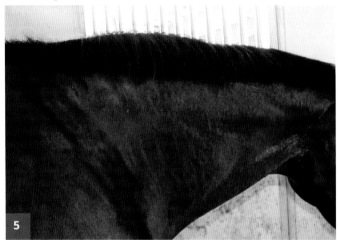

### Hunters

**5** The mane for a hunter needs to be around 4 inches long. It is important that the mane lies flat and straight across the bottom on a show hunter. Hunters must look pristine at all times, so even when they are not braided the mane must look well kept. The type of braid used on a hunter is very specific, in fact, most people refer to the style as simply a "hunter braid" (see p. 139). There are often as many as 30 braids that are very neat, which means the mane has to be well taken care of to ensure it stays even in length and thickness.

### Pleasure Riding

**6** Personal preference is all that matters for pleasure riders. Some owners keep the mane short and tidy; others allow it to get long.

## Daily Care

**1** Whenever you groom your horse, the mane should be combed or brushed out to keep it free of tangles. After bathing, always comb down the wet mane to encourage it to stay on the same side. For the most part, a mane is "trained" to the right side of the horse; however, breeds with manes naturally to the left—Friesians, Andalusians, Lusitanos, Morgans, and Arabians, as well as any dressage horse—are allowed to leave the manes where they are.

### "Training" the Mane

There are a couple of ways to train a mane to stay on the right side of the neck and to lie flat. In the long run you may never fix issues like manes that stand up or lie on two sides of the neck, but getting it to lie down correctly for a couple of days  will allow you to pull, thin, or trim it evenly.

Daily Care

Banding

## Banding

**1** Wet the mane and comb smoothly on the right side of the neck.

**2** Section off a 2- to 4-inch piece of mane and wrap a braiding band around it until it is snug.

**3** Repeat this all the way down the neck.

## Braiding Down to Train

Depending on how "wild" the mane is, you might need to braid it down.

**1** Wet the mane and comb it smoothly on the right side of the neck.

**2** Section off a 2- to 4-inch piece of mane and start a loose braid.

**3** Make sure you do not pull the side pieces in tightly since this can cause irritation, as well as damage the mane.

**4** Braid only 3 or 4 "crosses," then rubber band the end.

**5** Leave these braids in for as long as the horse is comfortable; when he starts to rub his neck, they need to be taken out.

**6** Wrong: Some horses will take offense and start to rub them out immediately, so always be on the lookout for this.

Braiding Down to Train

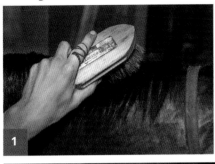  

Pulling

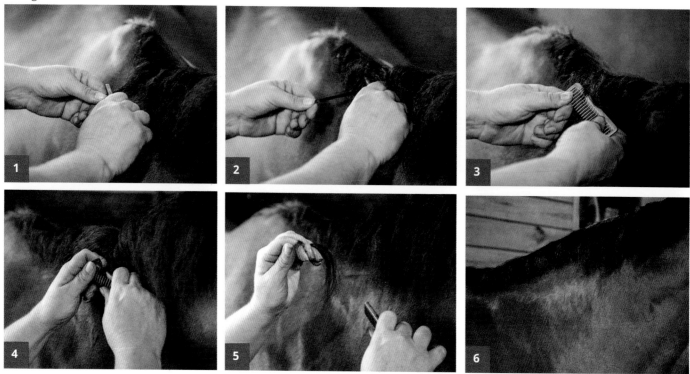

## Shortening the Mane

**1** There are three ways to maintain the kept look of a pulled mane: either the mane is pulled in the traditional manner; or it is trimmed with scissors or a special tool; or a combination of the two. Pictured here is (left to right) a sharp pulling comb, a solo comb, and a razor thinning comb.

Some horses fall asleep while you are doing the job; however, a horse might object by shaking his head, dancing around, or even biting or kicking. If the misbehavior is mild, try to move with him to keep pulling. If you pull, and he shakes his head and you stop, he has now learned that misbehaving gets a reward (the pulling stopped!). Oftentimes, a horse will shake his head or dance for a minute when you start, but settle down if you just quietly continue pulling. If he gets dangerous, however, it is best to ask a professional to pull it or use one of the alternative methods.

Shortening Tools

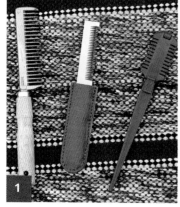

## Pulling

The "old-fashioned" way of shortening the mane is with your fingers and a pulling comb.

**1** Take a small section of mane at a time, approximately one-half inch, and back comb the mane—base to crest.

**2** This will separate the long hairs from the short hairs. Grasp a small number of long hairs...

**3** ...and wrap them around the comb...

**4** ...and pull sharply toward yourself. The hair comes out more easily if you pull outward rather than downward.

**5** Slowly work through the mane, remembering to take small sections at a time.

**6** You can avoid stressing the horse by spreading the procedure over two or three days.

**7** A completed, pulled mane.

## Cutting with Scissors

You will see some manes that have obviously been cut straight across the bottom. Although they are sometimes seen on show jumpers, we do not approve of the "banged" mane look! If you or your horse dislikes the pulling process, you can use scissors, and there is a method that leaves more of a pulled look as opposed to a cut one.

**1** Take a section of mane, comb it with a regular (not pulling) mane comb.

**2** Take the scissors at a 45-degree angle to the bottom of the mane and cut vertically into the mane. Remember to start low—you can always take more off if need be.

**3** Comb the mane out and repeat this step down the whole length of the mane until it is even.

**4** The effect is a natural, pulled look.

**5 A & B** Wrong: If you cut straight across the mane, it will leave a straight line, which is not what we are aiming for!

Cutting with Scissors

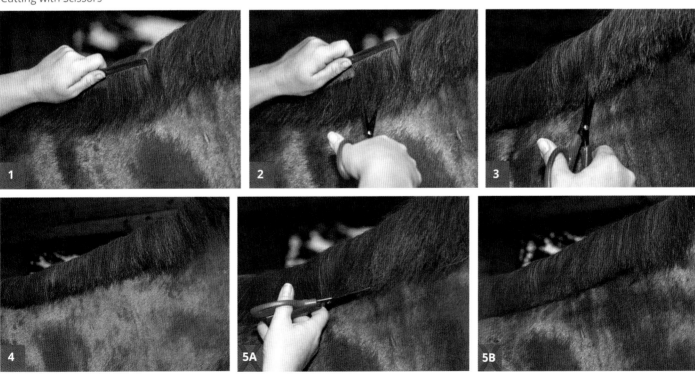

"Solo Combing"

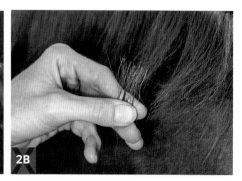

Razor Combing

## "Solo Combing"

A SoloComb™ is a comb with a razor on the inside that has a cutting action. It is used to easily cut a mane while maintaining a natural look.

**1** You back comb the mane, which separates the long from the short hairs. Take the long hairs that are left down and again comb down, deploying the razor as you go.

**2 A & B** Wrong: If you deploy the razor and simply pull toward yourself without the combing action, you will create a straight line that looks unnatural.

## Razor Combing

Use a razor comb for a thin mane that needs to be shortened, but not thinned out.

**1** Comb the mane down with a regular comb.

**2** Starting about an inch from the bottom of the mane, sandwich the hair between the razor and your thumb. Your thumb will keep the hair pressed against the razor.

Comb down the mane with the razor and the hair will cut in a natural shape.

**3** A mane well-trimmed rather than pulled. This mane is trimmed to a short, eventer length but this method can be used to create a natural line on any length mane.

## Long Mane Care

**1** A long mane can be more work than a short mane, so be prepared!

**2** First a long mane needs to be kept clean, well-conditioned and without tangles. Once you have shampooed, use an oil-based conditioner. A leave-in conditioner like those developed by SoftSheen-Carson® and formulated for ethnic hair are best; you want it to restore oil to thick, dry hair.

**3** The silicone in a product like Absorbine's® Show-Sheen® creates a moisture barrier that can build up

Long Mane Care

over time, so it is best avoided for daily use. It is a good product for show-day detangling.

**4** Finally, add a leave-in detangler. Note: never comb a wet mane because you can cause breaking and other damage. Wait until it is dry. We recommend eZall's® Shine & Detangler: it has natural ingredients, which don't build up over time.

**5 A** The tangled long mane of a horse that lives out can be intimidating.

**5 B** Simply start at the bottom of the mane, as you would your own long hair, and gently comb through small sections of the mane, gradually moving up toward the crest...

**5 C & D** ...until the entire mane is tangle-free. If you have used a good detangler, it will be done with minimal headache!

## pro tip

Many Baroque horses have loose braids put into their manes for everyday care. This is the most effective way to maintain a tangle-free mane, especially while riding. Friction of the reins can easily cause tangles and breakage. However, there are arguments against leaving loose braids in a horse overnight, since the braids themselves can cause a horse to rub and break the hair. One solution is to put a loose running braid during daily workouts and take it down again after you ride (see p. 140).

## BRAIDING MANES FOR COMPETITION

There are three main types of braiding for competition:

• *Button braids* are the neat, round knots that are seen on eventers, show jumpers, and dressage horses. They are accomplished the same way in all three disciplines, with the only difference being the amount of hair gathered in the original braid. How much hair you gather will determine the size of the "button" at the end of the job.

• *Hunter* or *flat braids* are worn exclusively by show hunters. These braids should lie flat on the neck with a very small, raised knob at the top of the braid.

• A *running braid* is a single continuous braid that runs down the length of the horse's neck. It is used on horses that are kept with a full, long mane.

### Gather Your Tools

**1** You will need the following:

• Yarn or crochet thread (for sewing braids). When preparing your yarn or thread for braiding, grasp the end of the yarn in the fold of your thumb and pointer finger, then wrap around your elbow and back up, repeat this until you have the desired number of pieces. Cut the loops you have created near your hand. This should result in yarn strands 25 to 30 inches long.

• Rubber bands (for braiding with bands).
• Wax or Exhibitor's™ Quic Braid™ spray (to help secure the braids).
• A fine-tooth comb.
• Small, sharp scissors.
• A pull-through (available through most tack shops or at a craft store as a "rug hook").
• A large-eye blunt yarn needle.
• A "crocodile" hair clip (to hold hair out of the way).
• A stool.

Braiding Tools

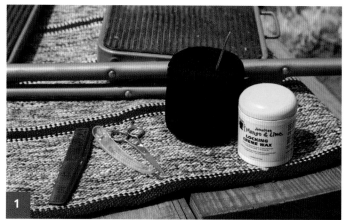

### Braiding Down

*Braiding down* in this case is different from the method used to train the mane on page 125. Here, we are talking about the process of braiding a tight, even braid down from the crest and securing it. It is the most important part of all braiding steps. Without a nice, tight, smooth braid, no final design will look good. First, we discuss how to braid down, then show you how to finish off with rubber bands, yarn, or thread, plus tell you the correct way to remove the braids. Note: We are using white-colored thread, yarn, and rubber bands to help demonstrate the steps. When in competition, use a color that matches

Braiding Down

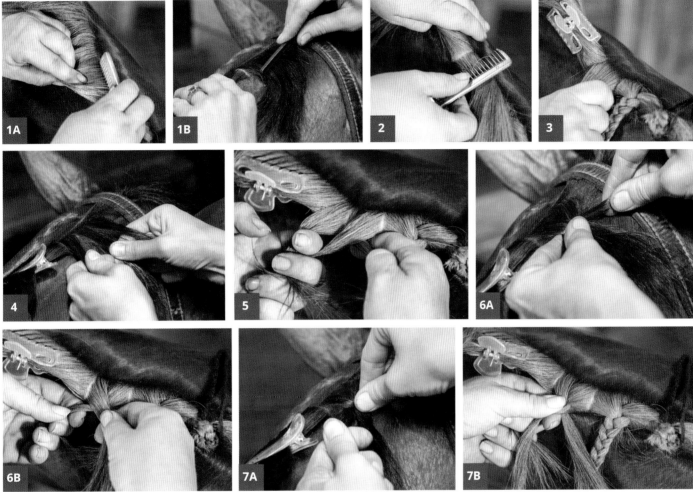

1A   1B   2   3
4   5   6A
6B   7A   7B

your horse's mane. We are using two different-colored manes for demonstration on this page.

**1 A & B** Separate the mane to be braided. The amount of hair will depend on what type of style you are creating: *button braids* can be small-, medium-, or large-diameter. *Dressage* horses use large-diameter braids, so separate 5 to 6 inches of hair (about the width of your palm). *Show jumpers* wear medium-diameter braids, so separate 3 to 5 inches of hair (about four fingers). *Eventers* go in small-diameter braids, so separate 2 to 3 inches of hair (about two or three fingers). *Show hunters* should have very narrow braids, so no more than 2 inches of hair should be separated.

**2** Make sure the part is straight.

**3** Sections can be secured either by using rubber bands or a crocodile clip.

**4** Separate the section into three equal portions.

**5** Cross the right strand over the center strand, using your thumb to keep it lying flat and down.

**6 A & B** Next cross the left side over the right, pulling the center piece to the right. Again use your thumbs to hold in place and smooth.

**7 A & B** Continue crossing right to left and left to right down the braid. Make sure to pull across, not down.

Using Rubber Bands

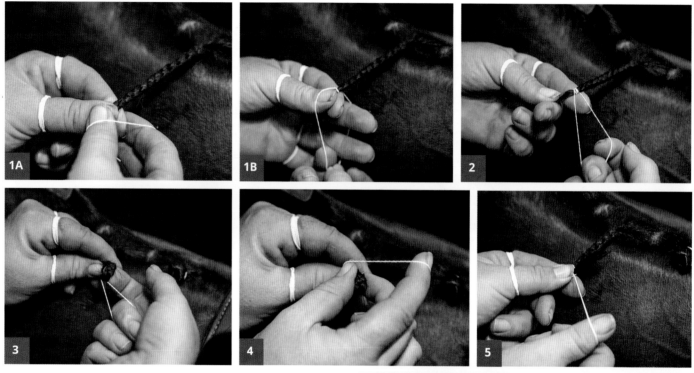

Now the technique continues, but varies according to the equipment used: rubber bands, thread, or yarn.

### Using Rubber Bands

**1 A & B** When using rubber bands, braid as far down as you can.

**2** Wrap the rubber band several times around the braid, leaving yourself a large amount of rubber band held in a large loop.

**3** Fold the braid up, using your middle finger to hold the rubber band and your pointer finger to create a smooth fold.

**4** Holding the braid steady, loop the rubber band around the folded braid.

**5** Continue holding the rubber band out; you will now have a folded end and a "tail" of hair lying parallel to your braid.

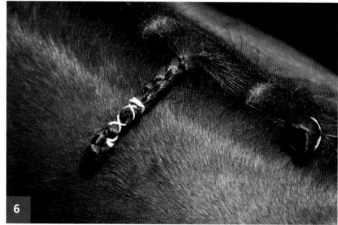

**6** Repeatedly loop the rubber band up the braid until all the loose ends are tucked away.

### Using Thread or Yarn

**1** When you get two-thirds of the way down the braid, or are 2 to 3 inches from the end, take a piece of your thread (or yarn), fold it in half, and incorporate half of it with the piece of hair about to be braided.

Using Thread or Yarn

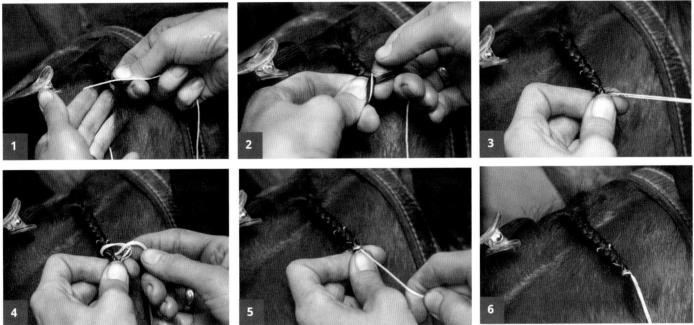

**2** Braid the next piece of hair over, and incorporate the other half of the thread, as shown.

**3** Continue braiding with the thread as if it is another strand of hair for four or five crosses. Then, separate the hair into one hand and thread into the other.

**4** Loop the yarn around the braid and through the loop.

**5** Pull snugly to tighten the knot.

**6** All finished.

## Finishing Braids with Rubber Bands

This form of braiding is a great way to learn and for more experienced braiders, it's a quick and efficient method. Follow the steps on page 132 to braid down to end using a rubber band.

**1** Fold the tip under toward the crest of the neck.

**2 A & B** Fold in half again and place a rubber band around the entire button.

Finishing Braids with Rubber Bands

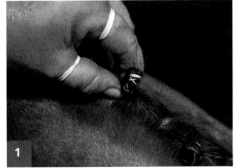 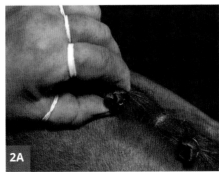 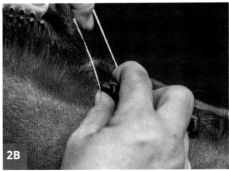

*Continued* ▶

Finishing Braids with Rubber Bands (Cont.)

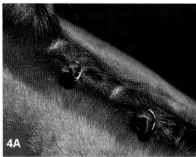

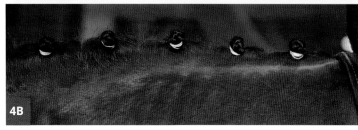

**3** For extra security place a second rubber band around the button.

**4 A & B** They can look quite professional when done correctly.

### Removing Rubber Bands

Leaving a mane overnight braided with rubber bands is not ideal: some horses find the bands "pull" too much on their crest and try to rub them out.

**1** Put your thumb and forefinger on the top and bottom of the braid.

**2** Pull the braid toward you and it will unfold.

**3** Remove the bands.

## Finishing Simple Sewn-In Button Braids

This form of braiding is the classic hunt braid, and for good reason. It is very customizable and will stay tight no matter what the weather or activity. Use cotton crochet thread or waxed-cotton braiding thread in the braid. Nylon crochet thread is hard to knot.

**1** Using a large-eye, blunt, yarn needle, thread both hanging ends through the eye.

**2** Push the needle through the center of the braid.

**3** Pull up on the string until the braid folds in half.

**4** Holding the needle in your hand, split the thread and put one strand on either side of the braid.

**5** Roll the braid up and push your needle through the lowest point of the "roll."

**6** Pull up on the thread until quite tight, removing the needle.

**7** Split the strands again, and wrap the outside of the braid.

**8 A & B** Cross the thread twice then pull tight.

**9** Cross the thread once more to secure the knot.

**10** Cut the ends close to the neck.

**11** Finished sewn-in button braids.

Removing Rubber Bands

Finishing Simple Sewn-In Button Braids

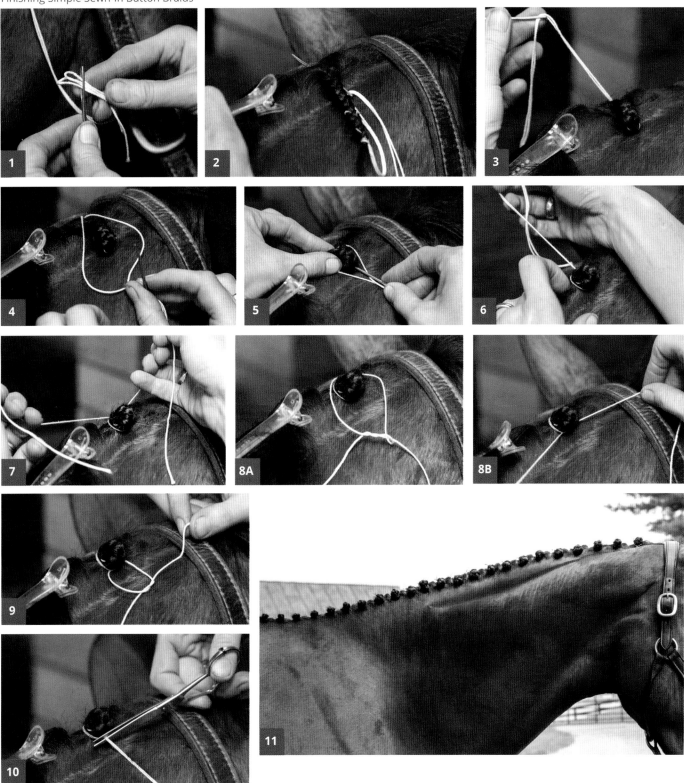

Removing Sewn-In Button Braids

 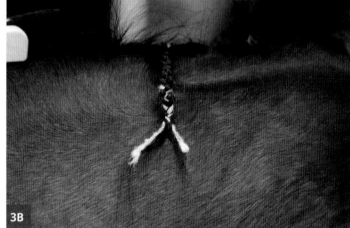

## Removing Sewn-In Button Braids

**1 A & B** To remove, simply cut the knot at the bottom of the button.

**2** Pull the braid down...

**3 A & B** ...and cut the knot at the end of the braid.

**4** When a horse's braids have been removed, the mane will look as if it's had a bad perm!

It is not a good idea to leave a horse's mane like this for any length of time. Do not assume the mane will just flatten on its own; if the braids were sewn in it can take several days for the mane to "un-crimp." Prior to undoing your braids, simply take a damp sponge and wet the mane. This will make removing the braids faster and will help to smooth the mane down. Once the braids are pulled out, run the sponge over it again and use a fine-toothed comb to smooth it out.

Yarn Button Braids

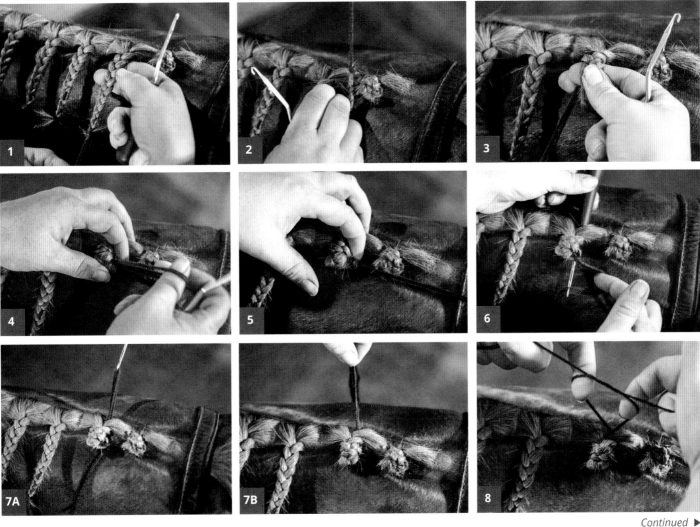

*Continued* ▶

## Yarn Button Braids— The Emma Ford Way

Very similar to sewn-in braids, this braiding method stays in very well and works on a variety of manes.

**1** Place your forefinger and middle finger of your right hand on the underside, close to the crest.

**2** Using your left hand, twist the braid to the right and over the top of the crest.

**3** Using your fingers to maintain the loop, grab the yarn.

**4** Push the yarn into the loop you have created then pull the entire braid through the loop to the right.

**5** To keep it tight, use your left hand at the base to help feed it through the loop.

**6** Insert a pull-through down through the center of the braid, close to the crest.

**7 A & B** Pull the loose yarn back through the braid.

**8** Separate the two pieces of yarn, wrap one piece to the left and the other to the right. Maintaining the loop, cross the yarn ends twice.

Yarn Button Braids (Cont.)

Removing Yarn Button Braids

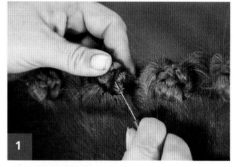

**9** Pull the loop tight at the bottom of the braid.

**10** Cut off loose yarn close to the knot.

**11** Emma Ford button braids.

### Removing Yarn Button Braids

To remove these braids, use a seam ripper. Note: You need good light to make sure you don't rip out the hair by mistake.

**1** Look under the braid and there should be a "cross" of yarn.

**2** Cut the cross carefully.

**3** Unknot the braid.

**4** Use the seam ripper carefully at the end of the braid in a downward motion to release the original knot that holds the long braid in place.

**5** Pull out the yarn and undo the braid.

# Hunter Braids

**1** This type of braiding is primarily seen in the hunter ring—anywhere from 30 to 50 even braids down the entire neck. This takes time to learn; however, when done well, it looks beautiful.

The key to proper hunter braids is a very evenly pulled mane. Use a comb with tight teeth when combing out the hair; this helps to smooth down any errant hairs.

**2** When braiding down, the braids should sit no more than half an inch away from each other. You want the braids to almost touch when done, so start with a braid no wider than your index finger.

**3** Using a pull-through, put it down the very center of the braid at the crest.

**4** Hook both ends of yarn with your pull-through.

**5** Pull the loose strings through the top of the crest.

**6** Pull the end of the braid into the bottom of the crest but not all the way through. It should make a flat fold that lies on the neck.

**7** Separate the pieces of string. Make a loop by crossing the ends over themselves twice.

**8** Using your fingers to hold the braid up slightly, tighten the knot down. This will create a small knob.

**9** If necessary, straighten the sides so the knob lies perpendicular to the crest.

Hunter Braids

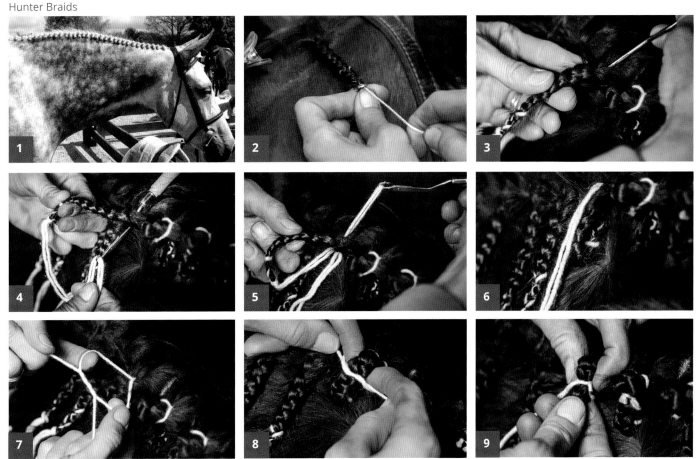

Continued ▶

Hunter Braids (Cont.)

**10** Finish the knot with another cross-over.

**11** Cut the thread close to the braid.

**12** In this photo, we've demonstrated a couple of common mistakes, plus included a correct braid for comparison, from right to left.

Wrong: Braid One has a decent knob, but the loop has slid apart. This is generally caused by braiding down with uneven sections of hair.

Wrong: Braid Two has a knob that is a bit too large, and it sits too far off the neck. You can catch this before the knot is finished and bring a little less hair into the braid.

Braid Three is just right.

**13** Finished hunter braids.

When deciding how far down the neck to go with your braids, set your saddle pad in the correct position.

Mark with a rubber band or clip where the saddle pad hits, then braid to that spot. Some horses can be fussy about braids on their withers, so be gentle and braid a slight bit looser than you do the rest of the mane. Hunter horses that will be jogged and event horses braided for the formal jog should have all of the mane hair braided.

## Running Braid

Essentially a long, single French braid, you only see this form of braiding on dressage horses with long manes, especially Baroque breeds, such as Friesians and Andalusians. These manes are braided on whichever side the mane lies naturally.

**1** Start at the poll and separate the mane into three sections. Cross the right over the center.

**2** Cross the left over the right.

**3** Next, start the "running" part of the braid. Cross the right over the center again.

**4** Section off a small amount of hair from the mane and add it to the section you just crossed over the center.

**5** Cross the left over the center, holding it almost parallel to the crest. Do not add any more hair.

**6 A & B** Using your left hand to support the braid, cross the right over the center again, adding new hair.

**7** Again, bring the left over the center without adding any hair.

**8 A–C** Continue this way down the neck, making sure to stay close to the crest.

**9 A & B** As you approach the withers, allow the distance from the neck to get slightly longer.

**10** When you reach the end of the mane, add yarn or thread by laying it behind the braid and grasping one strand in two sections of hair.

Running Braid

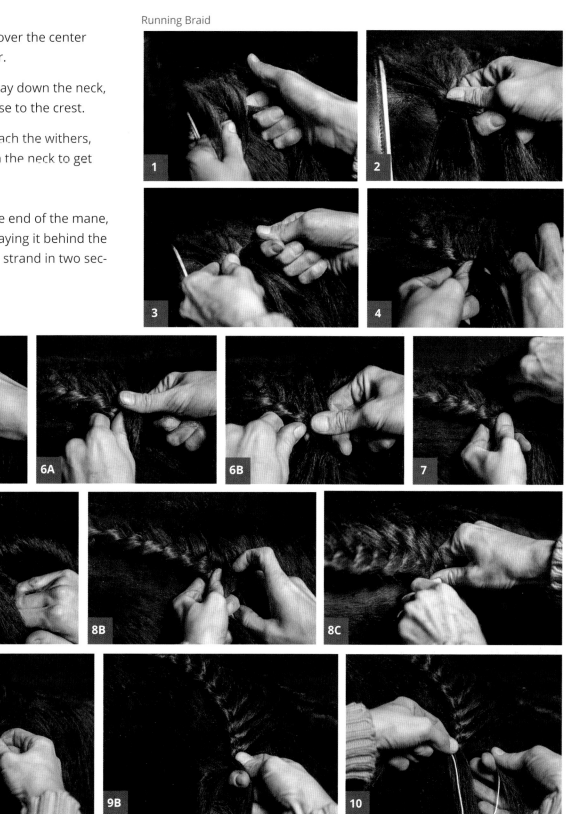

Continued ▶

Running Braid (Cont.)

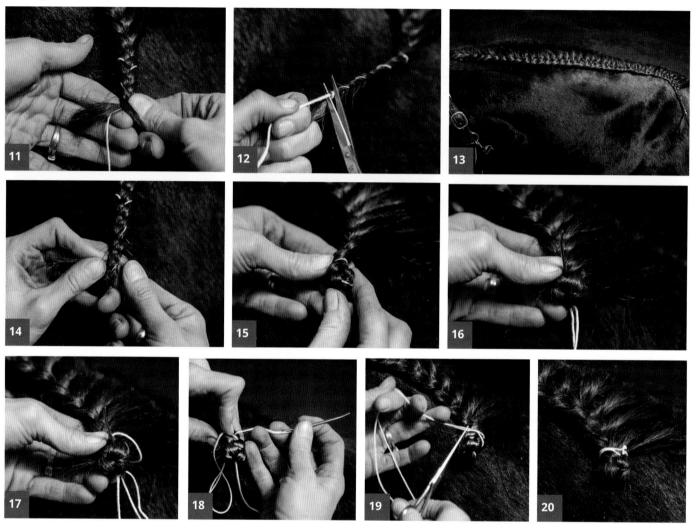

**11** Incorporate the yarn into the braid.

**12** Loop around the end, tying a knot. Cut the ends of the thread.

**13** Your braid should look like this. You can choose to leave it or to finish the end. For a fancier look, tuck the end up.

**14** Starting at the bottom of the braid, fold the end around your finger.

**15** Roll the braid toward the crest.

**16** When you reach the running part of the braid, insert a threaded needle through the roll.

**17** Pull the needle through and wrap it to the left of the braid.

**18** Thread the needle through the roll again and wrap this loop to the right of the braid.

**19** You will now have two ends of thread: one under the braid, one on top. Tie these in a simple knot and cut the excess thread.

**20** All tied up!

# BRAIDING THE FORELOCK

The finishing touch to your braided mane is a tidy fore-lock. There are two methods for braiding a forelock: a simple braid with a button and a French braid tucked away. The simple braid can easily be accomplished with a rubber band and looks nice as long as the horse's mane is not too thick or long. It should be noted that a rubber band braid is *not* appropriate for hunters. A French braid gives a really professional finish but is hard to accomplish on a thin or short forelock.

## Simple Forelock Braid

**1** Comb the forelock and separate into three equal sections. Have rubber bands on your fingers.

**2** Cross the right side over the center section.

**3** Then take the left over the center, making sure to pull nice and tight.

**4** Continue braiding until you get close to the end.

**5** Secure the end of the braid with your rubber band.

**6** Fold up the loose hair and use rubber bands to attach it to the braid.

**7** Roll up the braid and secure with a rubber band.

Simple Forelock Braid

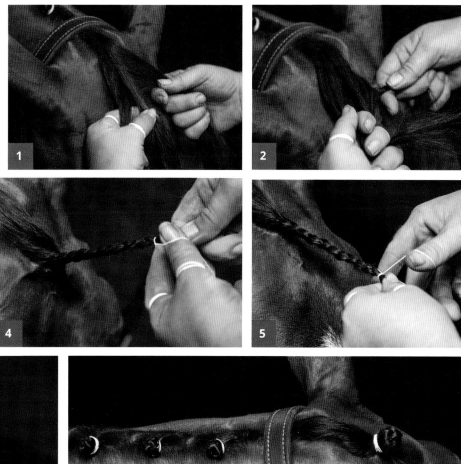

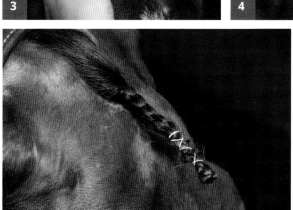

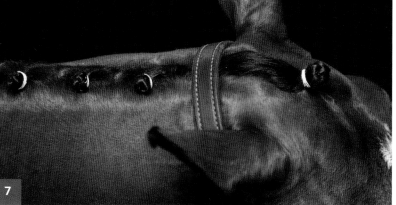

French Braid

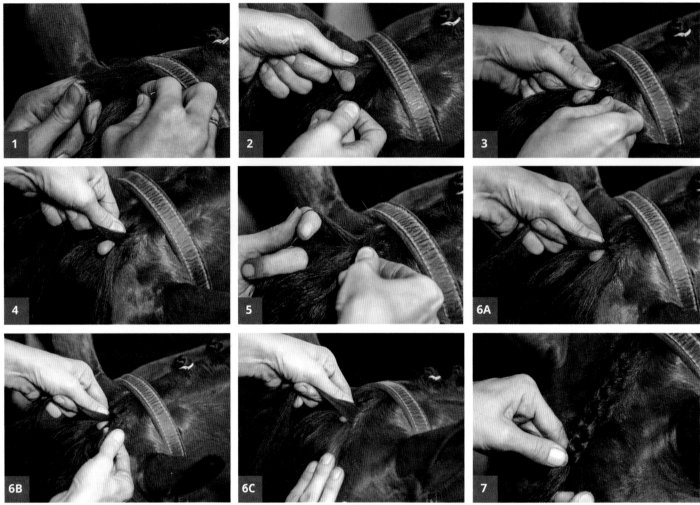

Continued ▶

## French Braid

**1** Comb out the forelock carefully. Use your large-eye, blunt-end yarn needle to separate out a section of hair from the top of the forelock.

**2** Divide this section into two even pieces.

**3** Cross the right piece over the left.

**4** Add a section of hair of equal thickness to the two you are already holding from the outside of the *right* side of the forelock. Cross this over to use as your third strand of braid.

**5** Separate out a narrow section of hair from the outside of the *left* side of the forelock.

**6 A–C** Each time you cross over, French braid by adding a narrow section of hair from only the outside.

**7** Continue adding only from the outside, until you reach the bottom of the braid, then gather up the remaining hair into the braid.

**8 A & B** Braid a half-inch below the end of the French braid and add your thread by crossing it behind the hair.

French Braid (Cont.)

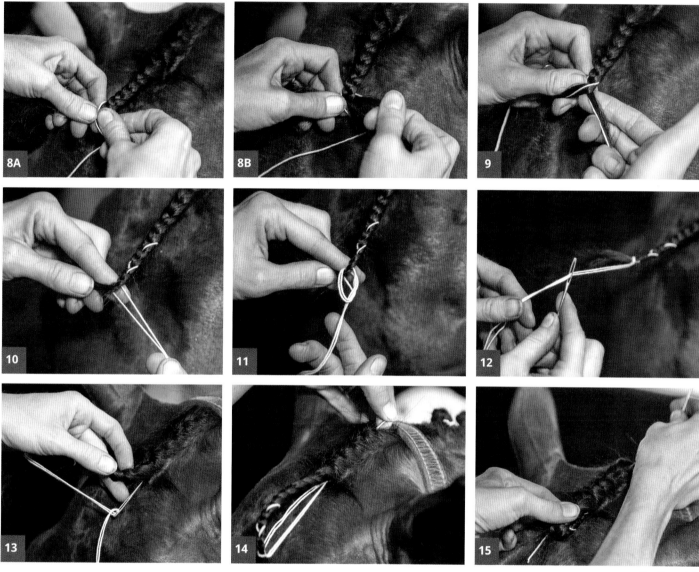

*Continued* ▶

**9** Incorporate the two strands of thread into the braid.

**10** Continue braiding until you have about one inch of hair left. Separate the threads into one hand and the braid into the other, holding the braid tight.

**11** Tie off the end of the braid with a simple knot.

**12** Thread both ends through your large-eye, blunt-end yarn needle.

**13** Being careful not to stab your horse in the head, thread the needle into the center of the French braid.

**14** You want it to emerge in the very top of the braid, dead center.

**15** Pull the braid up into the hollow area you've created by only pulling from the sides of the forelock in the French braid. You may need to use your finger to help guide it.

French Braid (Cont.)

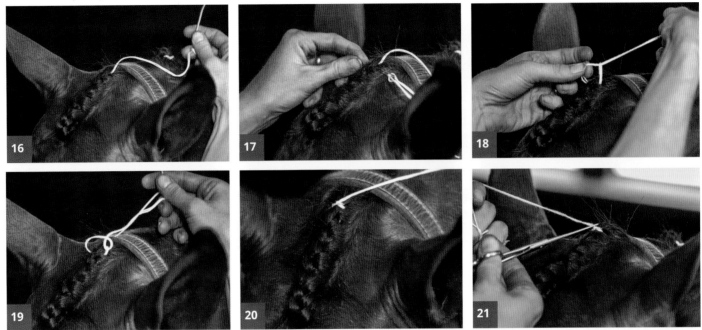

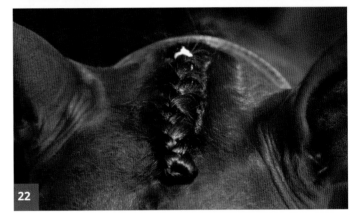

**16** It should fold in half and lie smoothly next to the forehead.

**17** Run your needle underneath the braid.

**18** Use the needle to thread through the loop you made on the right.

**19** Next thread through the loop on the left.

**20** Pull nice and tight.

**21** Cut the thread close to the forelock.

**22** You will end with a very tidy, tight French braid with no evidence of its end.

## CHAPTER TEN

# "On the Exit"

### *Emma says*

"Phillip Dutton's Woodburn was a supreme athlete and taken away from us too early. In the barn, I would describe him as the quarterback of the team: tough, strong, athletic, and very handsome with a personality that, at times, melted my heart. Even today I choke up thinking about him and can only hope that I get the chance to take care of another horse with half his talent in the near future. In 2007, Phillip and I made the trip to the Wits End CIC *** in Canada. Woodburn and another horse called Matchplay needed to qualify for Fair Hill CCI ***. Because of the trip being so long, we decided to take the Tahoe and two-horse trailer instead of our usual vehicle, a large combination van that had a living area in the front and a horse area in the back.

All went well throughout the weekend, apart from one small hitch. Woodburn's tail started to fall out on dressage day. I was horrified. I'm always very careful with tails, a believer in finger grooming rather than daily combing when not at competitions. But, it didn't matter how careful I was, the strands of hair just kept falling out. By Sunday morning he had half the tail he started with. Checking the stall it was obvious he hadn't been rubbing on anything.

For long trips I put a tail guard on rather than wrap since a too-tight tail wrap can cause hair loss. I finally figured out that he basically had "sat" on his tail the whole drive up to Canada—about 12 hours. The small bumper-pull trailer had much more movement than the large van he was used to, and he must have disliked the feeling, so he leaned against the butt bar for stability. For the trip home, I filled a grain bag with hay and tied it up behind him in the trailer to prevent any more pressure on his dock. At Fairhill that year, and throughout the next two years' competition seasons, I had to use a fake tail. But when I was preparing for Burghley in England, 2008, I made the mistake of packing the wrong fake tail—the chestnut color was too light! I had a go at dying it. Huge mistake! I got the color completely wrong. Luckily for me, another rider at the barn had the fake tail I needed so disaster was averted!

It would not have mattered to Phillip if Woodburn had gone into the dressage ring with no tail at all but for me, as his groom, I would have been mortified to have my horse enter the ring at one of the most prestigious four stars in the world without looking perfect."

# THE TAIL: ROUTINE CARE

Braiding

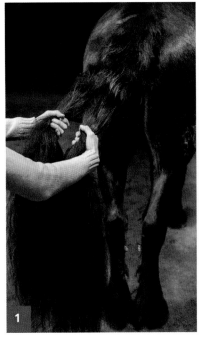

In any discipline, a good tail can make or break the look of a horse. While largely a cosmetic issue, there are a few practical details to note when it comes to tails. Remember that a very long tail can be stepped on when performing the rein-back, so care should be taken to make sure that the length is appropriate for each discipline.

For the average length of tail, routine care is very similar no matter the discipline. Your goal is to avoid breakage by preventing knots and not over-grooming; have the tail look decent by staying tangle-free and clean; and promote healthy hair growth through proper nutrition and conditioning. On bath days, make sure you scrub the dock really well, getting your fingernails into it, to help remove the dead skin and gunk that can build up close to the roots. *Never* comb a wet tail!

**1** A gentle conditioning shampoo like Motions® Lavish Conditioning Shampoo ensures that the tail is clean without becoming dry. A deep-treating conditioner like

Routine Care

one from SoftSheen™-Carson helps prevent weak hairs, and a non-silicone-based detangler such as eZall® Shine & Detangler makes sure the tail stays free of tangles.

## Long-Haired Horses

For Iberian and other long-haired breeds where a long, thick tail is desired, there are a few routine steps that are necessary to ensure a healthy tail. The tail should be protected from damage by being kept off the ground. There are three ways to do this: First, by simply *braiding* it; second, by *"bagging"* it in a tail bag; and third, *wrapping* it in Vetrap tape. Each method has its advantages so pick the one that works the best for you and your horse's lifestyle.

### Braiding

*Braiding* a tail helps to prevent it from getting caught and broken. This method is the simplest to do, but since it does not protect the tail from the outside environment, it is best suited for the horse that spends most of his time inside and protected from the weather.

Braiding (Cont.)

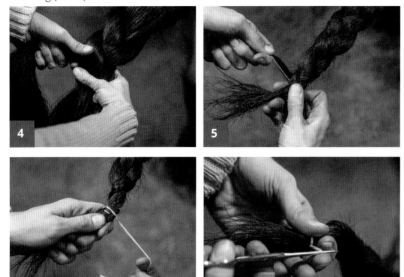

**6** Braid with the yarn for a few more crosses. Then wrap the yarn around the braid.

**7** Tie a knot in the yarn and cut the ends.

### "Bagging"

*Bagging* a tail refers to using a cloth bag to cover a braided tail. It has all the advantages of a braided tail with added protection from the elements. It also helps to prevent the tail from snagging and breaking off. A bag is easy to apply and can be reused over and over; however, the tail should be taken down, washed, conditioned and put back up at least once every week to 10 days. Mares often need to be done more frequently due to urine getting into the bags. You can purchase a nylon tail bag from most tack shops. Look for one about 30 inches long with either a top with a snap, or four ties. Avoid Velcro closures since they often come undone and break the tail. In our photos, we have used a bag with ties at the top.

**1** The tail should be clean, dry, and well combed. Use a leave-in conditioner, such as eZall's Show-N-Go to lightly coat the tail.

**2** Divide the tail into three equal sections.

**3** Start braiding 6 to 8 inches below the dock. If you braid too tightly, the horse will itch and end up pulling out all the hair, negating all your hard work!

**4** You want a braid with medium tightness, just snug enough to hold into place.

**5** Near the end of the braid add a piece of yarn.

First, shampoo and condition the tail. Allow to dry and apply a leave-in detangler. Braid the tail as described above.

**1** Take the tail bag, turn it inside out, and slide your hand inside.

**2** Hold the end of the braid with your hand inside the tail bag.

**3** Slide the bag up the braid.

"Bagging"

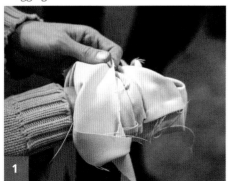

*Continued* ▶

"Bagging" (Cont.)

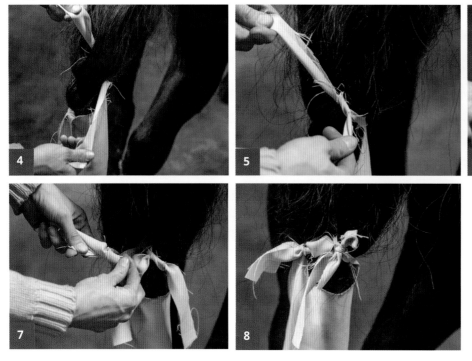

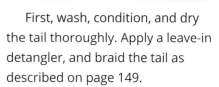

First, wash, condition, and dry the tail thoroughly. Apply a leave-in detangler, and braid the tail as described on page 149.

**1** Create a hole in the tail between the dock and the start of the braid.

**2** Take the tail of the braid and thread it through the hole.

**4** At the top of the braid, thread one of the bags ties through the loose hair at the base of the dock.

**5** Tie the right side.

**6** Thread another bag tie through the loose hair at the base of the dock.

**7** Tie the left side.

**8** Securely tied.

## "Wrapping"

A *wrapped* tail can be kept completely out of mud and muck since it is rolled up high away from the ground and completely wrapped in Vetrap. When the tail is well-conditioned and dry, this wrap can be left in place for the entire winter, which is especially useful for horses that live in cold climates where washing and conditioning the tail in January is not an attractive option. However, during the show season, wrapping is not as practical as *bagging* because it is more time-consuming and wasteful since the wrap can only be used once.

**3** Pull the tail through gently then thread the tail through again.

**4** Continue rolling like this until the entire tail is in a ball.

**5** Take a roll of Vetrap and begin at the top of the rolled braid.

**6** Roll all the way around the braid and back through the parted hair.

**7 A & B** Next go across the braid from side to side.

**8 A & B** Again, go back through the parted hair and wrap side to side from the other direction.

**9** Continue this pattern, up and down, right to left, left to right, until you are at the end of the Vetrap. You should have a neat, tight ball that sits well above the hocks.

**10** Take a strand of electrical tape and tape over the end of the Vetrap to prevent unraveling.

**11** Your tail should stay secure like this for the winter months if necessary.

"Wrapping"

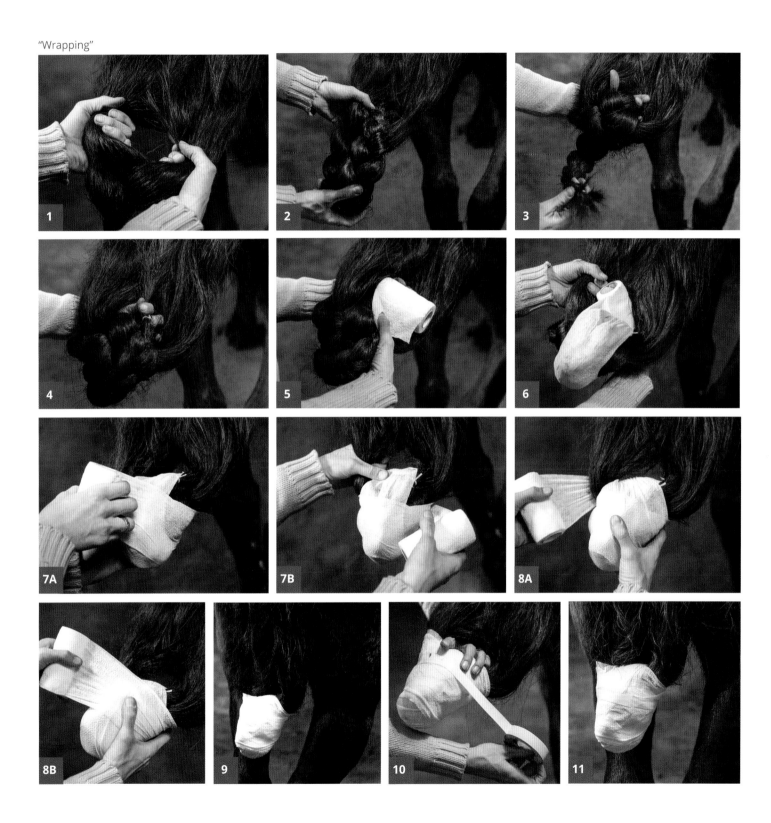

# PREPARING FOR COMPETITION

## "Banging"

*Banging* a tail is simply the term used for cutting a tail straight across. Every discipline has a length that is appropriate. Generally, hunter and dressage riders like a tail banged at the low fetlock. Jumpers like a tail at the lower end of the cannon bone. An eventer's tail is banged mid-to-high cannon bone.

Start with sharp scissors, a dry tail, and a rolled standing bandage.

**1** When a horse moves, he carries his tail up slightly higher, so remember that cutting to the length you want when he is standing still will be too short. To avoid this, either put a standing bandage under the horse's dock to help gauge length, or place your arm under the dock. (If your horse objects, skip this step and just cut the tail 3 to 6 inches longer than you think it should be. You can always trim more if it still looks too long when he is moving!)

**2** Comb the tail out, being careful not to yank through knots. Instead use your fingers to gently work them out.

"Banging"

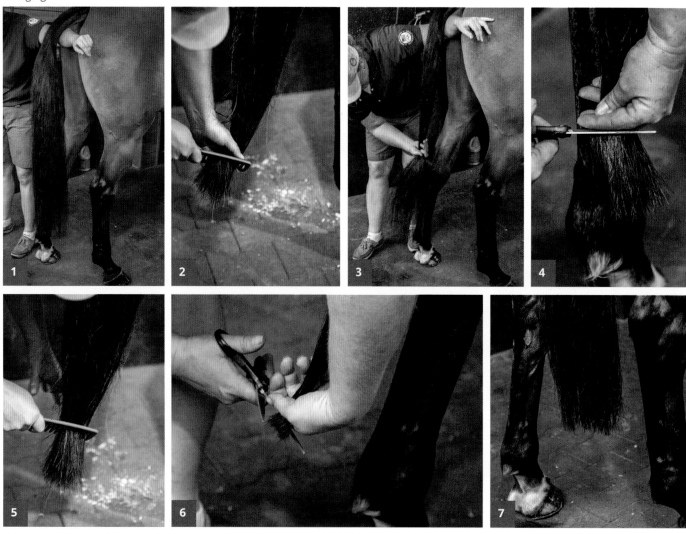

**3** Follow the last sweep of the comb with your hand and gather the tail into a smooth bunch. If tail is too thick, separate it into two bunches and use an alligator clip to hold one bunch up and out of the way.

**4** Without moving the tail, cut straight across the bottom by holding the scissors parallel to the floor. If you have divided the tail, pull down the second bunch, gather and cut at the same level as the previous bunch.

**5** Re-comb the tail, being careful not to pull through knots, instead work them out with your fingers.

**6** Re-trim the bottom to clean up any wisps.

**7** A nice, cleanly banged tail.

Note: When you pull down on the tail, it will spring back up an inch or so when you are done. So, cut a little longer than you think you should—it's easier to cut more than grow more!

## Clip, Pull, or Braid?

Depending on the discipline, the top of a horse's tail needs attention as well. Years ago, it was discovered that thick hair near the dock prevented a horse from cooling down efficiently after a good gallop, so tails got braided or pulled to make this easier. Nowadays, show-hunters' tails are braided as a nod to their foxhunting roots—also for the look. Event horses' tails are pulled about halfway down the dock because they need to be cooled down rapidly. Show jumpers are left with the tail naturally thick. Dressage horses have a small section clipped at the very top of the dock. You can easily start a war by walking into a room full of grooms and asking them whether—and why—they clip or pull their charges' tails! We will cover both methods and their pros and cons.

Clipping

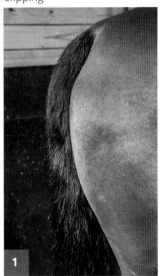 

Continued ▶

## Clipping

*Clipping* never looks quite as polished as a *pulled* tail, but it can be easier to execute and less dangerous when you have a horse who doesn't love the pulling procedure!

**1** Start with a clean, combed tail.

**2** Use rubber bands to contain any long hairs running down the center of the dock.

### pro tip

During the winter in the north, our horses have several months off competition. I like to bang their tails quite short after their last fall competition. I do this for two reasons: First, it keeps the tail out of icy mud that can damage and break it. Second, the tail gets a chance to grow in more thickly for the next season since I trim to above any split ends that cause a thin, wispy-looking bottom. I find my tails stay much thicker when I do this. —*Cat*

Clipping (Cont.)

**3** Next, hold the tail away from the body, and position your clippers parallel to the horse's dock.

**4** Being careful not to come to the front of the tail, run your clipper up the side only, clipping the hair on the sides of the dock.

**5** Use a smaller clipper to tidy up the edge between the clipped section and the long dock hairs.

**6** Move to the other side and repeat the process.

Pulling

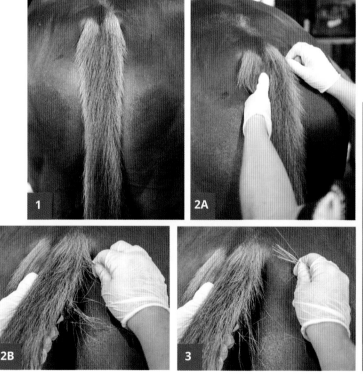

# Pulling

*Pulling* the tail creates a more natural look than *clipping,* and you can finesse its shape to suit each horse. This method must be done regularly. Be advised that you should not pull a tail that has never been pulled before all on one day; it can be too painful to have that much hair removed all at once. Work in brief sessions to make the horse more comfortable and proceed with caution because many horses do not like it being done!

**1** First, start with a tail that is clean and combed. Make sure it does not contain any silicone conditioner because it will be too slippery to grab. You may find a rubber glove helps to give you more grip.

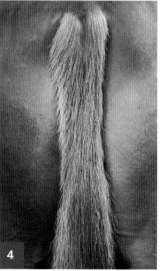

**2 A & B** Hold the tail up with one hand, grasp the long hairs along the side of the tail with your other hand, and yank sharply outward to pull the hairs out from the root.

**3** Make sure to pull straight *outward* not downward: this helps to release the hair.

**4** Continue working down the tail, pulling the long hairs as you go.

**5** You should end up with a tail that looks tidy from the back on both sides, but probably looks a bit frizzy and uneven.

**6** Don't panic! Simply put on a tail wrap (see p. 158) for about an hour then re-check your work.

**7** Most likely, it will look just right.

Pulling (Cont.)

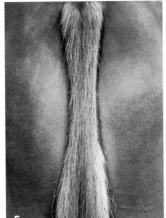
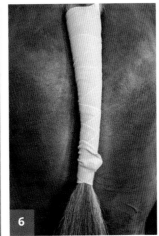
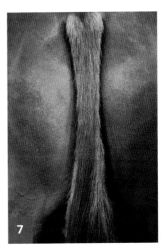

## Braiding

Braiding a tail is time-consuming and must be practiced, so make sure you hone your skill at home before heading to the ring. We use a combination of a French braid and a regular braid to create the look.

**1** Start by combing the tail down very well, especially the sides and back of the dock. There should be no conditioner at the top of the tail.

**2 A–C** Dampen a brush with a bit of water. Then brush the sides and back of the dock so the hair is damp.

**3 A & B** Separate out a small section of hair from the top corner of each side of the tail, bring to the middle, and cross right over left.

**4** Separate out another small section of hair from the left side of the tail and cross over the two strands in

Tail Braiding

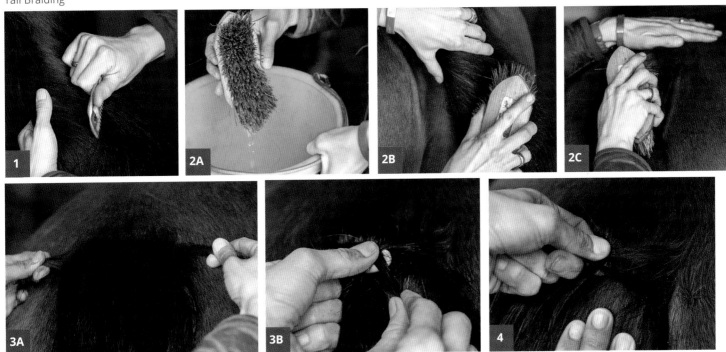

*Continued* ▶

Tail Braiding (Cont.)

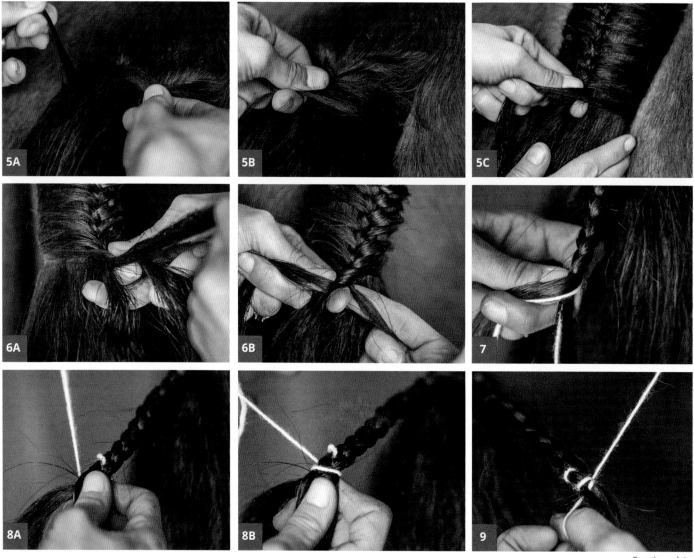

*Continued* ▶

the middle. These pieces will be your three strands to braid.

**5 A & B** Alternating sides, bring a very small section of hair from the outermost area of the dock into the middle and incorporate into the strand you are working with.

**5 C** This will create a French braid with very narrow strips of hair coming from the outside of the tail into the center of the braid.

**6 A & B** When you get to the bottom of the dock, drop a small amount of hair from each of the three sections. Do this by splitting the section as you cross it over the center.

**7** Continue with a regular braid for about 6 more inches; add in your yarn.

**8 A & B** Braid one or two more times, then tie the braid. First, cross one strand of yarn over the top of the braid...

Tail Braiding (Cont.)

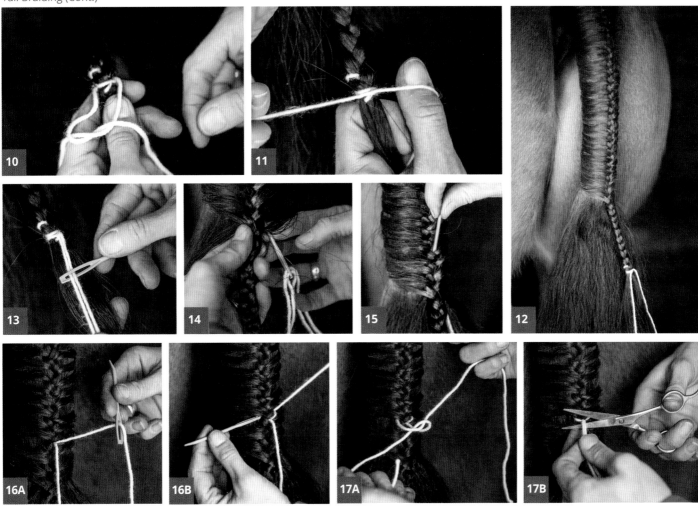

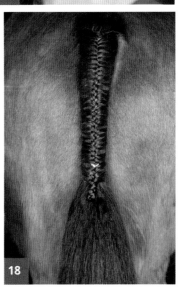

9  ...then the other way.

10  Cross your yarn over itself twice to create a surgical knot.

11  Tighten it down securely.

12  The braid should be tight and even.

13  Now thread the yarn through a large-eye, blunt-end yarn needle.

14  Push the needle behind the braid.

15  Come out the center of the braid about 3 inches up the braid.

16 A & B  Keep one piece of yarn in the needle and go straight behind the braid, coming out the other side.

17 A & B  Tie a secure knot and trim the ends.

18  A nice, tidy tail braid.

# Tail Bandaging

There are many times when you are going to need to bandage a tail: to protect a braid, train a pulled or clipped tail, or keep a full tail clean at a show. You must be very, very careful when bandaging not to put it on too tight because you can cut off circulation to the tail hairs

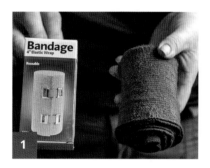

and cause them all to drop out. A tight tail wrap can also cause the horse to itch and if he rubs his rear end, he will rub out your nice, neat tail!

**1** You can use an Ace bandage or a tail wrap.

## Basic Method

**1** Start by putting your bandage all the way up under the dock, as high as it will go. It helps to put the tail over your shoulder to hold it up while you wrap.

**2** Pull the end of the bandage up and lay it above the tail.

**3** Cross over and gently pull both sides to tighten.

**4** Wrap under the tail once.

**5** Fold the excess down and bandage over it. This locks the top of it nice and snug.

**6** Continue to bandage down the tail, pulling snugly and consistently, but not tightly.

Basic Method

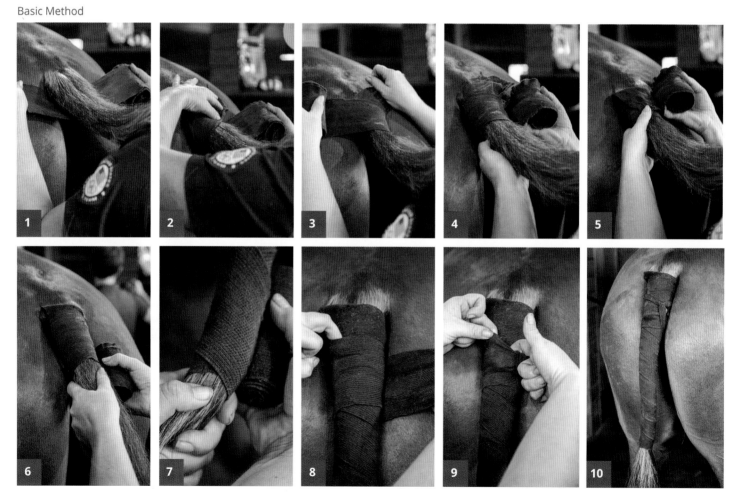

Advanced Method

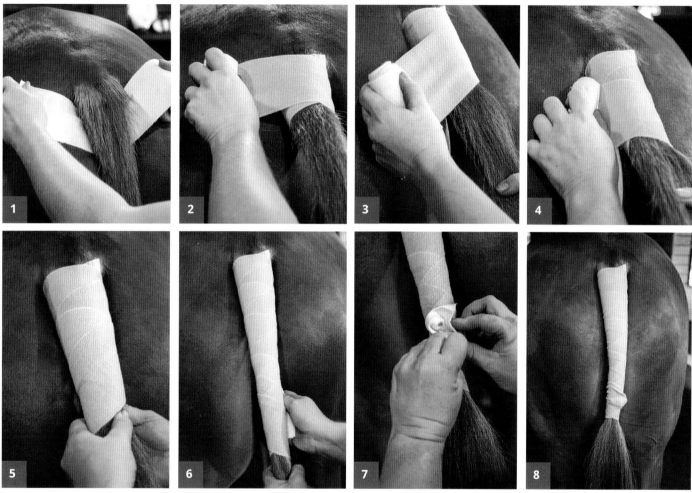

**7** When you get to the end of the dock, start back up the tail.

**8** Keep bandaging until you get near the end of the wrap. When you get to that point, make a pocket with one finger in the last wrap you made.

**9** Tuck the end of the wrap into the pocket.

**10** The bandage should be snug and even all the way down and back up.

## Advanced Method

This is the best method for bandaging a braided tail.

**1** Start by putting the end as high up the tail as you can.

**2** Cross over the tail of the bandage and tuck it under the side.

**3** Next wrap, angle down to the left.

**4** As you come around the back, head up to the left.

**5** Repeat this pattern each time you come around, down, then up.

**6** It should create a crisscross pattern across the tail.

**7** When you get to the end of the Ace bandage, tuck it into the last wrap.

**8** It should end just above the end of the dock.

Removing Bandage: Unbraided Tail

  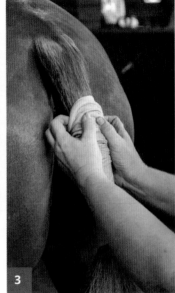 

Removing Bandage: Braided Tail

  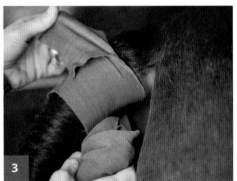

## Removing Bandage

### Unbraided Tail

**1** Simply work your fingers into the top of the wrap.

**2** Gently pull down on the bandage.

**3** Keep pulling as the bandage slips down the tail.

**4** The wrap just slides off the tail.

### Braided Tail

**1** Carefully undo the end.

**2** Hold the tail still with one hand and unwind the wrap with the other.

**3** Be extra careful at the top to hold the tail still and not loosen the fragile top of the braid.

## Attaching a Fake Tail–The Cat Hill Way

There are two kinds of fake tails: one type comes mounted to a piece of leather and another, more commonly seen, with a loop of string at the top. I'm going to deal with the latter—the loop of string version. In these photos, I have made the loop white-colored so you can see it: with a real fake tail, you would want the loop to match the tail. Make sure to check with the Rulebook of your discipline; tail extensions are illegal in some. Putting in a fake tail for the first time can be nerve-wracking because you don't want to go through the embarrassment of it falling out! To add to the problem, there are many ways to attach it. I grew up showing and grooming Arabian horses. Many of them wore dramatically long fake tails, so a very secure attachment was necessary. The method I learned then has served me well, and I have sent many a horse out on a jump course without the tail piece shifting.

**1** First divide a small section of hair from low on the horse's dock. You can use hair clips to keep extra hair out of the way.

**2** Braid the small section tightly down about 2 to 3 inches.

**3** Cross a piece of yarn behind the back of the braid and add it into the braid.

**4** Tie a secure knot and leave the tails of the yarn.

**5** Grab your fake tail, which should be well brushed and conditioned.

**6 A & B** Thread the braid through the loop at the top of the fake tail.

Attaching a Fake Tail

Continued ▶

Attaching a Fake Tail (Cont.)

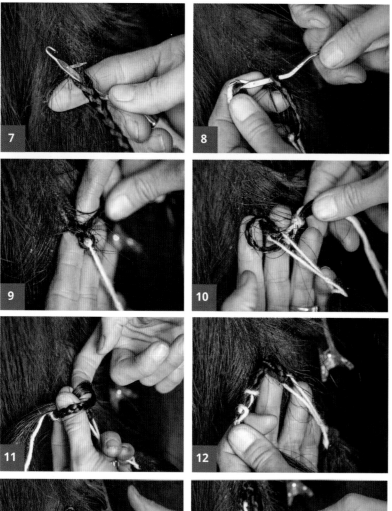

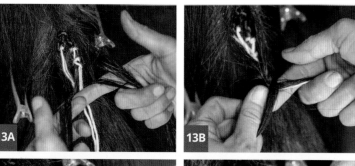

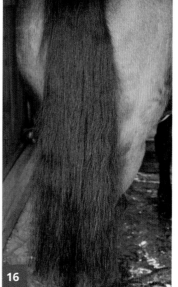

**7** Thread a pull-through at the base (top end) of the braid. In this picture, you can see that the mechanism that closes the hook of the pull-through is open.

**8** Hook both the braid and yarn ends through the open hook, then close the mechanism. (The loop for the fake tail should be hanging in the middle of the braid.)

**9** Pull the tool—with the braid and yarn ends— through the braid, until the fake tail's loop is tightly in the center.

**10** Cross the braid behind the extension, creating a loop.

**11** Push your thumb and forefinger through the loop you just created.

**12** Pull the braid down into the loop until it is snug.

**13 A** Now collect a strand of hair from each side of the dock, two strands from the top of the extension, and the braid end with the yarn.

**13 B** Braid all of the pieces together for just two or three crossovers.

**14** Use the yarn to tie the braid off tightly.

**15** Snip the yarn.

**16** Brush the tail with your fingers. The extension should be invisible, and it will move with the horse's natural tail.

# CHAPTER ELEVEN
# "Down to the Wire"

## Emma says

In 2010, Phillip had four horses at the Rolex Kentucky CCI\*\*\*\*: Woodburn, Waterfront, The Foreman ("Chip"), and Kheops Du Quesney ("Danny"). As you can imagine it was a rather busy event! Thanks to Kelley Merrett and Lizzie Olmstead we got through the weekend without too many hitches. Danny was number one to go, which was okay with us: he could get very nervous in the ring so the fewer spectators around the better. The morning of dressage day, Phillip always pre-rides before his test time then returns the horse to the barn to get tidied up. So I sent him to the ring without his full competition attire, plus I still had the last quarter of his mane to braid (I always leave this till last so the mane stays tidy and does not get rubbed out). Danny had settled well during this pre-ride so Phillip made the decision not to take him back to his stall because sometimes going back could wind him up.

Phillip called me and I had to get down to the warm-up area with braiding equipment, show pad, and necessities to have Danny looking "ring ready." I'm not going to lie—I panicked a little! I scrambled to get everything together and with Kelley's help we got to the warm-up and did the makeover session while Danny ate grass! Afterward, Danny put in one of his best tests. Although Phillip's decision was stressful for me, it was the right one for the horse. Part of a groom's job is to make competition less stressful for the horse, and when it's not you, the rider, too. No matter how strange some requests might seem to you, if the rider feels it helps the horse's performance, you have to find a way to get it done.

## TACKING UP FOR COMPETITION

We have discussed in previous chapters how to take care of your horse at home and while at the show. Now, we'll look at what brings it all together to get a neatly turned-out look.

### Bridle Number

Dressage horses, show jumpers, and eventers are assigned a bridle number when they get to a show. This number has a small metal strip on the back of it, and is usually oval. There are two ways to put on the number: you either attach it to the bridle or to the saddle pad. Occasionally, you will see the number attached to the center of a breastplate, but this method has a problem; as soon as the horse sweats the number gets wet and can fall off the metal strip, leaving the rider with no number at all. Attaching to the bridle is simple, but some horses find it annoying when it touches their ears. We use the number on the bridle for the lower levels

Attaching Number to Bridle

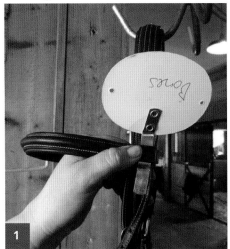  

but prefer to attach the number to the saddle pad for championships and upper-level competitions. It's a more professional look, but it takes a few minutes of planning since it needs to be done before tacking up.

## Attaching Number to Bridle

**1** Thread the number through the loop at the end of the browband on the left side.

**2** Fold the bottom of the metal up tightly.

Tools for Attaching Number to Saddle Pad

**3** Then fold the number down to below the browband. Be careful about creasing the number, which is made of paper; handle it by its metal parts.

## Attaching Number to Saddle Pad

**1** To attach the number to the saddle pad, you'll need the following tools:
- Heavy-duty quilter's thread
- Sturdy needle
- Extra-large safety pins

### Using Safety Pins

**1** Coming from the back of the saddle pad with a large safety pin, poke through the underside of the pad.

**2** Come back through the pad and close the pin

**3** One inch below the first, attach another pin parallel to the first pin.

**4** From the front of the pad, you should have two parallel pins.

**5** Thread the number through both pins.

**6** Fold up the bottom of the number.

**7** Fold down the top of the number so it lies flat.

Attaching Number Using Safety Pins

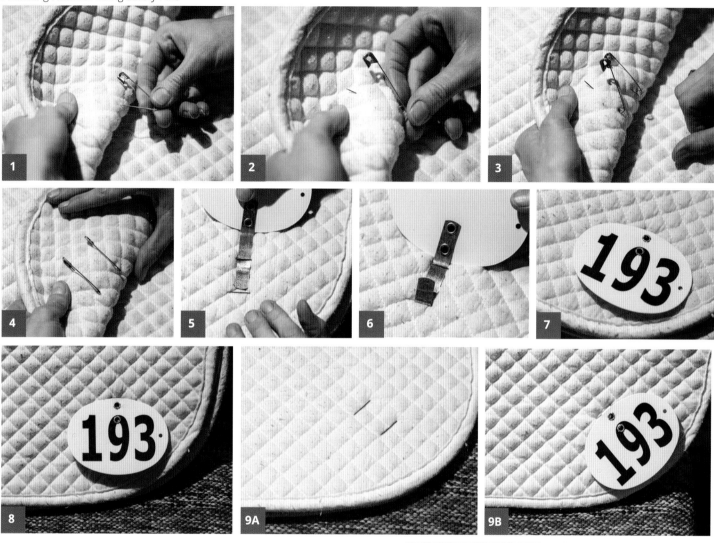

**8** In *dressage*, the number should be on the left side in the bottom rear corner, parallel to the bottom of the pad.

**9 A & B** In *show jumping*, the number should be on the left side, clear of the rider's leg, at a 45-degree angle to the bottom of the rear corner of the pad.

**10** Wrong: Don't just attach to the sides of the number as shown—the visible pins look unprofessional.

Attaching Number Using Needle and Thread

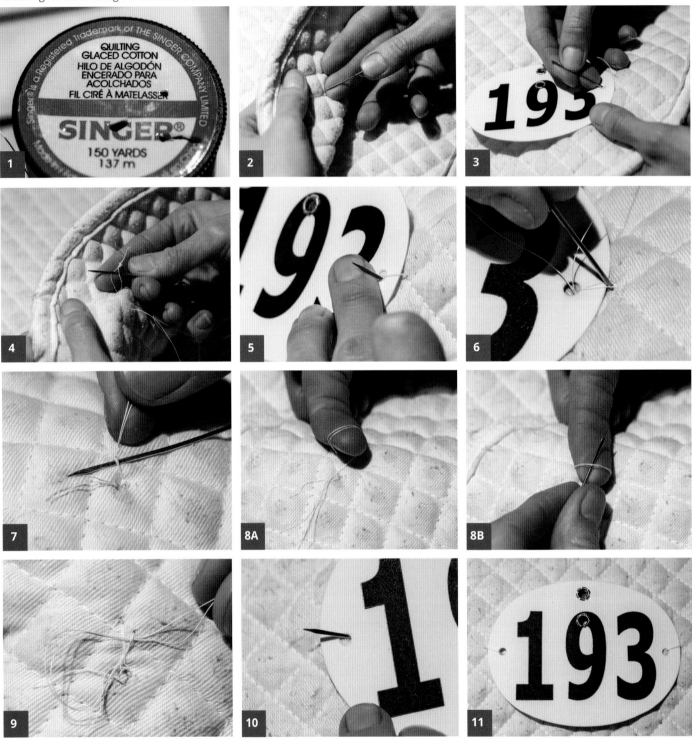

## Using Needle and Thread

For the big competitions, sewing the numbers makes certain there is no unnecessary movement.

**1** Use a large needle and sturdy thread. Waxed quilter's thread holds tight even in wet conditions.

**2** Thread the needle and tie both ends of the thread together in a sturdy knot. Begin on the underside of the saddle pad.

**3** On the top of the pad, thread through the small hole on the right side of the number and push the needle back through the pad.

**4** Before you pull tight, thread the needle through the end of the thread on the underside of the pad. This prevents the knot from accidentally slipping through the pad and releasing the number.

**5** Come back up through the pad and through the hole of the number.

**6** Back to the underside as close to the same hole as possible.

**7** Pull the thread tight and insert the needle through the loop of thread on the back of the pad.

**8 A & B** As you pull the needle through, use your finger to keep a small loop free, then thread the needle through the loop.

### pro tip

I have often had several horses competing back to back at the larger competitions. To make my life easier, I use thick crochet thread to sew loops onto the show saddle pads. This way, I never have to look for safety pins and can always quickly and easily attach a number to a pad. —*Cat*

**9** Pull tight to create the knot and snip the ends of the thread.

**10** Position the number correctly and repeat the process on the other side.

**11** When all sewn on, the number should sit tight and flat on the saddle pad.

Hoof Oil

## TIPS AND TRICKS BY DISCIPLINE

Each discipline has its own style, and it's important to make sure you look the part. As you do the final preparations before sending your horse into the ring, use this section to ensure you have the right "look."

### Hoof Oil

**1** One pre-competition tip for all disciplines is *hoof oil*. Before you leave the barn, make sure to add a swipe of hoof oil. Be careful to start below the hair so you don't make the coronary band look dirty.

### Tips for Dressage Riders

You have braided your horse, shined his bit, and brushed out that amazing tail. To finish off the look, spray some oil sheen onto a body brush and vigorously brush his coat to bring up the shine.

**1 A & B** One tip gained from top dressage rider Silva Martin's groom, Gracia Huenefeld, is to use anti-static spray on a soft finishing brush, then rub it over your horse. This prevents dirt and sand from getting into his coat and gives him a better shine.

## Putting on the Bridle
### Snaffle
*Dressage* has very strict rules about the bits that are allowed at each level. Consult the most recent Rulebook to make sure the bit you are using is legal.

**1** Once on, the bit should not hang low in the mouth; with a snaffle there should be two to three wrinkles in each corner of the mouth, as shown.

Anti-Static Spray

1A

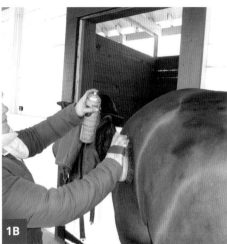

1B

**2** A crank noseband has to be threaded through a metal loop called a roller. When going through the roller, make sure you do not pinch the skin. In this photo, you can see my right hand guiding the skin to make sure

Dressage: Snaffle

1

2

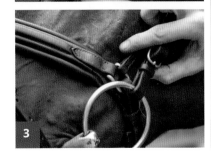

3

4

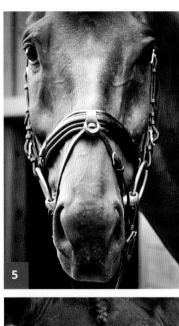

5

6

it doesn't get sucked into the roller. (My left hand is simply holding the bit out of the way so you can clearly see the noseband.) It's easy to pull a crank noseband too tight, so be aware of this.

**3** The noseband should sit straight and snug. It should lie one-finger-width down from the bottom of the cheek bone.

**4** The horse should look quite comfortable in the bridle, with room to flex his poll in the throatlatch.

**5** To finish, the bridle can be gently rubbed over with a soft cloth and glycerin soap to bring out the shine.

**6** Make sure that browband is shining!

## Double Bridle

**1** A correctly fitted double bridle should have the bridoon bit sitting on top of the Weymouth.

**2** Once on, the bridoon bit should sit at the same height as a regular snaffle bridle. The Weymouth should then sit approximately one-half inch below this. Each horse is slightly different; therefore, this changes from horse to horse.

**3** The noseband should be snug, with two fingers width between it and the horse's skin.

**4** The curb chain should be rotated to lie flat against the horse's chin.

**5** Once fitted, the horse should look comfortable and be able to move freely. The bits should lie in his mouth without causing gaping or discomfort.

Dressage: Double Bridle

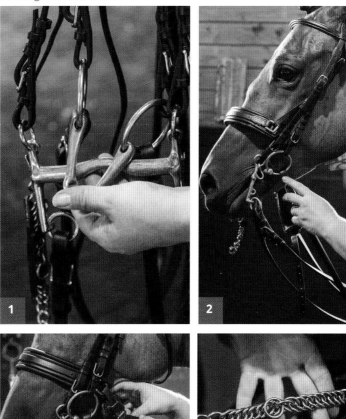

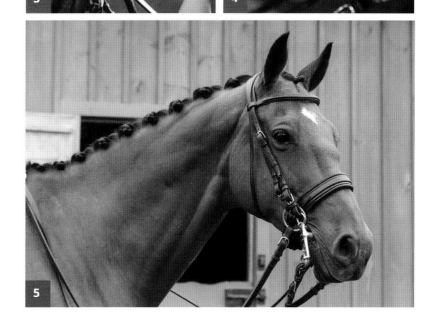

Dressage: The Overall "Look"

## Dressage: The Overall "Look"

**1** The saddle pad should fit the saddle and the horse. There are a few pad options, including square pads that come in either a dressage or an all-purpose shape. Make sure you buy the appropriate pad for the saddle you use. Pads also come in many different sizes, so measure the saddle and check the measurements of the pad prior to purchasing. An overly large pad on a small horse does not look correct; having one inch of pad in front of and behind the saddle gives a very neat look.

A square pad is often paired with some form of half pad. Half pads add a layer to help protect the horse's back and come in sheepskin or a shock-absorbing material covered in fabric.

**2** Wrong: A correctly fitted half pad should not hang out over the edge of the saddle pad.

**3** When you are competing at the lower levels in dressage and do not own a dressage saddle, don't worry. A neat, tIdy horse with a brown bridle, a square all-purpose or jumping pad, and jump saddle is perfectly appropriate and will not cost you points. This horse is also wearing a half-pad that fits just right.

**4** Wrong: A black bridle paired with a brown jumping saddle and square dressage pad looks distracting and will mark you as a "newbie"!

## Dressage Warm-Up Secrets

*Kit: Towel*

According to Gracia, most riders want to head straight into the arena from the warm up area without a pause. So, beforehand, arrange to give a friend the signal to come and do a mid-warm-up cleanup. If you, like a lot of riders, prefer to warm your horse up in

Show Jumping: Open-Front Boots

fuzzy boots, make sure your helper is ready to yank them off at the agreed-upon moment.

Have your helper:
• Assist you with your horse's boots.
• Towel off the horse's mouth, nose, bits, and reins. (Some horses are a bit fussy in a double bridle. If that's the case, leave his face alone—don't risk upsetting the delicate balance!)
• Towel off your boots.

**2** Start with the top strap and put it on just snug enough to secure the boot.

**3** Next take the bottom strap and cross it to the middle buckle, again securing it snug but not tight.

**4** Next, take the middle strap and cross it to the lowest buckle, snug but not tight.

## Tips for Show Jumpers

Your horse is perfectly groomed. Now put in studs, if needed. Then put on the horse's boots.

### Open-Front Boots

Open-front boots offer impact protection without padding in front, which can make a horse dull to the rails. There's a variety of open-front brands and designs. We'll focus on how to put on classic leather three-strap boots. Positioning is the same on all brands, but the style or straps can differ.

**1** The boots go around the back of the leg, with the larger pad at the bottom, and the straps come across the front of the leg.

## Running Martingale

A running martingale is a good way of providing a little extra control without increasing the severity of the bit.

**1** If you are using a running martingale, make sure you have rein stops on the reins.

**2** Wrong: Not only is it illegal to have a running martingale without rein stops, it's also quite dangerous. Should the rings slip down to the bit, they can get bound up on the ends of the reins and cause the horse to panic or fall.

Show Jumping: Ankle Boots

## Ankle Boots

These small boots offer impact protection for show jumpers. The boots should be placed low on the leg, with the round part down. The straps come across the front and the buckle to the back.

**1** Secure the top strap first, making sure not to crank it too tight.

**2** Next secure the bottom strap.

**3** All set.

# Figure-Eight Noseband

Figure-eight nosebands are quite popular in both the show jumping and eventing disciplines. Since this type of noseband goes over the jaw and below the bit, it can assist in preventing a horse that crosses his jaw. It must be fitted properly to prevent rubs and discomfort.

**1** From the front, the center of the "eight" should be high on the horse's face, well above the delicate ends of the nasal passages.

**2** Wrong: Here the noseband is too low, which could easily damage the delicate nasal passages.

The cheekpiece of the noseband should lie parallel to—that is, on the same line as—the bridle, and the noseband should sit high above the end of the cheekbone.

**3** Wrong: This noseband is sitting high enough, but the cheekpieces are not in line.

**4** Wrong: Here the noseband is too low, and will cause rubs, but the cheekpieces are in the correct position.

**5** Correctly fitted, the noseband should look like this, well above the cheekbone, with the cheekpieces in line with one another.

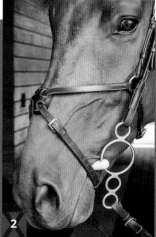

Show Jumping: Saddle Pads

## Saddle Pads

**1** Square jump pads in a neutral color are the correct style for show jumping. The pad should sit with only one inch of pad showing in front of the saddle. Not only does this look tidy, it also makes sure there is nothing in the way of the rider's hands. Many show jumpers also use a half pad for its shock-absorbing properties; it should also sit well back and away from the rider's hands.

**2** Wrong: This is a square dressage pad paired with a jumping saddle. Notice how the front of the saddle pad is too far in front of the pommel. It not only looks silly but can be in the way of your hands as you jump.

# Protecting Ears

Ear plugs and bonnets are allowed in some disciplines; check your current Rulebook. Try both at home first because some horses do not tolerate them well.

**1** Take the ear plug, in your thumb and forefinger.

**2** Use your finger to gently push the ear plug into the ear canal.

**3** It should sit very deep in the ear or else the horse will shake it out.

**4** An ear bonnet can help to drown out noises as well as stop pesky flies and gnats from biting. If you use ear plugs, a bonnet actually helps to make sure they stay put. The ear bonnet is placed over the ears before putting the bridle on. Make sure the forelock is lying flat underneath the bonnet.

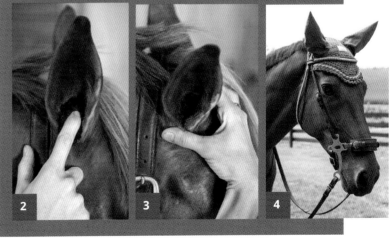

Show Jumping: Heading to the Ring

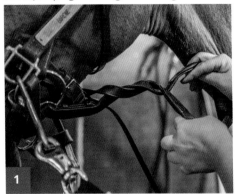

## Heading to the Ring

Each course at a show jumping competition is different and needs to be walked first. Depending on the size of the class, there might not be time to get back to the barn to collect your horse after walking the course. In this situation it's helpful to have a friend

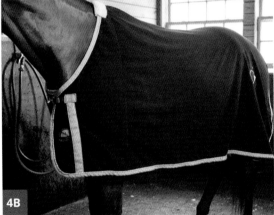

who can hold your horse near the ring. Use a halter over the bridle to hold the horse so the reins are safely out of the way and the horse's mouth isn't being pulled on.

**1** Twist the reins around each other several times.

**2** Thread the throatlatch of the halter through the reins. This prevents the reins from falling over the horse's head.

**3** Buckle your halter.

**4 A & B** Depending on the weather, a *net, scrim,* or *wool cooler* could be required while the horse waits ringside.

## Show Jumping Warm-Up Secrets

*Kit: Brush, comb, towel, hoof oil, fly spray*
Jumper riders may want to be jumping right before heading into the ring, so discuss beforehand what the

plan will be. If you want to head straight into the ring, ask your helper to do a quick polish a few rides ahead. Your helper should:

- Towel off the horse's nose, mouth, bit, and reins.
- Apply fly spray if necessary.

## Tips for Hunters

**1** For show hunters, the horse must be shining to within an inch of being reflective! Once braided, shined, and re-shined, it is appropriate to use a white, fitted saddle pad. (A square pad is not acceptable.) When a half pad is necessary, it should be close-fitting and white.

**2 A & B** A padded leather girth is preferred. If the horse has sensitive skin, a girth with fleece on the inside is acceptable, but the fleece should not be very visible, and must be clean.

**3** A hunter's bridle fashion changes regularly, but there are a few items that remain in style: a raised, padded, fancy stitched snaffle bridle in brown leather with a D-ring is the most classic look. The bit should sit comfortably in the corners of the mouth, with one to two wrinkles.

**4** A matching standing martingale is used in the over-fences classes. It must be removed for the hack classes.

## Hunter Warm-Up Secrets

*Kit: Towel, alcohol, sheepskin mitt, spray shine, brush, hoof brush, hoof oil, baby powder, fly spray, baby oil, comb*

Take your time. Once the horse is warmed up, "park" him near the entrance for a minute and ask your helper to shine him up:

- Wipe any slobber off the nose, mouth, bit, and reins.
- Spray alcohol on a rag and rub any sweat marks down.
- Brush down legs and belly.
- For white legs, sprinkle a little baby powder on a brush and go over the legs.
- Brush off hooves and oil them.
- Comb out tail.

Tips for Hunters

**barn gossip**

After years of showing Arabian horses at breed shows, I got a job grooming at a major hunter barn in Buffalo, New York. I prepared the first horse to go to the ring and was quite proud of how he looked that is, until his rider came around the corner and started asking what on earth I had done! I had used my shiny, hard, nail-polish-style hoof polish, and I had rubbed a large amount of grease all over the horse's eyes, nostrils, and inside his ears. I didn't realize that in show hunters, while they must gleam, it is meant to look like a more natural beauty than in the Arabian show world. I had basically decked my horse out in evening clothes to head to a garden party. I spent a frantic few minutes wiping off the grease and scrubbing his feet with sand to wear the shine down a bit before sending them into the ring. I learned my lesson that day about looking around and paying attention to how the other grooms were turning out their horses, rather than just doing what I thought was right! *—Cat*

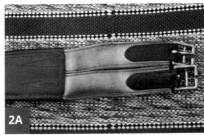

2A

2B

1

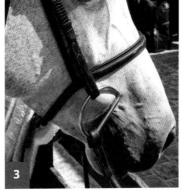

3

4

## pro tip

For *light-colored* horses, a bottle of dry shampoo is an absolute must! An inexpensive way to make your own is to put one-half teaspoon of "bluing" shampoo and three cups of rubbing alcohol in a spray bottle. This will come in really handy for manure spots, grass stains, and last-minute spot-cleans. A light-colored horse is notorious for not getting a good shine, and he can often look a bit dull. Use the bluing shampoo alone every two days, more often can cause skin irritation, but bathe him every time he works, even a few times a day. For last minute touch-ups, use a dry rag: a damp rag leaves a dark mark on his skin.

Dark-colored horses pose an entirely different problem—their hair shows every little bit of sweat and dust. Many dark horses suffer from dry skin so try to keep a "2-in-1" shampoo and conditioner on hand. Always do a conditioner rinse after a good scrub, which will help in two ways: first, it keeps dandruff to a minimum; second, it repels dirt.

On dark bay and black horses, a light spray of a Shapley's™ coat shine product Magic Sheen will help to repel those tiny dust particles that cling to black hairs. Always have a damp rag in your back pocket for last minute wipe-downs, since black retains shine when wet.

- Spray shine onto a cloth and rub all over the body.
- Rub a *small* amount of baby oil onto your hands and rub into the area around the horse's eyes and nose; you can also rub onto any leather bits looking dull or dirty.
- Fly spray if necessary.

## Tips for Eventers

If you are at a one-day event you need to be organized and efficient. Your horse has been given a final groom and then a decision on studs needs to be made. When you have starting times in phases that are close together, there is no harm in putting in studs that will suit for all three phases. However, at a championship or three-day event, you want to pull out all the stops and make sure your horse looks and feels his very best (see p. 192 for more on studs).

### Dressage Phase

As with "pure" dressage, you want your horse to be well turned out. Follow the dressage guidelines, starting on page 167, when preparing for this phase.

### Show Jumping Phase

When turning out the event horse for the show-jumping phase at a one-day event, please refer to the show-jumping guidelines on page 171. At a championship or three-day event you may want to braid for show jumping.

### Breastplates

Breastplates are commonly used by eventers in both jumping phases. Many event horses are kept thinner than in the other disciplines since they must run cross-country. Because of his light frame, an eventer may have trouble carrying a saddle reliably in the correct spot. A well-fitted breastplate prevents the saddle from sliding back and shifting around.

# Micklem Bridle

The Micklem bridle is a special type that is very popular in the eventing world for the dressage phase, and in the show jumping world, too. It was designed by William Micklem, a rider, instructor, and horse anatomist, to fit the skull differently than a traditional bridle, so horses that are fussy about their mouth or have problems with pressure points on their poll or jaw can benefit from wearing one (williammicklem.com).

**1** One of the main differences is the way the bit hangs in the horse's mouth: the bit is attached to the cheekpieces with an adjustable strap that should be tightened so that there are two to three wrinkles in the corners of the mouth. You should be able to visualize a straight line from the cheekpiece to the corner of the mouth.

**2** The Micklem has a throatlatch that sits on the horse's jaw that should be buckled first.

**3** It should be buckled snugly, with one finger between the jawbone and the buckle.

**4** Next, do up the noseband portion of the bridle, which sits below the bit. It should be fitted snugly with two fingers between the lips and the band.

**5** Be careful not to crank down on the noseband strap because you might catch the lips in the buckle.

**6** Here's the Micklem bridle properly fitted. Note: each strap, including the browband, sits close to the horse's head but is neither tight nor restrictive.

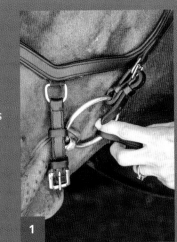

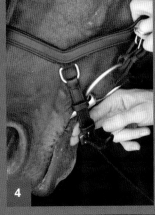

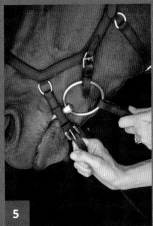

Eventing: Breastplates

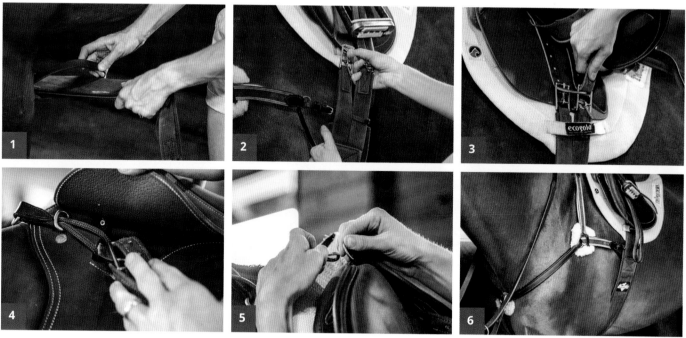

One year, Emma was unable to go to an event with Phillip. I was going with Mara DePuy with only one horse so I volunteered to help out. Phillip had a working student with him and was riding five horses. One of the horses was a very sweet stallion and such a light gray he looked silver. It so happened that Phillip needed to be getting on the stallion right at the same time as Mara was getting on her horse, and the working student was at the ring with Phillip's other ride. I got the stallion all tacked up, shined, and tied him in his freshly cleaned stall. Then I went over to get Mara's horse ready. Just as I put Mara in the tack, Phillip appeared. He pulled the stallion out of his stall to find he not only pooped, he lay down in it. His entire right hindquarter was brown! Mara looked at me and said, "I don't need you for another 15 minutes…good luck." She headed off to the warm-up. I dumped an entire bottle of dry shampoo on the offending stain and scrubbed with a towel as we made our way to warm-up. By the time Phillip went in the ring, you couldn't even see the slightly damp spot on the stallion's hindquarters and a fashion crisis was averted! —*Cat*

**1** Put the breastplate on, then the saddle. Thread the girth through the bottom breastplate loop before doing up the top straps.

**2** If using a five-point breastplate, thread the side attachment under the first girth elastic, and around the second.

**3** Buckle the girth snugly, but not tight. You can tighten it later.

**4** A breastplate should be hooked directly to the saddle's tree. Just hooking to the front D-ring on the saddle can be dangerous: it might get pulled out, leaving you with a loose breastplate. To hook it to the tree, use a D-ring extender. Thread the extender through the saddle D-ring then loop it around the stirrup bar.

**5** Hook the breastplate to the D-ring extender.

**6** The breastplate should sit above the point of shoulder, across the muscle. The center should sit well below the windpipe.

## Cross-Country Phase

### Tacking Up In the Best Order

This can take some time. Whether at a one-day or three-day show, hay should be removed from your horse at least two hours out so he is not galloping on a full stomach. You want to have all your boots, tape, studs, Flair® Equine Nasal Strips, and tack in order so that you don't waste time looking for odd pieces of equipment. Your horse should not stand in cross-country boots for extended periods of time: his legs can heat up, then be irritated, so using your time efficiently is a must.

Here is an outline of the correct order to address extra needs for this phase:

- Groom horse.
- Prepare the nose for nasal strips when using.
- Put stockings or Tubigrip® on legs when using.
- Put in studs (see chapter 12, p. 192).
- Put on galloping boots.

### Apply Flair Nasal Strips

**1** Flair Nasal Strips help a horse breathe, which in turn helps him recover more quickly after he has galloped.

**2** Wipe off the nostril area with rubbing alcohol. This removes dirt and oil from the skin, both of which affect how well a nasal strip will stay on. Doing it early makes sure the nose has a chance to dry before you get to the application step.

**3 A–C** To put on the nasal strip, first follow the directions to bend each side with the handling strip still in place.

**4** Remove the center strip protection on its back.

Apply Flair Nasal Strips

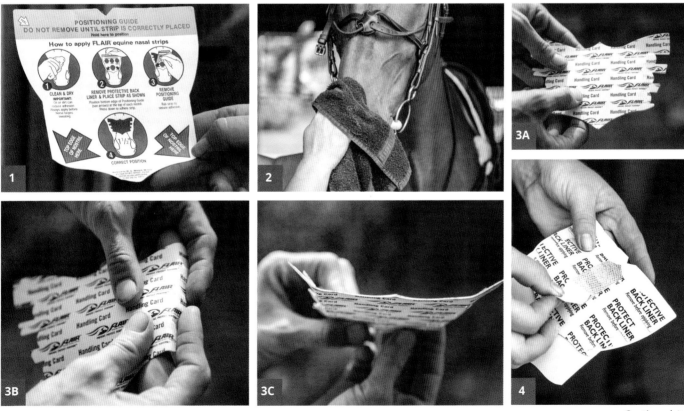

Continued ▶

Apply Flair Nasal Strips (Cont.)

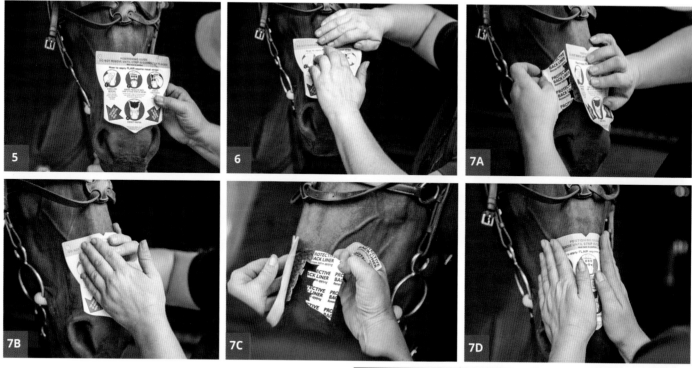

5 Using the guide, position the strip in place so that the outside edge is at the top of the nostrils. Make sure the strip is straight.

6 Rub the center of the strip firmly to activate the glue.

7 A–D Remove either side of the back, one at a time and rub firmly onto the nose.

8 Remove the protective covering and firmly rub strip onto the nose one last time.

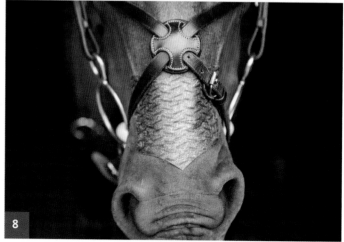

### Preventing Leg Friction

When your horse has sensitive skin, he's just been clipped, or is prone to boot rubs, use stockings or a Tubigrip underneath the boots to prevent injury. This basically acts the way a sock in your shoe works to provide a barrier to friction. To use stockings, buy knee-high trouser socks and cut off the toes to create a hollow tube.

1 Tubigrip is an elasticized tubular bandage that is sold in a long piece that is then cut to the desired length.

2 It must be put on prior to putting studs in. Bunch the fabric over your hand.

3 Pick up the hoof and stretch the stocking over it. You can leave the stockings pulled up over the knee while you do the studs (see chapter 12, p. 192).

Preventing Leg Friction

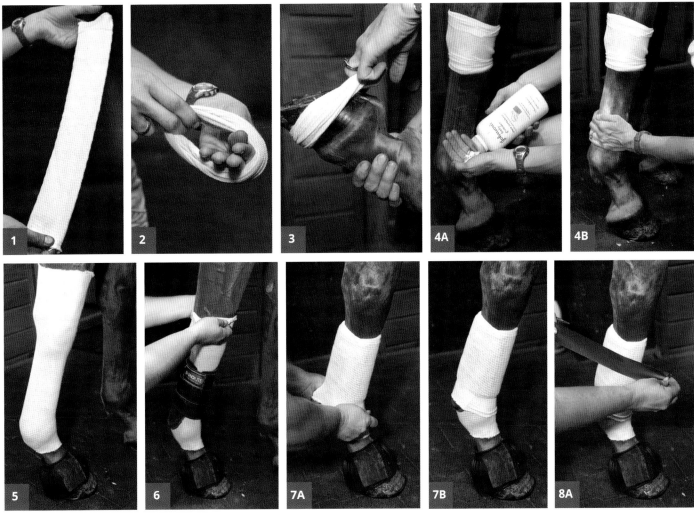

**4 A & B** Once studs are in, rub some baby powder into the leg.

**5** Pull the stocking down over the leg. Make sure you only pull it *down* since pulling up can cause the hair to get caught and to rub.

**6** Put on the horse's boots as directed on page 182.

**7 A & B** Take the stocking and fold it down over the boot.

**8 A–C** Using either electrical tape in your colors or black duct tape, tape over the top two straps of the boot that is covered with the stocking.

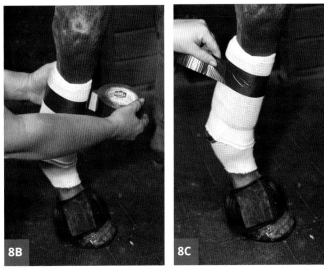

*Continued* ▶

Preventing Leg Friction (Cont.)

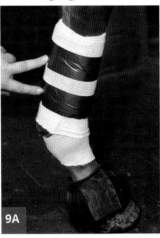  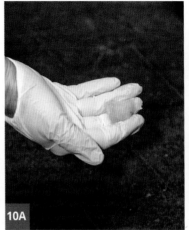 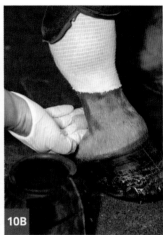

**9 A & B** End both pieces of tape in the same spot. This is to help when removing the boot: you'll know where to find the end.

**10 A & B** If you have a sensitive horse, chances are the bell boots will also cause irritation, so rub Vaseline into the pastern to reduce friction.

### Boots

There are many varieties of cross-country boots. Most come with some form of tendon guard in the front and a cannon-bone guard in the hind.

**1** Start with very clean, dry legs.

**2** Begin with the front boots: Set the boot slightly higher than where it should be, place the boot on the leg. Do up the center strap first...

**3 A & B** ...followed by the top and then bottom straps.

**4** Push the boot down the leg until it sits in position just below the knee.

**5 A & B** Re-tighten the straps using quite firm pressure.

**6** Now you should be able to push quite firmly down on it and not have it shift.

**7** For the hind boots: Start by placing the boots a bit high on the leg, making sure the cannon-bone protection is centered over the bone.

**8 A–C** Do the straps up top to bottom.

**9** Push the boot into its correct placement, with the protection on the inside extending to the bottom of the fetlock joint.

## pro tip

When using electrical tape to secure straps, fold the end of the tape back on itself to create a tab that is easy to find to remove the tape.

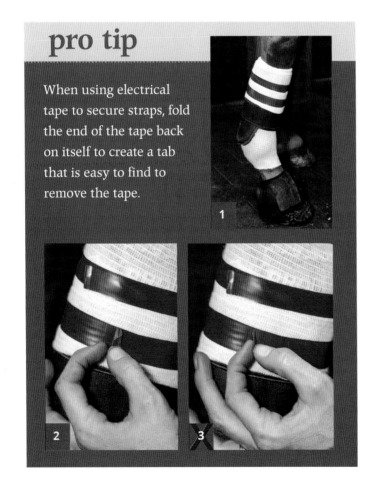

Eventing: Boots

Continued ▶

Eventing: Boots (Cont.)

   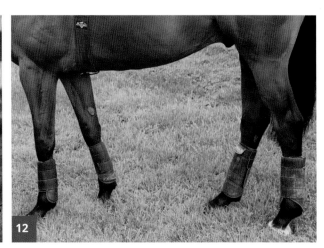

**10 A & B** Starting at the bottom, tighten the straps down until they are quite snug.

**11** You should be able to push on it with no movement.

**12** Booted up for cross-country.

## Saddle, Bridle, Breastplate

Next, put on saddle pad, saddle, and breastplate (see p. 178). Double check the fit of the breastplate and its attachments. You don't want anything popping undone halfway round the course.

Saddle, Bridle, Breastplate

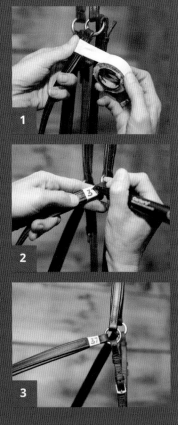

**pro tip**

At a CIC or CCI you must have a number on your horse at all times or risk being disqualified. We use white tape and a permanent marker on the horse's halter to ensure this never happens. We also put tape on the breastplate on cross-country day so we can save the "paper number" for the jog the next day since it often gets destroyed when it gets wet or covered in sweat.

Knot the Reins

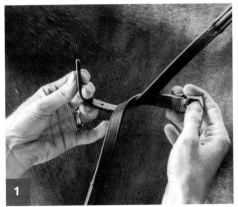

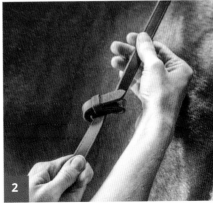

Check Girth

Many riders like to knot the ends of their reins for cross-country. This ensures they won't come undone and also makes a knot to grab onto should the horse pull down the reins on a big drop fence. To knot:

## Knot the Reins

**1** First, unbuckle the reins and cross the ends.

**2** Then, buckle up the reins and pull the knot tight.

## Check Girth

**1** At this time, also make sure the girth is quite tight, walk a couple of loops and recheck it. You should then pull the legs forward to prevent pinched skin between girth and the horse's elbow.

## Eventing Grease

**1** This is a thick, slippery substance that helps to prevent scrapes and scratches as a horse goes through a brush jump or skims a bit too close to a solid jump. It also contains a mild antiseptic that helps prevent red, angry welts when a horse just barely scrapes the skin. At the lower levels it is not necessary, but at CCIs and CICs we prefer to use it. When you do, use a latex glove because it's tough to wash off.

**2 A–C** Starting from the top of a front leg, run the grease down the entire length of the leg.

Eventing Grease

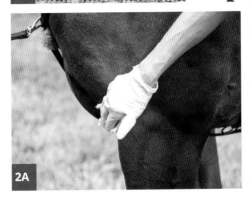

Continued ▶

Eventing Grease (Cont.)

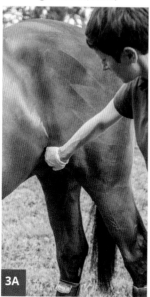

**3 A–D** With a hind leg, start from the top of the stifle and move down the entire leg. Some horses can get edgy when you do this so always be mindful of where you are standing. Don't get kicked!

Be very careful not to get grease on the tack, saddle, reins, and especially your boots! Wash the horse after cross-country with a grease-cutting soap so there is no grease left on his skin.

**4 A & B** Groom Sara McKenna with Harbour Pilot, Hannah Sue Burnett's ride at the Pan American Games in Mexico, 2011.

## Cross-Country Warm-Up Secrets
### One-Day Event
*Kit: Towel, halter, and lead*
Most riders will need very little at the cross-country warm-up. Fences need to be set, and a cheer out of the start box is nice!

If a very hot and humid day or a wet, rainy one, you may need your reins toweled off before you head to the start. Ask your helper to have a halter and lead with her in case you want the horse walked back at the end of cross-country; this way, she won't have to pull on the horse's mouth by the bridle.

### Three-Day Event
*Kit: Towel, ice water, sponge, scraper, gloves, grease. There is no shining up. Instead, you cool the horse down after warm-up and grease him up. Even on chilly days, the horse can get quite hot galloping. It is vital for a quick recovery that he head out* onto the course as cool as possible. If he is sweating and his veins are up, use a sponge to run ice water down his neck, keeping the reins away from the water. You need the reins to stay dry.

Scrape the water off because leaving water on actually creates an insulation layer that can cause heat. Sponge between the horse's hind legs. Some horses appreciate a sponge squeezed into their mouth. If yours does, go ahead and do it now. Repeat until the horse is cool. Towel the reins off.

Eventing: Quarter Marks

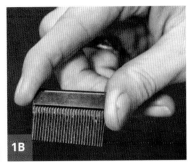

## Event Horses: Getting the "Look"

### Quarter Marks

At the major competitions, event horses often sport "quarter marks" on their rump. These brushed-in designs show off a horse's movement, muscling, and coat. They are fairly simple to do, but require practice to get even and consistent.

**1 A & B** First, assemble your tools:

- Short-bristle brush
- Fly spray
- Coat shine
- Comb cut to 1.5-inch length.

Quarter Marks: Checkerboard

**2** Next, spray with fly spray the entire area from the spine to the stifle.

**3** Use the short bristle brush to smooth all of the hair in one direction.

There are three basic designs for the hip:

### Checkerboard

**1** One popular pattern is the checkerboard.

**2** Using your comb, start in the center point of the hip and carefully pull down, ending 1.5 inches down to make a square.

**3** Move your comb so that the upper right corner just touches the bottom left corner of the mark you just made, make another square.

**4** Move your comb so that the upper left corner just touches the bottom right corner of the first mark, make another square.

**5** Repeat until the checkerboard is the desired size. A small checkerboard creates the illusion of a larger, more

Quarter Marks: "V"

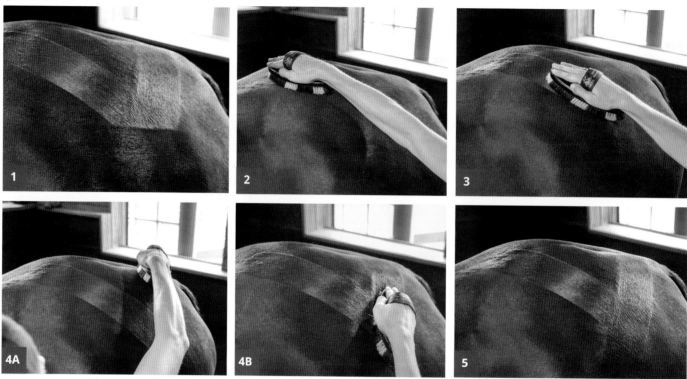

muscular hind end, and a large checkerboard can help slim down a powerful rear.

"V"

**1** Alternatively, you can use your stiff brush to make a "V" on the horse's rump.

**2** Start to one side of the highest point of the hip.

**3** Pull slowly and careful on an angle toward the horse's hock.

**4 A & B** Next start equidistant from the highest point of the hip on the back side and carefully drag the brush toward the point where you ended the first line.

**5** You will have a "V" with a messy bottom.

**6** Then pull the brush parallel to the horse's back to create a neat, squared off line at the bottom of the triangle.

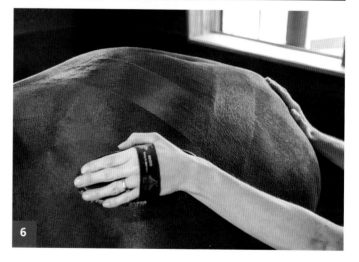

Quarter Marks: Stencil

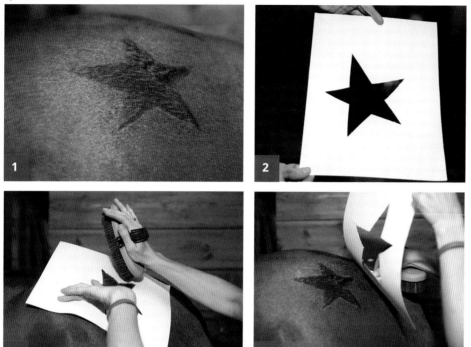

## Stencil

**1** You can put a logo on the hip by using a stencil.

**2** Create the stencil using a stiff piece of plastic, available at most craft stores.

**3** Carefully lay the stencil on the horse's high hip, and brush the hair up, holding the stencil very still.

**4** Lift your stencil up and away.

## barn gossip

When I first got hired by Mara DePuy, I was woefully unprepared to be a groom for such a top-level rider, but I felt I would make it since Mara had a small number of horses and was very involved in their care herself. I had also managed barns of all sizes and worked as a groom at various shows in every discipline. However, it is an entirely different level of responsibility to groom a horse being looked at for the US Eventing Team. As soon as I even thought about presenting the horses at a show I got nervous. To make matters worse, the man who had groomed for Mara before me was exceptional at the details, like perfectly round braids and quarter marks.

I had this silly thing in my head that if I could do proper quarter marks, I would have it made. So with no one to show me how, and not wanting Mara to know I couldn't do them, I practiced in secret. We had a horse named Jos Ambition who, conveniently, was bright chestnut, making it easy to see the quarter marks, and also a very patient boy. Eventually, Mara caught me. We had a good laugh about it, so I asked for her input. I ended up sending "Ambi" out to hack with quarter marks for months before I felt my work was up to snuff.

That year at the Fair Hill International CCI 3***, I finally felt prepared. It poured with rain the entire day of dressage. I ended up taking a picture of Mara's horse, Nicki Henley, all groomed with quarter marks done, standing in the tent before heading out into the rain, just so I would have a record of my work!

*—Cat*

## Shark's Teeth

**1** This design goes on the horse in addition to and below the checkerboard, "V," or stenciled design.

**2** Begin with your stiff brush at an angle, with the front of the brush just below the point of the hip and the back pointed to the hock. Drag the brush back following the line between the hip and hock.

Quarter Marks: Shark's Teeth

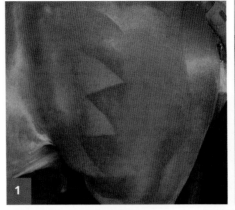

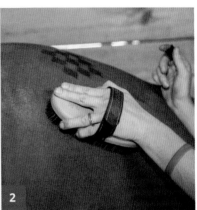

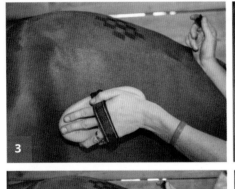

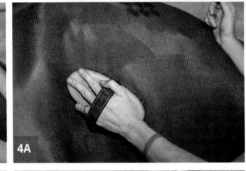

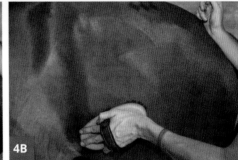

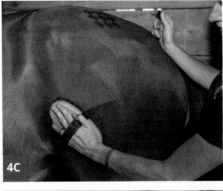

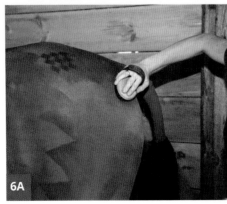

3 Next, move one-brush-width lower, and move the brush parallel to the ground. Drag the brush back on the parallel plane.

4 A–D Alternate Steps One and Two until you reach the stifle.

Switch sides: with the first side done, head to the other side and repeat. Look from behind (carefully!) to make sure the design is equal on both sides. Once you have your hip design and Shark's Teeth finished on both sides, it's time to finish the look.

5 Drag your brush straight down the spine until you reach the tail.

6 A & B Make a curve starting at the tail head and ending at the end of the muscle on each side.

7 Stand back and admire!

# The FEI Jog

All three Olympic disciplines have a formal jog at FEI competitions. The purpose of the jog is to make sure the horse is sound enough to participate in the competition. The three sports all have a different "feel." I like to compare them to a party: Show jumpers are at a garden party, dressage riders are at a cocktail party, and the eventers are at a gala.

The show jumper is not normally braided. The dressage horse tends to be braided, and the event horse has two jogs and is turned out immaculately: braided and groomed like crazy. The second event jog tends to be a nerve-wracking affair since it often attracts a large crowd of spectators and the horses must jog sound after having jumped around the cross-country course the day before. A horse should head to the jog with his boots on, and when a chilly morning, a cooler will to keep him tidy and warm.

1 Here is Shannon Lilley's mount, Ballingowan Pizzazz, at the Pan American Games in Mexico, 2011.

2 And Gina Miles and her team getting McKinley ready for the jog at the Pan American Games in Brazil, 2007.

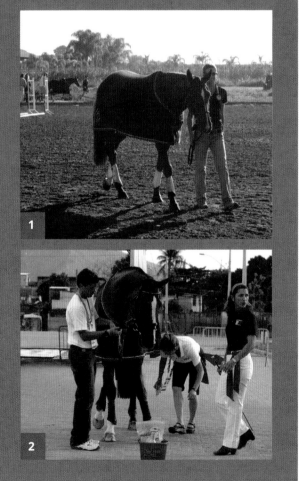

# CHAPTER TWELVE
# "Get a Grip"

## Cat says

"I used to work at a show-jumping yard in Ireland. Most of the shows there take place on turf footing, so studs are vitally important to prevent sliding through the corners. One of the girls took her horse to a one-day show, and she needed big studs for the tight turns in the jump-offs. Since she was doing several classes, she left her mare saddled, booted, and with studs in the trailer while she waited and spectated. We will never know what happened, but her dead quiet, sweet mare did something and ended up stepping on herself behind, tearing a huge hole in her coronary band and pastern. It took months to heal enough for her to be turned out, let alone ridden. I learned my lesson about using big studs that day, and I always put them in at the last second and take them out the minute I can."

## STUDS

### Why Stud?

Most horses competing at any level wear shoes, which leads to studs being used in almost every discipline where there is grass footing. A barefoot horse has his own natural traction due to the hoof's shape, but by adding shoes we take away the ability for the foot to flex and grab the ground. A metal shoe does add protection to the sole, but it causes a loss of traction by creating a more slippery, less flexible interface with the ground.

### General Guidelines

Note: When we pick out studs, we commonly set them on a magnetic dish in the way that they will go into the hoof. In the following photographs, when there are four studs in a dish, they are set up exactly as if they are in the horse's hooves: the top two sets are front studs, the bottom are hinds. The studs go, from left to right, outside-inside-inside-outside.

**1** Always put two studs in the foot; the stud closest to the opposite leg is the *inside* stud, the stud farther from the opposite leg is the *outside* one. This makes sure the foot remains balanced upon landing. Studs must penetrate the ground in order to prevent unnecessary concussion on the foot and stress to the lower leg.

**2** You can use different size studs on the inside and outside of a hoof as long as the difference in height is minimal. In this photo, the taller *grass tip* is safe to use on the outside with a smaller *bullet* on the inside because the *grass tip* will penetrate farther into the ground.

To help prevent injuries, sharp studs must not be placed on the inside of the shoe. A horse can step on himself or kick himself. Studs in the hind shoes should be of an equal or greater size to those in the front shoes. *Never* leave a horse without leg protection when studs are in.

**3** When you have a horse that tucks his knees in tight, check his belly for punctures or scratches from his studs. If he can touch himself, he may need to jump wearing a girth with a stud-guard on the belly.

General Guidelines

## Studs for All Disciplines

### Dressage

In "pure" dressage competition (not the dressage phase in eventing) the use of studs is very rarely seen. Nowadays, dressage shows from lower levels to Grand Prix are normally held on good arena footing where studs are not required. At eventing competitions, though, the dressage is often held in a grass arena, where you need studs to prevent slipping.

### Show Jumping

Show-jumping competition can be held in arenas with good footing, or on grass, so studs are still necessary.

Show Jumping

Some riders use studs on good arena footing too, as a precaution in case the horse hits the base of the footing or slips on a sharp turn.

**1 A & B** The major difference between show jumping and the show-jumping phase in eventing is that show jumpers have *three* stud holes in the hind shoes. This is to provide extra traction on those sharp turns—especially in speed rounds and jump-offs.

### Eventing

It is very common for eventers to have studs all around—that is, two studs in each foot. You will often need to use studs in all three phases due to the

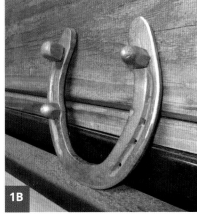

surface being grass. Whenever choosing studs, it's important to keep the footing in mind.

### Show Hunters

Show hunters very rarely find the need for studs, since the sport competes at a relatively slow speed and most often on arena footing. However, some new Derby events are held on grass, and making an "inside" turn is often advantageous in such courses. Derby horses are now showing up with studs in behind. Equitation horses also occasionally appear with studs since these classes require quite a bit more complicated footwork than a standard pleasure round.

## Choosing Your Studs

There are three main factors that dictate your stud choice: *individual horse*, *level of competition*, and *the footing*.

### Individual Horse

No matter what the discipline, some horses get nervous on wet footing and require a larger stud, while other

> ## barn gossip
>
> At the 2012 Olympics in London, we had the event horses outfitted with three stud holes in their hind feet for cross-country. We knew that there were steep slopes with sharp turns and that the turf was going to be a more "golf-course" type. The variety of stud used in that third hole changed as the day went on: the quality of the footing changed due to hot weather and the number of horses galloping on it. US Team member Boyd Martin, riding Otis Barbotiere, went out on course first and started out with more of a small bullet, but by the time Phillip went out on Mystery Whisper, as the last American on course, I put him in a large grass tip. *—Emma*

Bar Shoe

horses do not like to have large studs in because they feel restricted, especially in the dressage arena.

**1** Another consideration is the horse's shoes. When your horse wears bar or heart-bar shoes you will have to find the right balance: you need to keep the studs small enough to prevent the shoes from being pulled off if the hind feet catch the front studs, but big enough to give you traction. Using a heart-bar shoe dramatically reduces the amount of foot traction since the hoof loses its ability to "dig in," instead "skating" on top of the ground. When a large stud is deemed necessary because of the footing, it is common to see event horses at the higher levels wearing a plain shoe with studs for cross-country to increase traction. They will then be put back into the heart-bar shoes at the end of the day.

### Level of Competition

The faster you ride, and the bigger the jumps, the more control you want when the horse's foot hits the ground. While at the lower levels speeds are slower and turns not as sharp, and the horse is less likely to lose his step, a small stud helps to make sure that in less-than-perfect footing, your horse has just the right amount of traction to feel confident enough to push off the ground.

## Footing

Ultimately, the type and quality of the footing will be your final deciding factor when selecting your studs.

• What type of footing—arena, grass, or mud? Arena footing is a more consistent surface than grass, and in mud, all bets are off.

• Has the surface been rained on recently? Even when a bright, sunny day, if it has been raining for weeks, the surface must be walked on in order to determine if it has had a chance to drain. Arena footing that has been soaked can get deep and slippery as the horse punches through the top layers to the base. And, grass footing that has not had a chance to drain will have slick sections that will get torn up and turn to mud as horses move across it.

• Is it variable terrain or the same throughout? At a major jumper show in Upperville, Virginia, the show jumping is held in a grass arena with a fairly significant grade. The flat sections at top will have quite good footing and the hilly sections will be slippery.

When answering these questions you must decide which stud is appropriate. Too large and the lack of penetration will cause more harm than good; too small and you will have no extra traction.

## Which Stud to Use?

There are an enormous variety of studs available; however, to keep things simple, we will stick to the three main types: *road studs*, *grass tips,* and *mud studs*.

**1** *Road studs* are good for a variety of conditions: damp grass paired with firm ground, wet arena footing, and for the lower levels, most general good footing. For most riders these will be the go-to studs, with just the right amount of traction to help prevent slipping. They can be either square or hexagonal, and are either flat or have a small bump in the center.

**2** *Grass tips* also come with a square or hexagonal base, but these tips have a sharp point to pierce through grass and hard ground. These tips can cause damage if the horse stands on himself so it is recommended that they are only used on the outside of each foot along with a road stud or small *bullet* on the inside.

**3** *Mud studs* are used for deep footing. They come in either a square "block" or a hexagonal "bullet." *Bullets* have smooth edges and a rounded tip so they are perfect for use on the inside of the foot. *Blocks* provide the best traction in deep mud but have sharp, square edges so should be reserved for the outside of the foot. They should not be used on hard footing as they will not penetrate the ground and will cause bruising to the foot.

Which Stud to Use

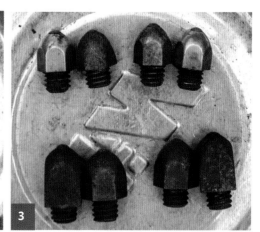

Stud Kit

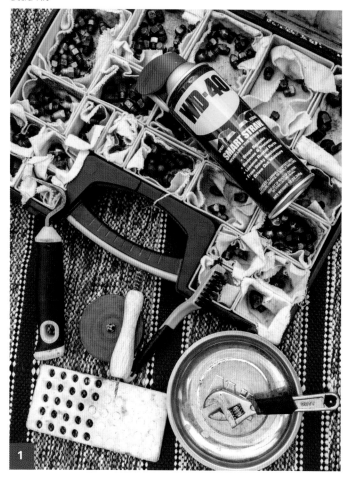

## Stud Kit

**1** A typical stud kit includes:

- Large horseshoe nail (for cleaning out stud holes).
- Magnetic plate (safely holds your selected studs so you don't have to worry about them falling in the shavings—to be lost forever).
- Hoof pick.
- Stud-hole plugs (white item in photo) of which there are various choices: rubber, cotton, metal, and foam (pictured). It comes down to personal choice and what you find is most efficient.
- Wrench. If it's all metal, covering the handle with Vetrap provides better grip, especially in really cold, humid, or wet conditions.

- Tap (red item in photo), properly the flathead round tee tap. The flathead tee tap is much safer to use: suppose you have a fidgety horse that pulls his foot away from you, he can stand on this tap without breaking it. This type of tap also gives you more control when tapping the stud hole, lessening the chance of cross-threading.
- Wire bristle brush (helpful in removing loose dirt from the threads).
- WD40® to oil the studs.
- A selection of studs.

**2** Your studs should be kept in a watertight container. If possible, have a different section for each style of stud. Line each section with newspaper or soft cloth and spray this base with WD40. This helps to keep the studs from becoming rusty.

## Preparing Stud Holes

It is always a good idea to clean out the stud holes the day before a show. This way there is no panic at the show when you realize you have cross-threading or there's a small annoying stone stuck in the hole.

Preparing Stud Holes

Putting in Studs

*Continued* ▶

**1** Using a nail, remove as much dirt as you can.

**2** Take the wire brush and use counterclockwise in the stud hole. This helps to remove dirt in the threads.

**3 A & B** Next use the tap, twisting into the hole in a clockwise motion.

**4 A & B** Take your stud plug and using your large nail, push into the hole until it is flush with the shoe.

## Putting in Studs

**1** Pick out the feet.

**2** Using a nail, remove any stud plugs and/or dirt from the stud hole.

**3** If you prepped the hole the day before, and your stud plug is in place, go straight to your studs. If not, tap the hole first. Be aware that repeated tapping can strip the threads. Grab your stud.

**4** Tighten the stud by hand as much as possible.

**5** Then take your adjustable wrench to tighten it further.

It should be snug enough so that you cannot release it by hand; however, don't pull so hard on the wrench you won't be able to get the stud out at the end of the day!

## Removing Studs

Clean out the hoof. Leave the horse's boots on until *all* the studs have been taken out.

**1** Stabilize the hoof with one hand while using a wrench to turn the stud to the left.

**2** Repeat on the other stud. Immediately plug the holes with stud plugs.

**3** Remove the horse's boots.

**4 A–C** Wash and towel dry the studs and put them back into your kit, spraying them with WD40. They should now be ready to go the next time.

Putting in Studs (Cont.)

Removing Studs

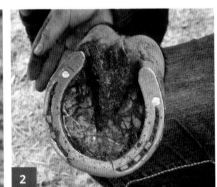

# CHAPTER THIRTEEN
# "The Final Leg"

## Cat says

*In my early career, I secured a working student position for dressage rider Tina Konyot. I had worked for a number of large, busy, lower-level barns prior to going to her so I was pretty sure I knew how to do everything. Tina was trying for the Olympics that year on a horse named Anna Karenina, as well as having several other upper-level competitors in the barn. I was unfamiliar with the level of care that horses of that caliber received and struggled to sort out my place. Tina's management was very good, and her horses lived like royalty. She insisted on perfection in the barn, and was a strict task-mistress. Since I was an overconfident kid, I chafed under her insistence that every little thing mattered. Many of the horses required standing wraps every night, and my wrapping was below par. She would sit and watch me wrap each leg every afternoon at the end of the workday, and if it wasn't absolutely*
*perfect I would have to unwrap and start over. One night, I rewrapped one horse 23 times before it was good enough, and I was in tears by the time I finished.*

*I ended my stint as a working student with her rather suddenly due to some family issues and never quite realized just how much I had learned until a couple years later when I found myself standing over a working student telling her to unwrap and start over. It took me a long time to be aware of the great opportunity I had; Tina may have been tough on me, but she instilled a real belief that the only way to do things in a barn is the correct way. She was tough because she had seen what happened when people were careless or cocky about horse care. Even now, I find myself looking at a standing wrap I don't like, then unwrapping it and starting over—until it is just right.*

## COOLING OUT

No matter which discipline or at what level you are competing, cooling down your horse efficiently after exertion is paramount to his health and happiness. How much time this process takes depends on three variables: *the outside temperature*, *the horse's fitness*, and *the day's workload*.

### Colder Climates

Obviously, cooling out a horse in cold weather is different from hot weather. In the cold, you want his muscles to stay warm and relaxed, so putting on a quarter sheet, or simply a woolly or fleece cooler folded back around the saddle, can help. Take your time to walk your horse out: he might not be breathing hard, but you still need to

Cooling Out: Colder Climates

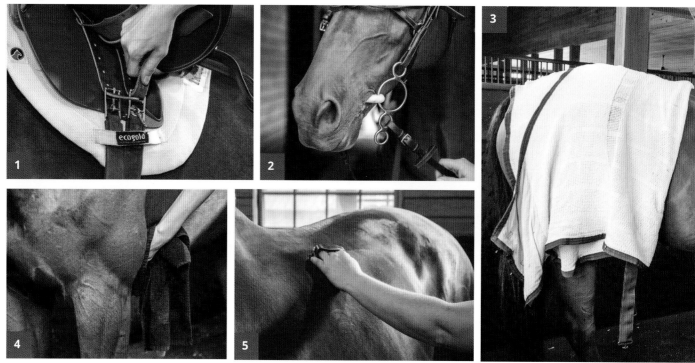

allow his muscles to slowly process the toxins that developed during exercise. You are helping to prevent severe muscle cramps, a condition known as "tying up."

**1** It's a good idea to loosen the girth during the cooldown process; it helps the horse to relax and know that he is done with work for the day.

**2** At the same time also loosen the noseband, and with a drop or figure-eight noseband in particular, simply tuck the ends into the cheekpieces to prevent them from flapping around.

**3** While untacking, throw a woolly or fleece cooler over the horse's hindquarters and back to prevent the horse from getting a chill. If there isn't one at hand, leave the saddle pad in place on his back to prevent the sweat under the saddle from creating a chill.

**4** When the horse is not sweating heavily, follow the directions on page 66 to use rubbing alcohol and towels to dry him and remove any saddle, girth, or bridle marks.

**5** Once dry, he can be fully curried and groomed, have his normal blankets put on, and go in his stall.

## Sponging

**1** When the horse comes in sweating, take a bucket of warm water and mix some alcohol in it.

**2** Sponge the horse down to remove sweat and dirt. Keep his hindquarters covered while you work, in order to prevent a chill.

**3 A & B** Don't neglect the face. Accumulated sweat can cause hair loss.

When you bring your sweating horse into a very cold barn, you need to make sure you help him dry without him getting chilled or allowing the sweat to dry on him. When it's below 45 degrees F, skip the sponging and follow the directions on page 202.

Sponging: Colder Climates

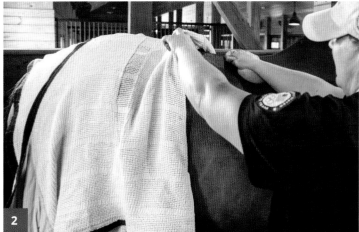

## pro tip

Hydration is important in winter months in cold climates. If at all possible, I try to give the horse a lukewarm bucket of drinking water—in the winter, I find horses will drink more this way. If your barn or showgrounds doesn't have hot water but does have electricity, fill a bucket with water and add a water heater to it before you go for your ride so you will have warm water available when you get back. —*Cat*

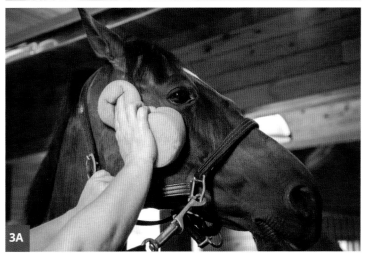

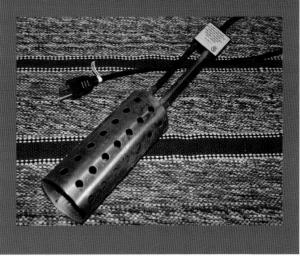

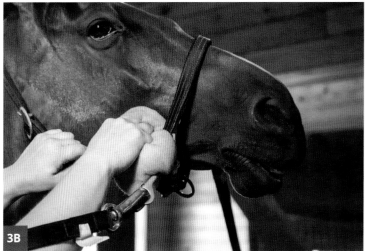

## Hot Towel

**1** First, get a small amount of hot water and put a couple drops each of baby oil and dish soap into it.

**2** Swirl your towel around in the mixture and wring out almost completely. Vigorously towel your horse all over, then put him away with an Irish knit underneath a wool cooler. This double layer has a great wicking effect by allowing water vapor to breathe through the layers, and the Irish knit remains dry next to the horse's skin thus preventing him from getting chilled. It is important to check for dryness, however, and you may need to exchange the top layer once you see the moisture sitting on top of the wool.

Hot Towel: Colder Climates

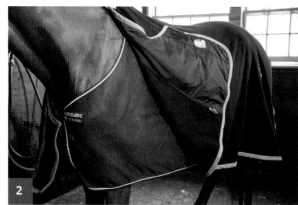

## Hot Climates and Strenuous Exercise

When a horse finishes a really hard workout or is working in hot conditions, he will be blowing hard and his internal temperature will have risen. First remove all tack.

Hot Climates and Strenuous Exercise

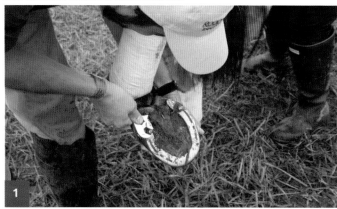

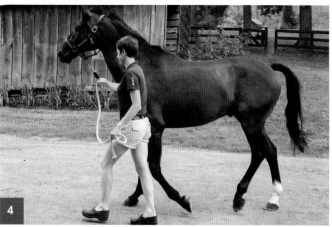

**1** Leave boots on until any studs have been removed. Although you want his legs to cool down quickly, a stud injury to a tendon is the fastest way to withdraw yourself from competition.

**2** Wash your horse down with cold water.

**3** Immediately scrape off the water.

**4** Then walk the horse.

Alternating between washing and walking is important to promote air cooling by evaporation. Walking increases blood flow to the skin; the blood carries heat from the internal organs to the skin. Washing with cold or icy water then cools the blood, which is returned to the internal organs, and the cycle is repeated until the horse's temperature returns to normal. If possible, all this should be done in the shade, or where there is a breeze. This process of wash, scrape, walk, should be repeated until the horse has stopped blowing and his temperature is back to normal. A horse's rectal temperature usually peaks about 10 minutes after completing his exertion.

Here's a tip: When no thermometer is at hand, you can touch his chest to feel how much he is cooling. The water being scraped off will become cold when the horse is cool.

## Misting Fans

**1** This picture shows Phillip Dutton's Connaught standing in front of the misting fans at the Beijing Olympics in 2008. These fanning stations were set up at the end of cross-country. Once the horse finished, we would start washing and scraping in front of the fans so that we could cool the horses out as quickly as possible since it was so hot there.

For a hunter, jumper, or dressage horse in extremely hot or humid weather, his temperature must be taken after completing exercise. For the event horse running cross-country in anything above moderately hot conditions, his temperature must be taken at the finish. A body temperature above 104 degrees F is dangerous, so a horse showing this needs to be taken into the shade and washed down with ice water. Scraping the water off *immediately* after putting it on is imperative because leaving water on his body just heats him up more—a negative effect on the cooling-out process.

## Cool and Calm

**1** Pay attention to the horse's mental state. A horse who is "amped up" sometimes will keep himself in a hyperactive state if still surrounded by intense activity. It's important with this horse to find a quiet spot and

Misting Fans

Cool and Calm

Rehydration

be very calm with your movements. Teaching him a cue to lower his head will help to bring his heart rate down, which, in turn, lowers his respiration and temperature.

Watch a horse carefully after you think he has cooled off. Sometimes, the respiration rate climbs again and he'll start to sweat again. If you notice this, you will need to start the cooling-out process again until the horse is comfortable with all

## pro tip

It is common practice at the Advanced level of eventing competition (FEI *** and ****) for horses to receive fluids the evening after cross-country. For the most part, this is to help the horses hydrate their muscles efficiently so that they feel at their best for the Sunday jog and show jumping. Here, Angie Cooney is sitting with Ballingowan Pizzazz while he gets fluid and has his legs iced after cross-country at the Mexico Pan American Games.

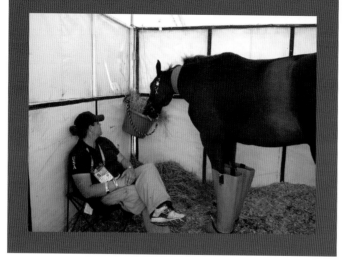

vital signs back to normal. If this doesn't happen within one hour, you need to call a veterinarian.

Hay can be fed one hour after cooling out; grain should not be given until at least two hours have passed.

### Rehydration

When you are working your horse hard in hot temperatures, he can lose up to 4 gallons of sweat per hour; even if you only ride for a half hour, that's 2 gallons lost. His sweat is comprised of mainly water, sodium, potassium, and chloride. In fact, the horse loses more electrolytes than water when sweating. This is a problem since the feeling of "thirst" occurs when the water level drops below the electrolyte level in the blood.

**1** So, once the horse is finished offer him small amounts of water quite often to encourage him to drink. Make sure there is fresh clean water in his stall. You can add electrolytes to one water bucket if the horse likes the taste of them. Some people will add Gatorade® to a bucket to try and pique a horse's interest in drinking. For the really "picky" drinker, try adding small handful of sweet feed and cut up apples in his bucket.

**2** Provided your horse is not showing signs of serious dehydration, correctly cooling him out should be enough to get him back to normal. Giving him wet feed such as a bran mash or soaking his hay are good ways to replace what he has lost.

However, serious dehydration and exhaustion can be seen at the higher levels of competition, especially when competing in hot, humid conditions. And, unaccustomed exertion at any level can also produce these symptoms, so watch carefully if you've had an unfit horse out for a harder ride than you intended. A horse that panics and runs in a field on a hot day can also do himself harm.

Serious signs of dehydration include:

- Excessive sweating.
- Muscle twitching.
- No sweat when he is still working or in hot conditions. Stop immediately if you notice this and cool your horse with cold water right away.
- Lack of gastrointestinal (GI) sounds; the GI tract can slow down with dehydration, possibly causing signs of colic.

Should any of these symptoms occur, call the vet. Normal treatment is intravenous (IV) fluids, with serious dehydration cases being given up to 80 liters of fluids. When the horse has not passed urine after receiving 40 liters, blood samples will need to be taken and checked for unusual renal issues. Providing his kidneys have not been affected, a horse tends to recover well from overexertion.

## AFTERCARE FOR THE COMPETITION HORSE

No matter what discipline, once the horse has cooled down and is comfortable, a good aftercare routine is important to keep your horse ready for the next competition. This is where knowledge of your horse's legs and other normal lumps and bumps is imperative.

You must go over your horse thoroughly and inspect him for any new marks or scratches as well as heat or swelling in the legs. Any minor cuts should be cleaned and antibiotic ointment applied. And, any cuts that are deep might need to be seen by a vet to be flushed out and stitched. Depending where the issue is, a standing wrap might be required to keep the cut clean and prevent swelling.

### Legs

The decisions you make for your horse's aftercare come down to a variety of factors: the big ones are the *discipline and level you participate in*, *your horse's age*, and *the amount of time and money you have available*. For the most part, a pleasure rider does not put on the miles or stress her horse's legs like a competition rider. And, horses being ridden at the lower competition levels in all disciplines do not need the leg-care routine that an upper-level horse needs. That being said, there are many retired, advanced-level horses now competing at the lower levels. The ex-Grand-Prix jumping horse carting around a junior may come with a history of leg issues that need regular care to maintain soundness, and dressage horses are not exempt from leg care either: Lateral

## pro tip

I am fortunate to have use of a Multi Radiance Medical® ActiVet Laser. This is a cold laser that I can use on most injuries. Cuts heal more quickly, and by using the blue-light application, bacterial infection is greatly reduced. *Reactive* muscles can be treated effectively to reduce spasms and remove those sore, sensitive areas. —*Emma*

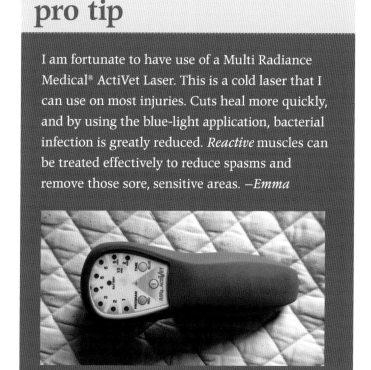

---

Tubigrip and Loose Ice

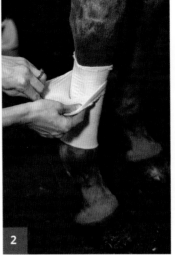
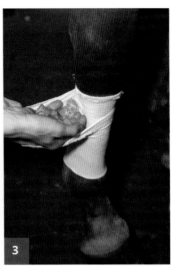
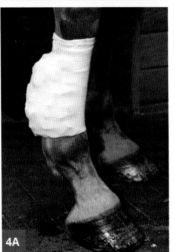
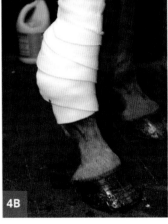

work and collection puts stress on the tendons and joints just as surely as jumping does.

Your leg-care routine can be very basic with dry wrapping to very complex with extensive icing. We'll start with a discussion of many icing therapies and follow this with the other ways to treat legs, like dry wrapping, liniments, and poulticing after icing, or after strenuous exercise where icing is not necessary.

## Cold Therapy

*Cold therapy* is probably one of the most common forms of treatment to help legs recover after strenuous exercise. Quickly getting rid of heat and minor swelling in the soft-tissue structures is important in preventing future injury. There are multiple ways to use cold therapy. There are pros and cons to all of them but, at the end of the day, personal preference wins over. Research shows that standing a horse in ice for longer than 20 minutes can actually damage his blood vessels; it is safer to ice twice with a 20-minute break in between than it is to ice continuously for more than 20 minutes.

## Cold Hosing

The most common form of cold therapy is cold hosing. Cold water is run continuously over the horse's legs to help pull heat away it. It can be very useful for a horse that doesn't like to stand in ice of any type. Simply turn the cold water on and run it down the legs.

## Tubigrip and Loose Ice

The most inexpensive way to ice legs involves using a piece of Tubigrip folded double on the horse's leg. Tubigrip is an elasticized fabric bandage that comes in a long tube that you can then cut to the correct length. This is great for icing small areas such as a splint or hematoma.

**1 A & B** Pull the Tubigrip on the same way you would a rubber bell boot.

Ice Packs

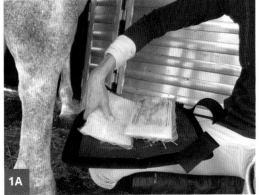 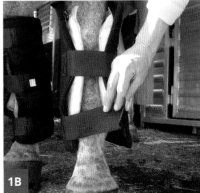 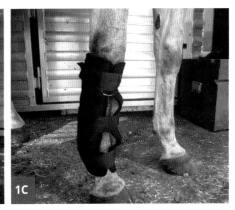

**2** Double the Tubigrip over so the fold is at the bottom of the leg and the ends are at the top. This should create a pocket.

**3** Place ice in the pocket. This keeps the ice away from skin thus preventing burning.

**4 A & B** Use a polo wrap to keep it all in place

You do need to keep an eye on the time. Obviously, once the ice starts to melt the wrap will loosen and begin to slip down the leg. To be more effective, crush the ice first. This gives maximum contact around all parts of soft tissue.

## Ice Packs
**1 A–C** There are many versions of ice packs that are reusable by placing in the freezer. They are simple to use, and most of the time you do not need to stand with the horse. You don't have to worry about leaving them on too long because they do not remain frozen very long: the horse's body temperature thaws the ice. Many of these ice packs can be molded to a leg, then you can bandage them to keep the pack in place. The added pressure of a bandage is beneficial in reducing swelling, too.

When using an ice pack, wet it and the horse's leg before putting them on. This improves the transfer of the cold pack to the leg since water conducts temperature better than air. For an inexpensive ice pack you can get gel ice packs from your local drugstore—they are reusable and only a bandage is needed to keep them in place.

## Zip-Up Ice Boots
Made out of flexible plastic or canvas, these boots are inexpensive to use after the initial purchase. The boot easily fixes around the leg with a zip. Most types have a large piece of sponge around the bottom and that snugly fits around the pastern and prevents ice from falling out.

**1** First, you adjust the buckles around the pastern, which should be on the outside of the leg toward the front.

**2** You want them to fit evenly and snugly so ice can't sneak out of the boot.

Zip-Up Ice Boots

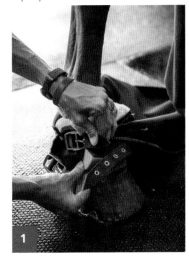 

*Continued* ▶

Zip-Up Ice Boots (Cont.)

 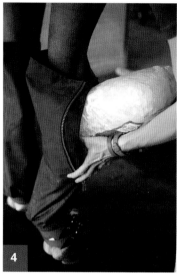  

**3** Zip the boot up about a third of the way.

**4** Fill the bottom with ice, using your hands to make sure it goes all the way around the leg.

**5** Fill the rest of the way as you zip up the boot.

**6** Spray a bit of cold water into the boot to help settle the ice and ensure contact with the leg.

You have to be careful when getting your horse used to these. If he tries to walk, he may take a severe dislike to the ice moving around, so introduce them slowly and at home. The first time, put them on without any ice and let him move around. Once he's done that, start to fill them with ice but put only small amounts in on a daily basis. Eventually, he will become a pro at hanging out in his boots with ice up to his knees!

Pocket Ice Boots

### Pocket Ice Boots

**1** Generally made out of neoprene, these boots can have four pockets, if short, or eight pockets when they go above the knee. They are efficient and inexpensive to use after the purchase cost. For a horse that does not tolerate the zip up boots, these are a good alternative.

**2** The most effective way to use these boots is to soak them in water first, then fill each pocket with ice.

**3** Be careful not to overfill the pockets otherwise it is difficult to put the boots on tightly enough to mold to the leg.

Whirlpool Boots

 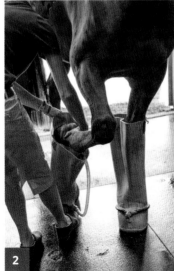 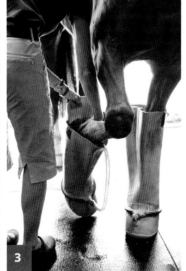 

Throw water over the ice pockets before putting them on as this helps the temperature transfer between the leg and boot. Some people put the ensemble in the freezer beforehand to make it extra cold.

## Whirlpool Boots

These tall rubber boots are possibly the most effective form of icing that also treats the feet at the same time. You can buy them with an air compressor: the motor aerates the foot and coronet band, and also massages up the lower limb. This action provides good pressure to help circulation. Many people also use these boots without the motor.

**1** To ensure that the horse steps onto the bottom of the boot and not onto the back of it, place the toe of the boot just behind his leg and angle it forward.

**2** Lift his leg and direct it to the center of the boot's opening.

**3** Slide the boot forward as you lower the leg, guiding it into the boot.

**4** You want him to stand centered in the boot.

**5** Slowly pour ice into the boot.

**6** Fill the rest of the way with cold water.

**7** Ice for 20 minutes, no longer.

Ice Bucket

1

Teaching your horse to stand quietly in these boots takes time. Start by placing your horse in the wash stall, but not on cross-ties. Have a helper hold him, then place one leg into an empty boot. If he is happy and doesn't react, slowly place the second leg in. Once your horse becomes comfortable standing in the empty boots for several minutes—and this might take several training sessions—you can start to add water. Only partially fill the boots to start with. Add ice one handful at a time. Expect some spilled ice the first few times, and be ready with a reward when he stands there! Some horses do really well with a hay net in front of them while they are being iced.

## Ice Bucket

**1** If you don't have whirlpool boots, you can use a trash can or a muck tub and stand your horse in it. Ideally, you want the ice to reach the bottom of the knee to make sure all the soft tissue is fully covered. While this is cheaper at the outset than whirlpool boots, getting the tub cold enough requires two to three times as much ice, so be prepared to spend a lot on ice!

## Game Ready® Equine

This icing method maintains a constant water temperature while using a pressurized leg-wrap system. The pres-

Hock Compression Boots

1A

1B

surized leg wrap has ice water circulating through it so the water never touches the skin. It is quite an expensive machine and for some may be cost-prohibitive for regular use, but for an injury such as a bowed tendon, many veterinarians have them available for rent. You only need one bag of ice, and since the water never touches the skin, you can use alcohol to lower the water temperature. For a horse with a skin condition that needs "dry" icing this is a great method. There are many hoses connected to a single motor, so note that a horse must be supervised while connected to minimize the chance of him spooking and possibly breaking the machine.

## Compression Boots

**1 A & B** In the last few years, companies such as Equi-fit® have introduced a product that allows you to add compression to the leg. It consists of some freezable inserts and a boot with a detachable pump similar to a blood-pressure machine. You pump up the boot to add some pressure ensuring good contact between the leg and cold therapy source, and in addition, the compression helps to reduce inflammation.

## Dry Wrapping

**1** As implied, you should be sure that the legs are dry

and feel normal to touch before you apply standing wraps. Refer to page 21 for complete instructions on application. For older horses that stock up when they stand in overnight, or for lower-level competitors, such as Training Level dressage horses, Level One jumpers or Low hunters, this may be all your horse requires to remain comfortable

Dry Wrapping

throughout his competition life.

## Liniments

There are many liniments on the market, all of which promote reduction in swelling, inflammation, and pain. Your cheapest forms of liniment are rubbing alcohol and witch hazel. If you are on a budget and need something extra, first rub some arnica gel into the horse's legs before wrapping up your horse for the night. It is paramount here to try a new product on your horse at home (and on a small area) before a competition; many horses are sensitive and can react to the use of certain products.

Liniments

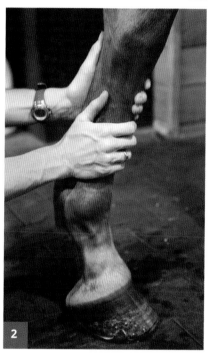

**1** Sore No-More® Liniment is one of the best products on the market today. The ingredients are herbal and very effective at reducing pain and swelling after any serious exertion. The manufacturer now makes a line that is FEI compatible called Sore No-More Performance Liniment—a product that is both capsaicin- and lobelia-free (both banned substances on the FEI list).

**2** When applying a liniment it is important to use so it that can be thoroughly massaged into the lower leg. Just spraying it on *is not* enough. Once applied you must place a hand on both sides of the leg and rub the liniment into the limb for at least 30 seconds.

Poulticing

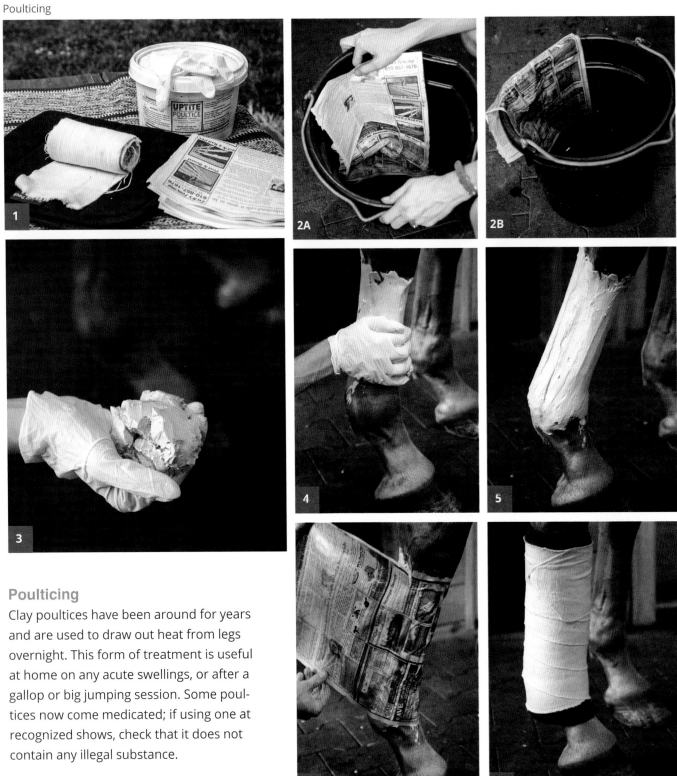

## Poulticing

Clay poultices have been around for years and are used to draw out heat from legs overnight. This form of treatment is useful at home on any acute swellings, or after a gallop or big jumping session. Some poultices now come medicated; if using one at recognized shows, check that it does not contain any illegal substance.

**1** The Poultice Kit
- Poultice
- Thick paper (newspaper, brown paper bags, or any unwaxed paper)
- Standing bandage
- Flannel wrap
- Water

**2 A & B** Get your paper wet and hang it to drip.

**3** Wearing a latex glove, scoop out a small amount of poultice.

**4** Apply to the leg about 1 centimeter thick. Too much and it will not dry, which makes for a lot of scrubbing in the morning, plus it won't have done the job you intended it to do!

**5** The poultice should cover from the fetlock to the knee.

**6** Using paper cut to size, wrap around the leg (always front to back!).

**7** Apply a regular standing wrap on top (see p. 21).

If your horse has a cut or scrape on his leg, wash this clean and apply either a piece of gauze or Animalintex® over the area so that the poultice does not cover the cut. Poultice material can irritate skin, so if you have a sensitive horse, try plain witch hazel, which has the least likelihood of causing any problems.

**barn gossip**

In 2008, Connaught, aka "Simon," won the Rolex CCI**** in Kentucky with Phillip Dutton. This was an amazing time for me and all his "family." However, the night after cross-country was the most nerve-racking time for me. He had pulled up well with no obvious signs of injury and after fluids and icing, he jogged up great. I still couldn't leave anything to chance; we were standing in second place so coming out on Sunday morning with all cylinders firing for the stadium phase was a must.

That night the barns stayed open until 11:00 p.m. Even though he looked great at 7:00 p.m., I could not put him away for the night not having done all I could to make him comfortable. So, I left him alone until around 9:00 p.m. when I came back and iced him, then hand-walked and grazed him for another 45 minutes. We jogged again a little after 10:00 p.m. for Phillip and our vet, which went well. I decided one more icing, then I would poultice, and wrap up his feet for the night.

I returned in the morning at 5:00 a.m. and after feeding, I immediately unwrapped him only to find a completely wet poultice. Because I had wrapped him so late the night before, the poultice did not have enough time to dry so it had pretty much acted as an insulator rather than withdrawing heat.

As you can imagine, I was mortified. Simon's legs had fill in them, so after cold-hosing the poultice off, I stood him in ice while I braided. Phillip arrived at 6:00 a.m. to jog him. Fortunately, although slightly stiff, he was sound. I put polo wraps on to add some compression while Phillip took him for a long-and-low walk, trot, and canter. The rest is history: the quirkiest horse I have ever worked with jumped his way to the Rolex trophy.

Since then I have always followed my own rule of no poulticing after six. If I need to wrap a horse after that, I use a liniment instead. —*Emma*

Poultice Removal

# FEI and USEF Rules

As you progress through the levels there are rules and regulations that come into effect both from the national (USEF) and international (FEI) federations when you are competing at recognized competitions. It is important to understand the implications of these rules because they can affect the most simple product in your barn—fly spray, for example. You need to be very aware of any ointments you use for skin conditions and wounds. Even something as benign as Panalog® has a steroid in it, so cannot be used 10 days before a competition.

You can ask your vet about products or easily access the FEI website at www.feicleansport.org. For USEF rules, go to www.USEF.org, and look under drug rules for banned substances and withdrawal periods. For those of you who are not in sole charge of your horse, make sure your barn manager knows your competition schedule. When a decision needs to be made about applying certain ointments or liniments, a manager needs to be aware of any products that may be "testable" at your competition. Make sure you are always asked or informed before any product is used.

Poultice Removal

**1 A & B** To remove, use the dried paper and scrub off as much of the clay as you can.

**2 A & B** You will then need to shampoo the legs to remove the remaining dust.

**3** Rinse well to prevent irritation.

**4** Towel dry the legs and check for any unusual heat or swelling.

## A Good Poultice Alternative

**1** Stayons® Poultice Leg Wraps.

**2** This form of poulticing takes away the messiness of regular poulticing and still has the good benefits. It's a great product for horses with sensitive skin or any cuts that you don't want to actually cover with the clay.

**3** Just wet the sheet of clay, either in a bucket or with a hose.

**4** Wrap around the leg.

**5** Apply a standing wrap.

**6** Done! No gloves, no wetting paper, you remain clean.

**7** To remove, just take off the standing wrap and peel the paper sheet away from the leg.

**8** One dry, clean dust-free leg.

Poultice Alternative

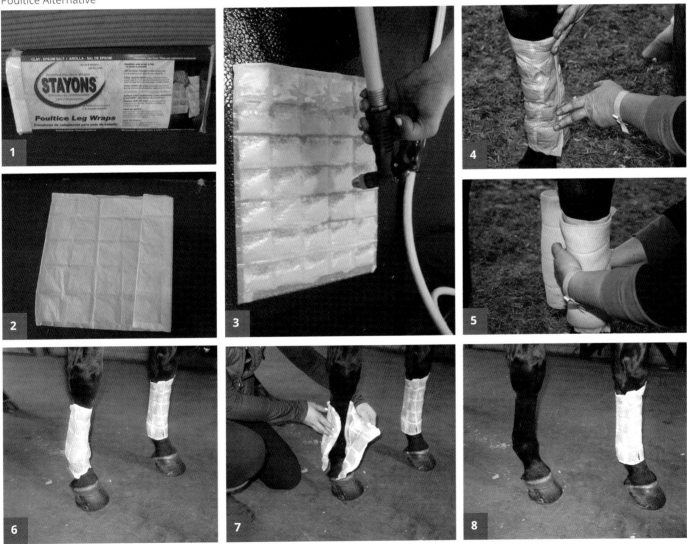

Packing Feet

Continued ▶

## Packing Feet

If your horse has a stone bruise, is prone to sore feet, or has just jumped on hard ground, you should consider packing his feet for the night to improve his comfort. It's good to know how to check your horse's hoof pulse. There is a large vein that runs down the inside of the horse's fetlock; it normally has a weak pulse, being so far from the heart and low on the body. When a horse has been standing quietly but has a throbbing, fast pulse, it can indicate there is a problem brewing in the hoof. Wrapping the horse's feet is a good idea.

**1** To find the pulse, glide your fingers slowly around the back of the fetlock. You will feel a slight depression in the joint directly above the inside bulb of the heel. When the pulse is strong and throbbing, you probably have a problem. When it's weak or hard to find, it's most likely the hoof is okay.

**2** The most basic form of hoof packing consists of Epsom salts and Betadine.

**3** First, you need to make your duct-tape "bootie." Place about 8 inches of duct tape across your leg.

Packing Feet (Cont.)

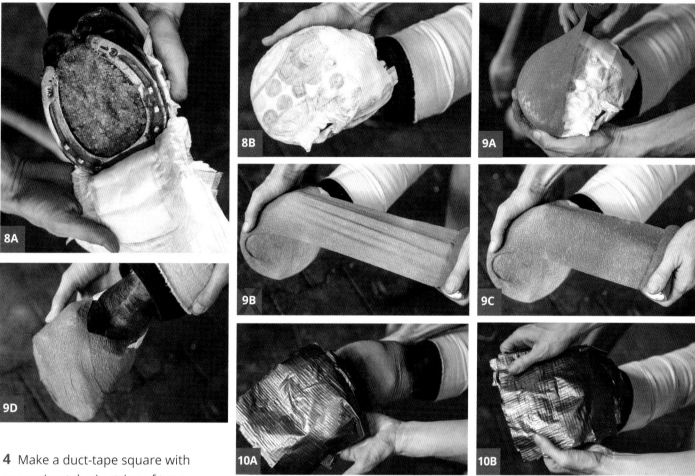

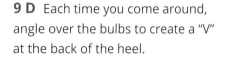

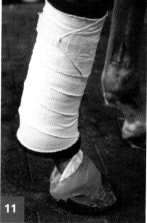

**4** Make a duct-tape square with approximately six strips of tape.

**5** Repeat the process, but go in the opposite direction—this helps to strengthen the bootie.

**6 A & B** Mix the Epsom salts and Betadine together until they have the consistency of wet sand.

**7 A & B** Pack into the foot.

**8 A & B** Apply a disposable diaper.

**9 A** Beginning at the toe, wrap the Vetrap around the hoof and toward the bulbs of the heel.

**9 B** Wrong: When going over the bulbs of the heel, do not pull too tight.

**9 C** Instead, pull only enough to snug the wrap as you pass over the soft tissue.

**9 D** Each time you come around, angle over the bulbs to create a "V" at the back of the heel.

**10 A–C** Finally, apply your pre-made duct-tape bootie.

**11** A leg poulticed and foot packed for the night.

Commercial Alternatives

### Commercial Alternatives

**1** Commercially marketed products, such as Absorbine's Magic Cushion® and Rebound Hoof Pack are simple to use and work quite well. With these products, use a latex glove to pack the foot then apply Vetrap and a duct-tape bootie as described on page 217. Note: The diaper will absorb the healing properties of these products, so you should skip that step when using a commercial alternative.

Animalintex hoof packs come as a sheet that can be trimmed to fit, soaked, and wrapped on with Vetrap. Since it has a drawing-out property, it is a great form of packing if you suspect an abscess or stone bruise.

## pro tip

When using Absorbine's Magic Cushion, apply a layer of Vaseline to the bulbs of the heels and the lower pastern to prevent the skin from getting irritated if the product seeps out of the wrap.

## Body Care

At the higher levels, whether dressage, show jumping, hunters, or eventing, some form of body care is helpful to keep your horse comfortable. For the equine athlete to maintain peak condition after competition, regular bodywork is generally carried out. Many options are available—here are a few of our favorites:

### Magnetic Blanket

**1** A magnetic blanket can be put on the horse and automatically complete its cycle within 20 to 30 minutes. The two most popular brands are from Respond Systems and Sport Innovations. These blankets contain pulsing magnetic coils that help the circulation in the horse throughout his body. They are great for warming up prior to a workout, as well as relaxing the muscles after completing a day of competition. It has been shown that magnetic therapy can be beneficial in bone healing and degenerative joint injuries, as well as helping to improve inflammation and swelling.

Magnetic Blanket

The Sport Innovations' magnetic unit also includes a massage function, which can be used alone or in conjunction with the magnetic function. While it is expensive, this piece of equipment is easy to use and most horses visibly benefit from its therapy.

### Equissage®

**2** This physiotherapy massage system delivers vibrations throughout the horse's whole body. It can help in blood circulation, lymphatic drainage, relaxation, and joint mobility. It is easy to use, non-invasive, and great to put on your horse both pre- and post-workout.

### RevitaVet™

**3** A light-therapy system that uses light-emitting diodes (LED), it stimulates healing at the cellular level. It is non-invasive, portable, and safe. It is shown to be effective in wound-healing, soft-tissue injury, and stimulating acupressure points. Due to the fact it increases circulation, RevitaVet is great for pre- and post-workouts.

### Laser Therapy

**4** This therapy uses certain wavelengths to stimulate cell activity. There are a variety of hand-held lasers. The Multi Radiance Medical® laser is the only cold laser that has magnetism in its red light that helps the cells to absorb the light. This laser has four different wavelengths that allow you to work on wounds, soft-tissue injury, and deep muscle spasms. Since it is super-pulsed, there is no thermal buildup as with other lasers, which means you cannot burn the horse. It also has a blue-light function, which, when used on wounds, aids in reducing bacterial infection (see also p. 205).

Equissage®

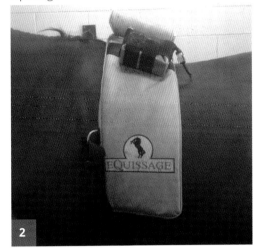

RevitaVet™

Laser Therapy

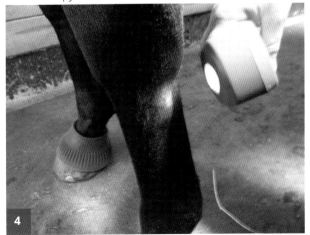

Chiropractic, Sports Massage, Acupuncture

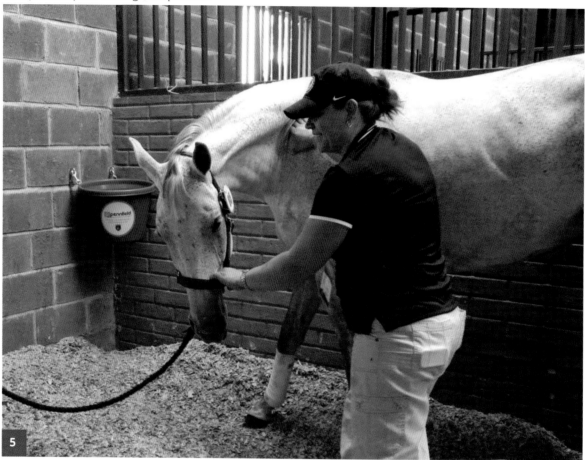

**5**

## Chiropractic, Sports Massage, Acupuncture

**5** Many times these forms of therapy are used in conjunction with each other; however, some horses benefit more from one than another. Use depends on the individual horse—whether he has specific issues and his competition schedule. In many states you have to be a vet to carry out chiropractic and acupuncture treatments.

Your horse will tell you what works for him. Some warm up easier and quicker after a massage, while others remain relaxed while working after acupuncture. If you are in the fortunate position of being able to afford qualified therapists to work on your horse, then any of these could be exceptionally useful in your care routine.

# Afterword

Over our many shared years of experience in all levels of the horse industry, we have come to one conclusion: It doesn't matter what manufacturer your saddle has stamped on it or what brand name is on the tag of your breeches, we are all in this sport for one thing—and that is the horse. This holds true, from the child learning to braid her pony's mane to the superstar winning the big bucks, and nowhere more so than the professional groom, whose care of horses of all breeds and in all disciplines supersedes *everything* else. We are all a little horse-crazy and as content to see our four-legged charges go out and jump or dance their way to a win as to tote around a toddler, as long as it makes them happy.

It is our sincerest hope that what we've provided in these pages helps to elevate the level of care that *all* horses experience and that through that sweat and time, the relationship between each horse and his caretaker gets a little stronger. From cleaning a stall *just right* so your horse has a clean place to sleep, to putting his mane perfectly in place to show off how handsome he is, we hope you walk away from this book with a desire to make your horse's world just a little bit better.

# Acknowledgments

One of the things we have learned through this process is how many people it takes to get a successful book off the ground! We would all like to extend the warmest thanks to Trafalgar Square Books for believing in our project and for helping us through the process; to the Wildisin family for opening up their farm and home to us for our main photo shoot; and to Mara DePuy, Bren Ryan ReSue, and Jean-Marie for the use of their lovely horses.

## From Cat

My journey to being a professional groom was not an expected one, and I would not have gotten to where I am without the help and advice of the entire groom community, and those who were always there to answer questions and help with late-night emergencies. I also wouldn't have gotten to where I am without the faith of Mara DePuy, who gave me a job when my credentials didn't fully qualify me for it! Mara taught me to never take sub-standard as acceptable and encouraged me to continue always putting my horses first.

    Thank you to my amazing husband who stood with me through the years of travel, long hours, and experience needed to write this book, as well as pushed me to take the time now to write it. I cannot give enough thanks to all the people who watched my daughter while I wrote, proofread, and rewrote. To my family who always stands behind my ideas with encouragement and love, and to Doug Payne, who pushed me over the edge, taking me from talking about writing a book to talking to a publisher and then to actually doing it! Of course, I also have to thank Emma Ford and Jessica Dailey for diving into this adventure with me, even though I'm pretty sure none of us knew what we were getting into! Thank you so much!

## From Emma

If someone had asked me 15 years ago, "What will you be doing in 2014?" writing a grooming book would not have been anywhere close to an answer I would have given! This is for two reasons: At the time, professional grooming was still not a definitive career choice, and second, writing in general was not my strong point at school!

    The road leading to this project has been filled with support from so many people they are too numerous to list. However, I would be wrong for not mentioning three professional grooms who have inspired and supported me throughout my personal journey: Liz Corchran, who when working for Abigail Lufkin, taught me to always have my horses looking their best, whether at a show or in the barn. And my close friends Sarah Morton and Colby Bauersfield have helped shaped my career with their never-ending advice and encouragement when needed. I thank you all.

Without my family's support, my best friend Carol Anne listening to me stressing over trying to string sentences together, and my American sister Amy Ruth Borun who always helps to push me forward to take the next step in life (even albeit a scary one), my part in this book would not have materialized.

I have been blessed with awesome employers whilst grooming: Adrienne Iorio and Phillip and Evie Dutton have done nothing but encourage me to grow within my career choice. They've become my second family through the process. I thank you all for trusting in me to take care of some amazing, world-class horses. Without your belief in me, I would not have been able to continue as a groom, and then this book would not have become reality.

My last "thank you" has to go to Cat for asking me to join her on this journey. The book idea would never have crossed my mind, let alone actually summoning the nerve to try and put pen to paper, without Cat at the helm. Cat, thank you for putting up with my lack of technical knowledge and computer abilities. It's actually amazing you are still talking to me after all my computer blips!

## From Jessica

Never could I have imagined that I'd have the chance to work as closely as I was able to with the many gorgeous animals in this book. Their personalities, strength, and grace are stunning in every way. Thanks to Cat Hill and Emma Ford, I expanded my knowledge into areas I didn't know existed, and began to understand the beautiful relationship between a horse and the person who cares for him. For this unique lifetime experience, I am grateful.

I want to thank the lovely Cat for having confidence in my abilities as a photographer and for encouraging me to tackle this project. I also want to thank my husband and my daughter for inspiring and supporting me on a daily basis. Without my family, this book would not have been possible.

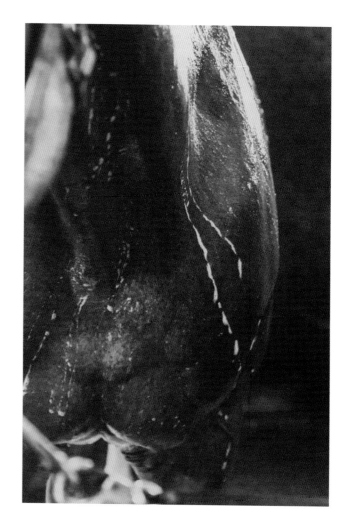

# Index